POPULATION GROWTH, EMPLOYMENT AND POVERTY IN THIRD-WORLD MEGA-CITIES

The ILO's World Employment Programme (WEP) aims to assist and encourage member States to adopt and implement active policies and projects designed to promote full, productive and freely chosen employment and to reduce poverty. Through its action-oriented research, technical advisory services, national projects and the work of its four regional employment teams in Africa, Asia and Latin America, the WEP pays special attention to the longer-term development problems of rural areas where the vast majority of poor and underemployed people still live, and to the rapidly growing urban informal sector.

At the same time, in response to the economic crises and the growth in open unemployment of the 1980s, the WEP has entered into an ongoing dialogue with the social partners and other international agencies on the social dimensions of adjustment, and is devoting a major part of its policy analysis and advice to achieving greater equity in structural adjustment programmes. Employment and poverty monitoring, direct employment creation and income generation for vulnerable groups, linkages between macroeconomic and microeconomic interventions, technological change and labour-market problems and policies are among the areas covered.

Through these overall activities, the ILO has been able to help national decision-makers to reshape their policies and plans with the aim of eradicating mass poverty and promoting productive employment.

This publication is the outcome of a WEP project.

Population Growth, Employment and Poverty in Third-World Mega-Cities

Analytical and Policy Issues

A. S. Oberai
Senior Economist
International Labour Office
Geneva

A study prepared for the International Labour Office within the framework of the World Employment Programme with the financial support of the United Nations Population Fund (UNFPA)

150th YEAR

M

St. Martin's Press

304. 6091724
012 p
1993

First published in Great Britain 1993 by
THE MACMILLAN PRESS LTD
Houndmills, Basingstoke, Hampshire RG21 2XS
and London
Companies and representatives
throughout the world

This book is published in *The Macmillan Series of ILO Studies*

A catalogue record for this book is available
from the British Library.

ISBN 0-333-59439-8

Printed in Great Britain by
Antony Rowe Ltd, Chippenham, Wiltshire

First published in the United States of America 1993 by
Scholarly and Reference Division,
ST. MARTIN'S PRESS, INC.,
175 Fifth Avenue,
New York, N.Y. 10010

ISBN 0-312-09973-8

Library of Congress Cataloging-in-Publication Data
Oberai, A. S.
Population growth, employment, and poverty in Third-World mega
-cities : analytical and policy issues / Amarjit Singh Oberai.
p. cm.
Includes bibliographical references and index.
ISBN 0-312-09973-8
1. Developing countries—Population. 2. Labor market—Developing
countries. 3. Poor—Developing countries. 4. Urbanization-
-Developing countries. 5. Economic assistance, Domestic—Developing
countries. I. Title.
HB884.O253 1993
304.6'09172'4—dc20   93-10561
                                                       CIP

Contents

List of Tables

List of Tables

Preface

The current trend in urban concentration and the growth of large cities pose a formidable challenge to many developing countries. Of particular concern is the fact that urbanisation has been, and is likely to continue to be, accompanied by growing urban unemployment and poverty, the proliferation of slum and squatter settlements, and urban environmental degradation. A vast majority of the urban poor in mega-cities do not have adequate access to low-income housing, urban transport, water, education, health facilities, family planning and other social services. The economic downturn of the 1980s and the debt crisis, particularly in Latin America and Africa, have aggravated the difficulties of providing and maintaining urban infrastructure. Structural adjustment policies have squeezed budgetary allocations to social sectors and impeded the ability of cities to service basic needs.

Several international meetings (Rome, 1980; Barcelona, 1986; Mexico City, 1989) on urban and city growth have urged governments to take immediate steps to reduce the pace of rural–urban migration and to improve employment and living conditions in large cities. Among national governments, however, the fear has been widespread that actions to alleviate poverty in urban areas will accentuate urban bias, increase rural–urban inequalities, and exacerbate rural–urban migration. Until recently, city authorities in many developing countries even justified reduced investment in urban services by arguing that the more houses, schools, hospitals and jobs were provided in the cities, the more migrants would be attracted to them.

The arguments against action to alleviate poverty in urban areas are not entirely persuasive. First, the focus of poverty is rapidly shifting to urban areas in many countries, so concern for overall poverty alleviation must increasingly deal with its manifestation in cities. The number of poor urban households living in absolute poverty in developing countries is projected to increase from 40 million in 1980 to 72 million by the year 2000, and that of poor rural households to fall from 80 million to 56 million during the same period (United Nations Development Programme, 1990). Second, although average incomes in urban areas are generally higher than in rural areas, the urban poor are as poor as their rural counterparts. In spite of living in cities, they are no better off than the rural poor in terms of access to social services such as health facilities and education. In some respects, such as the overcrowded and insanitary living conditions in urban slums, they are arguably even worse off. Moreover, the withholding of urban infrastructure or social services and the bulldozing of slum or squatter settlements have all been shown not to affect migration flows significantly. They do, however, seriously impede the efficiency of urban markets, destroy valuable capital stock, and wreak havoc with the lives and welfare of the majority of the urban population. In fact, measures designed to improve the efficiency of the urban economy, in particular the pricing of public services at marginal social cost and the elimination of subsidies for private investors, as discussed in this study, are more likely to have much more important, albeit indirect, effects on migration.

It should also be recognised that in developing countries cities are the prime place where wealth is created. They provide the basic infrastructure for economic growth and social transformation, and they continue to attract people precisely because they offer opportunities to share in that wealth and growth. The focus on today's cities must therefore move decisively towards better urban management, with past failures giving way to more appropriate policies and practices. Decrees to restrict land use, enforce building codes and demolish slums have often proved costly and irrelevant.

Major urban centres cannot, of course, absorb all the rural poor in developing countries. Nor can urban poverty be effectively tackled without moderating population growth in large cities. Issues related to achieving a more even spatial distribution of population by encouraging the growth of secondary cities, developing new growth poles and increasing employment opportunities in rural areas must not, therefore, be neglected. They must remain an important element of any strategy for employment creation and human settlement in the face of a fast-growing labour force in large cities. At the same time, however, one cannot simply wait for the situation in mega-cities to deteriorate further in the vain hope that this will act as a disincentive to migration from the rural areas and smaller urban centres. In addition, even if rural–urban migration does slow down, the absolute size of mega-cities, given the natural growth rate of their population, will still pose enormous problems. In most Third-World mega-cities, the rate of natural population growth is quite high among the urban poor and contributes more to urban population growth than migration. The urban poor generally tend to have large families both because of their limited access to social services and because of their dependence on children in old age in the absence of any social security system. Large family size in turn contributes to household poverty. Population growth and poverty thus reinforce each other in urban areas, particularly in large cities. Policies and programmes are therefore required to help break this vicious cycle of poverty.

It is in this practical context that the ILO initiated a comprehensive policy research programme at the beginning of 1988, with financial support from the United Nations Population Fund (UNFPA). As part of this programme, detailed background studies of eight large cities (Shanghai, Seoul and Bombay in Asia; Lagos and Nairobi in Africa; Mexico City and Rio de Janeiro in Latin America; and Cairo in the Middle East) were initiated.[1] The aim was to assist national and city authorities in reducing urban population growth and improving the conditions, incomes and productivity of the growing millions of urban poor by identifying policy options and alternative action programmes. The major focus of the city studies was twofold: first, to provide an analytical description of the ways in which cities have coped with urban problems; second, as the studies were undertaken in a comparative framework using a similar methodology, to find out why some policies have worked well in some cities and not in others and what are the conditions for their success or failure in a particular context.

City case studies involved the following individuals/national research institutions:

Bombay:	Dr S. Deshpande and Prof. L. Deshpande, Department of Economics, Bombay University.
Cairo:	Dr Nadia Farah, Department of Economics, American University in Cairo.
Lagos:	Dr T. O. Fadayomi, Dr A. O. Agunbiade, Dr G. O. Olaore and Dr D. Tobi, Nigerian Institute of Social and Economic Research, Ibadan.
Mexico City:	Dr Francisco Alba, Mr Crescensio Ruiz, Mr Boris Graizbord and Ms Ma. Eugenia Negrete, Center for Demographic and Urban Studies, El Colegio de Mexico.

Rio de Janeiro: Dr Hamilton C. Tolosa, Institute of Economic
                         and Social Planning (IPEA), Ministry of
                         Economy, Mr A. V. Villela, Dr J. B. Figueiredo,
                         Institute of Industrial Economics, Federal
                         University of Rio de Janeiro, and Mr L. A.
                         Villela, City Government.

Seoul: Dr Jong-Gie Kim, Dr. Kwan-young Kim and
                         Dr. Jae-Young Son, Korea Development
                         Institute, (KDI).

Shanghai: Institute of Human Resources Development,
                         State Planning Commission, Beijing, and
                         Institute of Economic Planning, Shanghai
                         Planning Commission.

Bombay and Seoul city case studies have been published in ILO's
World Employment Programme Research Working paper series. The
remaining studies were at various stages of preparation and could not
be completed for publication by the end of 1991 when the project
terminated. However, some core city- and national-level data gathered
through a structured questionnaire on request from ILO were provided
by all collaborating individuals/institutions for attempting a comparative analysis.[2]

From the point of view of presenting the results of the policy-
research programme, it was considered more appropriate to use an
integrated approach for the discussion of the problems and policy
options facing Third-World mega-cities. As such the present volume
containing specific themes in individual chapters was prepared based
largely on comparative analysis of core data made available by
national research institutions. The analysis provides a detailed
description of the changes that have taken place in the economic and
social structure of the cities as a result of rapid population growth and
the world economic crisis of the 1980s, and an assessment of the
implications of these changes for urban employment and poverty. The
volume thus provides a comprehensive account of the problems faced
by Third-World mega-cities, critically evaluates past and current
policies and programmes adopted by city and national authorities in
dealing with these problems, and suggests how those policies and
programmes might be changed in order to deal more effectively with
the problems faced by large cities. Whenever relevant, the study draws

upon the results of the individual city case studies with appropriate references.

Many people, in addition to the external collaborators of the city case-studies, have contributed to this volume. It is difficult to single out individuals, but a large number of government officials in municipal corporations, local and national planning agencies and ministries of labour and urban development have provided useful information on matters of policy and practice and on their experience in the formulation and implementation of urban policies and programmes. I am indebted to all of them.

Special thanks go to Professor Ajit Singh, Faculty of Economics, University of Cambridge (England), who generously provided intellectual inputs throughout the period of this study. He had also, at an earlier stage, prepared an overview paper on urban policy issues which was used, along with a paper outlining a conceptual framework for the analysis of urban policy issues prepared by the present author, as background material for commissioning the city case-studies.

Many colleagues at the ILO have contributed to the evolution of this volume through their comments and observations. Thanks are particularly due to Iftikhar Ahmed, Richard Anker, Ghazi Farooq, J. Krishnamurty, Eddy Lee, Salem Sethuraman, Hamid Tabatabai and René Wéry.

I am also grateful to Dr Sudharshan Canagarajah and Dr Ricardo Chica, both of the University of Cambridge (England), and Mrs Parul Subramanian for providing excellent research assistance in data processing and help in the preparation of the manuscript. The typing of the manuscript was handled by Mrs J. Robb and Mrs D. Rowe. I gratefully acknowledge their assistance.

Finally, I wish to express my thanks to the UNFPA for its support of this work.

Needless to say, the views and opinions expressed in this volume reflect those of the author and not necessarily those of the ILO or the UNFPA.

A. S. OBERAI

1 Introduction

Rapid urbanisation, and particularly the growth of large cities, and the associated problems of urban slums, environmental degradation, inadequate health services, unemployment and poverty have emerged as major socio-economic issues with potentially important political implications in many developing countries. By the year 2000, more than 45 per cent of the 5.1 billion population of developing countries will be living in urban areas, and more than 50 Third-World cities are expected to have a population of over four million (United Nations, 1991). Most population distribution policies designed to moderate the rate of rural–urban migration appear to have had limited success so far.[1] But even if such policies do succeed in future, large cities are likely to grow larger because of the high rate of natural population increase in urban areas. In 1980, of the 20 largest cities in the world, 12 were in the less developed regions. By the year 2000, their number will have increased to 17, and of the seven large cities with a population of 15 million or more, five will be in developing countries. (United Nations, 1991)

The implications of these demographic trends for employment creation, the provision of food and housing, social services and the protection of the urban environment are staggering. In many Third-World cities, nearly half of the population is living in slum and squatter settlements (Table 1.1). More than one-quarter of the inhabitants in most large cities are estimated to be living in absolute poverty. Some sections of city populations, such as recent migrants and women, are particularly underprivileged in terms of job access and incomes. Public investment often misses the urban poor, with expenditures biased towards the higher-income groups. Inadequate attention is paid to the water, sanitation, hygiene, nutrition, maternal and child health care, family planning and health needs of the poor, with new roads, hospitals and other infrastructure tending to bypass the slums. The lack of these services leads to higher fertility accompanied by high levels of infant mortality amongst the urban poor, particularly amongst slum dwellers.

Yet, despite these enormous problems, it would be wrong to regard urbanisation in the Third-World in entirely negative terms. Urban

Table 1.1   Proportion of population living in slums and informal settlements in selected cities (%)

City	%	City	%
Addis Ababa (1980)	85	Manila (1980)	40
Bombay (1988)	57	Mexico City (1980)	40
Cairo* (1984)	84	Nairobi (1986)	34
Calcutta (1980)	40	Rio de Janeiro (1980)	34
Dar es Salaam (1980)	60	São Paulo (1980)	32
Delhi (1981)	50	Seoul (1988)	12
Lagos (1981)	58		

* Informal housing (without licence).
Sources: ILO mega-city survey (1990); United Nations Center for Human Settlements (HABITAT), 1987, table 5.18; and several country reports.

areas, particularly the large cities, often make a disproportionate contribution to gross domestic product (GDP) because they enjoy economies of scale and consequently have higher incomes and productivity per capita than the rest of the nation. In Mexico in 1980, for example, 20.8 per cent of the nation's population lived in Mexico City, but it generated 34.3 per cent of Mexico's GDP (Table 1.2). Rio de Janeiro accounted for 4.1 per cent of Brazil's population in 1987 and 10.6 per cent of the nation's GDP. Shanghai alone contributed 4.8 per cent to China's GDP in 1988 even though only a little over 1 per cent of the Chinese population lived there.

Table 1.2   Cities' share in national population and GDP

City	Percentage of national	
	Population	GDP
Bombay (1985)	1.2	3.4
Cairo (1986)	12.5	17.8
Lagos (1981)	2.9	3.4
Mexico City (1980)	20.8	34.3
Rio de Janeiro (1987)	4.1	10.6
Seoul (1988)	24.6	26.5
Shanghai (1987)	1.2	4.8

Source: ILO mega-city survey (1990).

Notwithstanding the relatively high productivity levels in urban areas, urban poverty is a pervasive phenomenon in most Third-World mega-cities, as already noted. The manifestations of this poverty are low and insecure incomes from unprotected employment, poor health, and limited access to social services. An increasing number of the urban poor in mega-cities are unable to pay for social services, which constrains the ability of municipal governments to invest in infrastructure development. Lack of adequate infrastructure (electricity, telecommunications, water supply, urban transportation, etc.) creates bottlenecks for economic expansion. A recent study shows that 10–35 per cent of initial capital investments in new manufacturing plants in Nigeria is made solely to compensate for the inadequate supply of power and water in cities (World Bank, 1991). Longer travel time from home to workplace, costly transportation of goods, uncertain delivery of inputs, lower productivity, higher production costs, the lack of basic welfare, education, child-care and health services, and environmental decay, in addition to water and power shortages, are among the factors limiting economic efficiency and human resource development.

During the economic crisis of the 1980s, urban economies in developing countries suffered more than rural economies. The downturn in the world economy, with its catastrophic falls in commodity prices, rises in interest rates, reduced demand for developing country products and reduced capital flows, led to a large number of developing countries becoming severely constrained by balance of payments problems. As a result, a majority of countries, particularly in Africa and Latin America, sought rescheduling of their debts and accepted IMF conditions. This often involved measures (large devaluations, cuts in public expenditure, etc.) which had a more negative impact on poverty, employment and social services in urban than in rural areas. In sub-Saharan Africa, for example, where 'urban bias' had been conspicuous during the 1960s and 1970s, recent stabilisation and adjustment efforts may have contributed in correcting policy imbalances, but the impact on urban incomes has often been dramatic. In Tanzania, farm incomes rose by 5 per cent between 1980 and 1984 while urban wages declined by 50 per cent; in Ghana, farm incomes stagnated but urban incomes fell by 40 per cent during the same period; in Côte d'Ivoire, the ratio of urban to rural incomes fell from 3.5 in 1980 to about 2.0 in 1985 (World Bank, 1991).

The gigantic problems faced by large cities in the Third-World have thus been heightened by the economic crisis of the 1980s. Blair (1984) sums up the central issues very well when he says that the dynamic city of developmental dreams is a Problem City in search of solutions to a range of critical and interrelated factors:

1. unbalanced population, spatial and economic growth;
2. large-scale deprivation and unmet land, housing, employment and transportation needs;
3. deteriorating environments and inadequate basic services;
4. shortages of public fiscal resources and qualified manpower for effective plan implementation and management;
5. uncoordinated national and municipal urban policies and inadequate organisational structures;
6. costly imported finance and inappropriate planning ideas and technology;
7. an absence of meaningful public participation in the planning and development process.

The manner in which these problems have been dealt with by city administrations and national governments in Third-World countries and the prospects for the future were the focus of the policy research programme initiated by the ILO at the beginning of 1988 with financial support from the UNFPA. As part of this programme, as already mentioned, detailed background studies of eight large cities, focusing on the problems faced by individual cities and the cities' experiences in dealing with them, were initiated in collaboration with government planning agencies and established national research institutions.[2] Some core city- and national-level data were also collected through a questionnaire specifically designed to attempt a comparative analysis of the problems associated with rapid urban growth (hereafter called the ILO mega-city survey, 1990). The major objective of the ILO studies was to assess the scale and severity of the problems of urban population growth, unemployment, poverty, and the deterioration of urban services and to help develop a comprehensive policy response. Within this framework, the city case-studies concentrated mainly on the following policy concerns:

1. the urban or anti-urban bias of national economic and social policies and ways of reducing this bias;
2. trends in the age–sex structure of the population in large cities and their consequences for the provision of employment and social services;

3. problems of labour market structure and the access of marginal groups to employment opportunities;
4. the nature and extent of urban poverty and the scope for alleviating it through public expenditure and infrastructure investment directed towards meeting the basic needs of the urban poor;
5. access of the urban poor to social services and the pricing of public services;
6. the position of women in the labour market and the factors which perpetuate the exploitation of working, particularly migrant, women in the city;
7. attitudes towards family size and family planning among poor urban women, their knowledge and access to family planning services and education, and the effects of these on fertility;
8. the existing administrative arrangements for dealing with employment and social service provision and the reforms that are required for integrated population and socio-economic planning at the city level;
9. the problems of resource mobilisation to finance urban programmes.

This volume provides a comparative analysis of mega-city problems and experiences based on data gathered as part of city case-studies initiated by the ILO, and discusses the policy experiences of several other cities in developing countries. It also provides a conceptual and analytical framework for the analysis of urban policy issues, examines the success or failure of past and current policies implemented to deal with urban problems, and suggests the direction in which future policies need to be developed to deal more effectively with these problems. Whenever relevant, the study draws upon the experience of individual cities with appropriate reference to the city case study reports.

The study is divided into eight chapters. The rest of this introductory chapter is devoted to presenting a profile of mega-cities and discussing the nature and magnitude of the current problems facing them.

Chapter 2 discusses the structural features of urbanisation in relation to economic development. It also examines the major sources of urban growth and spatial concentration, analyses the conflict between economic efficiency and decentralisation, and discusses the extent to which decentralisation policies have been successful in mega-cities.

Chapter 3 assesses the implications of rapid urban growth for employment generation and poverty alleviation. In particular, it examines the effects of labour force growth on labour market structure and assesses the extent to which distortions in the functioning of labour markets contribute to unemployment and low productivity.

Chapter 4 attempts to identify institutional and other constraints on increasing employment and assesses the role of labour market interventions and anti-poverty programmes in employment promotion and poverty alleviation.

Chapter 5 discusses the relationship between urban poverty and access to housing and basic social services. It also deals with local expenditure patterns and their effect on the availability of urban infrastructure and social services.

Chapter 6 examines the way in which family size and structure affect and are affected by urban poverty. In particular, it considers how low incomes and higher dependency ratios lead to poor education, health and family planning, which in turn act upon and reinforce each other, thereby perpetuating low productivity and poverty.

Chapter 7 examines problems of resource mobilisation to finance urban programmes and finally, Chapter 8 brings together the major findings of the study and highlights their policy implications.

CITY PROFILES

Table 1.3 provides data on basic demographic, social and economic indicators for both the cities and the countries in which they are located. The data show that the rate of population growth in Third-World mega-cities, except for Cairo and Shanghai, is higher than the national population growth rate. In Nigeria, for example, during the 1980s the population growth rate of Lagos was 6.4 per cent per annum while the national rate was only 3.3 per cent. Similarly, despite the fall in the rate of population growth in Mexico City from the 1970s to the 1980s, the rate of growth there continues to be high (3.0 per cent) and exceeds that of the country as a whole (2.4 per cent).

The differences in the population growth rates of the mega-cities and the corresponding countries have occurred despite fertility rates being consistently higher at the national level than at the level of the mega-city. This clearly points to migration as a significant determinant of population growth in the mega-cities.

Cairo's low population growth rate in the 1980s relative to that of Egypt as a whole is due to the fact that the city-level data relate only to the Governorate of Cairo and not to the metropolitan region where population growth, particularly through migration, has concentrated in more recent years. In China, Shanghai has a relatively low population growth rate compared with the national average, largely because of the more effective implementation of the one-child policy and a strict control on migration from rural and other urban areas.

The high degree of urbanisation in Latin America (around 70 per cent), like that in the Republic of Korea, contrasts with the particularly low degree of urbanisation in India (26.0 per cent) and Nigeria (20.3 per cent). It is also interesting to note that in Mexico, more than one-fifth of the country's population is concentrated in Mexico City. This pattern of concentration is also found in many parts of Asia: more than one-quarter of the population of the Republic of Korea is concentrated in Seoul.

The different indicators of the quality of life (proportion of population in slum areas, etc.) reveal harsh living conditions in Bombay, Lagos and Cairo. In addition, infant mortality figures point to particularly severe living conditions and poverty in Bombay and Cairo, even though, on both these counts, conditions in the cities are better than those in the corresponding countries. The relative sex composition of the population in the city vis-à-vis the country in the Bombay-India case (where the proportion of males to females is higher in the city than in the country) contrasts with that of Mexico (where the proportion of males to females is lower in the city than in the country). This contrast reveals the differences in the patterns of migration observed in South Asia and Latin America, with relatively more males migrating in the former than in the latter region.

The Asian mega-cities have achieved a relatively high degree of industrialisation and that of Bombay is typically higher than that of India as a whole. In the case of Seoul, however, it is lower in the city than in the country as a whole. This is largely due to the successful implementation of industrial decentralisation policies in Seoul. The effect of the economic crisis of the 1980s on manufacturing, particularly in Latin America, has been to drive an increasing proportion of the labour force into the buffer provided by the services sector. This is reflected in the relative dynamism of employment in the services sector compared with the shrinking labour force in the manufacturing sector in both Rio and Mexico City.

In economic terms, big contrasts in GDP per capita can be observed among the mega-cities, with that of Bombay being less than US$500 and that of Seoul almost US$5000. The impact of the 1980s economic crisis on African and Latin American cities is indicated by the sharp

Table 1.3 City and country profiles: demographic and socio-economic indicators, 1988 (or recent estimate)

Indicators	Bombay	India	Cairo[a]	Egypt	Lagos	Nigeria	Mexico City	Mexico	Rio de Janeiro	Brazil	Seoul	Rep. of Korea	Shanghai	China
Total population (millions)	-9.9	853.1	6.0	47.9	4.1	104.9	116.8	78.4	10.9	144.4	10.3	41.9	12.6	1096.1
Males (%)	55.7	51.6	51.1	51.1	56.7	50.5	48.8	50.1	48.1	49.9	49.9	50.4	50.4	51.5
Females (%)	44.3	48.4	48.9	48.9	43.3	49.5	51.2	49.9	51.9	50.1	50.1	49.6	49.6	48.5
Sex ratio (males per 100 females)	126.0	107.0	104.7	104.4	131.2	102.0	95.2	100.3	92.5	99.6	99.8	101.6	101.5	106.3
Rate of growth of population (% p.a.)														
1970–80	3.2	2.2	2.6	2.2	7.7	2.8	4.5	2.9	2.4	2.5	4.1	1.7	0.9	1.6
1980–8	2.6	2.1	1.7	2.7	6.4	3.3	3.0	2.4	2.5	2.4	2.6	1.4	1.2	1.3
Percentage urban population	–	26.0	–	43.7	–	20.3	–	70.4	–	73.8	–	69.9	–	49.6
Density of Population (persons/sq. m.)														
City proper	16436	241	28258	917	–	122	6715	40	4775	17	–	423	19514	114
Metropolitan area							4270		1670		16990		1991	
Percentage slum population	56.7	–	84.0	–	72.4	–	25.2	–	34.2	–	12.1	–	–	–
Dependency ratio (0–14)+(60+)/(15–59)	55.6	85.4	68.6	85.2	74.5	86.2	66.7	89.8	60.3	75.0	44.9	52.7	45.8	59.5
Crude birth rate	22.2	32.7	29.5	38.0	–	46.6	24.4	30.2	15.0	28.6	–	16.5	13.2	20.8
Crude death rate	7.6	11.7	8.4	9.4	–	15.0	5.6	6.3	8.0	7.9	–	5.9	6.8	6.6
Total fertility rate	3.1	4.5	3.8	4.8	–	6.5	3.0	3.2	2.1	3.5	1.5	1.6	–	2.4
Infant mortality rate	61.0	97.0	52.0	88.0	–	105.0	36.0	47.0	36.0	63.0	–	13.0	14.0	32.0
Life expectancy														
Males	63.8	56.1	60.0	59.0	–	49.3	70.1	65.9	64.3	62.3	–	67.1	72.5	67.2
Females	65.7	56.9	64.0	63.0	–	52.9	75.1	72.5	71.8	67.6	–	73.6	76.8	72.9
Total	64.8	56.5	62.0	61.0	–	51.1	72.6	69.1	68.0	64.8	–	70.2	74.7	70.1
GDP per capita (US$)	432.2	168.1	1064.5	770.1	1635.3	241.5	2281.2	1636.3	2911.0	2146.0	4804.9	4457.0	1163.2	277.2
GDP per capita real growth rate (% p.a.)														
1970–80	0.9	1.3	1.3	2.4	-0.7	3.1	2.5	3.1	4.7	5.5	4.7	7.1	4.9	0.3
1980–8	-0.9	2.0	5.0	4.8	-4.5	1.8	-5.2	-1.1	-3.5	0.1	7.2	7.8	2.8	8.4
Degree of Industrialisation[2]	8.5	4.3	4.1	2.5	–	–	4.6	–	4.8	–	5.4	12.9	15.3	–
Rate of growth of unemployment [(in services)–(in manufacturing)] in 1980s	0.1	–	0.9	–	–	–	4.4	–	6.0	–	1.02	–	2.85	–
Per capita revenue in US$ (1988 prices)	91.2	–	87.7	–	68.7	–	303.8[3]	–	95.1	–	475.2	–	344.2	–

Literacy rate															
Males	73.9	46.9	77.3	62.2	79.1	65.6	—	—	88.4	75.1	—	—	—	—	82.0
Females	60.8	24.8	60.6	38.2	43.2	38.5	—	—	85.6	75.8	—	—	—	—	56.0
Total	68.2	36.2	69.2	50.6	60.9	52.0	97.7	97.0	86.9	75.5	—	94.7	—	—	69.0
Access to services[4]	93.1	—	92.1	—	58.9	—	89.2	—	81.3	—	96.1	—	—	82.0[5]	—
Hospital beds per 1000 population	3.7	0.9	3.9	2.0	—	—	1.6[6]	1.3[6]	7.1	3.9	10.0	2.8	—	5.4	—
Passenger cars (per 1,000 Population)	23.7	—	62.8	19.2	35.1	2.1	145.0	62.5	185.3	71.4	47.9	—	—	0.2	—

Notes: [1] Data relate to the Governorate of Cairo.
[2] [Share of manufacturing in GDP] × [Share of machinery and transport equipment in manufacturing value added].
[3] Refers to the Federal District only.
[4] [Percentage of households having access to water supply] × [Percentage of households having access to electricity].
[5] Percentage of households having access to water supply.
[6] 1980.

Source: ILO mega-city survey (1990).

decline in the rate of growth of GDP per capita observed for Lagos, Mexico City and Rio (-4.5, -5.2 and -3.5 per cent per annum, respectively), which contrasts with the increasingly high growth rate achieved by Seoul (7.2 per cent). It is interesting to observe that the economic crisis has had a far more severe impact on African and Latin American cities than on the countries as a whole, showing the former's vulnerability (contrast the GDP growth rate of -4.5 for Lagos with Nigeria's 1.8 per cent, Mexico City's -5.2 with Mexico's -1.1 per cent, and Rio's -3.5 with Brazil's 0.1 per cent). On the fiscal side, budgetary problems appear to be particularly acute in the African mega-cities (Lagos and Cairo).

PROBLEMS FACING THIRD-WORLD MEGA-CITIES

The major problems facing most Third-World mega-cities can be grouped into five categories:

1. rapid growth in the urban population;
2. unemployment and underemployment;
3. poverty and limited access to social services;
4. environmental degradation;
5. fiscal constraints.

Rapid growth in the urban population

As already mentioned, most Third-World mega-cities are growing rapidly both through migration and through natural population increase. Mexico City, already the world's largest city, adds over 500 000 migrants to its numbers annually, and is expected to reach more than 25 million by the year 2000 (United Nations, 1990b). In Brazil 35 years ago, 75 per cent of the population was rural; today about the same proportion is urban (urban areas being defined in Brazil as population centres of over 2000). Shanghai's growth rate of 1.2 per cent per annum during the 1980s was higher than in the 1970s. Nairobi is growing at more than 10 per cent per annum and Cairo's population is expected to swell by another 7 million by the end of the century (United Nations, 1990a).

High birth rates and declining mortality rates due to better health facilities in the cities contribute increasingly to the natural increase in population. The declining mortality rates are also leading to an ageing of the population in mega-cities. This has negative consequences for labour productivity, increases the dependency burden, and puts a strain on the social security system.

Governments everywhere are attempting to check urban growth by relocating public investment to attract labour away from large cities to smaller cities and new towns. As will be discussed in Chapter 2, Cairo proposes to construct a ring road around the main city with ten satellite towns to absorb 2.5 million people. Mexico is developing 168 national city systems and strengthening local and regional centres through changes in the constitution. China hopes to have 60 per cent of its urban population in 10 000 small towns by the year 2000. In Bombay, with its population of about 10 million, a twin city is being built on the opposite side of the harbour to house two million people.

To draw industry away from the economies of scale and the agglomeration benefits of cities, including infrastructure and services, they need to be provided with comparable facilities, otherwise relocation regulations impose an enormous burden on these enterprises, reducing both their productivity and their demand for labour (as has been the case in most countries). Relocation is itself a prohibitively expensive exercise. In Mexico, despite a strong commitment in principle, only a small number of industries have been successfully moved out in the five years between 1983 and 1988. Bombay provides incentives for heavy industrial units to move out and does not permit new ones into the city. In the Republic of Korea, much of the industrial growth and migration of the early 1970s was directed to areas outside Seoul but still close enough for the industries to take advantage of support services, supplies and markets in the capital. As a result, the annual rate of growth of Seoul's population dropped considerably while smaller cities around Seoul grew rapidly (see Chapter 2). Egyptian attempts to create new towns have had some success in attracting industry, but they have drained away huge resources without attracting enough people due to the lack of social infrastructure available in such towns.

Unemployment and underemployment

Most Third-World mega-cities are facing severe problems of unemployment and underemployment. During the economic crisis of the 1980s, there was also rapid growth in the urban informal sector, particularly in the Latin American cities (see Chapter 3). Seoul's unemployment rate is higher than that of the rest of the country. In

Nairobi, open unemployment, according to the urban labour force survey conducted in 1986 (quoted in Jamal, 1990), is almost 20 per cent. In Mexico City there has been virtually no real growth in GDP since 1981, and real wages are in fact at the level prevailing in the 1960s. Open unemployment is about 4–5 per cent, but underemployment and the informal sector are growing, with declining real wages. In Brazil's major cities in 1988, more than 35 per cent of the labour force was underemployed with more than 60 per cent engaged in the informal sector. In greater Cairo, home to almost half of Egypt's manufacturing workers, unemployment is estimated at about 10 per cent, although as many as one in three may be underemployed. Current policy calls for a moratorium on industrial investment in Cairo; if strictly enforced, it raises the spectre of rising rates of open unemployment, worsening the already extreme poverty. In Bombay, the industrial decentralisation policy and increasing capital intensity in the manufacturing sector have led to reduced demand for labour and growing urban unemployment.

Poverty and limited access to social services

At the root of the problem of urban poverty lies the inability of the poor to increase their earnings through gainful employment. Population growth worsens poverty conditions in the urban areas as labour absorption is unable to keep pace with the labour supply pressure created by migration and natural population growth. Poor labour absorption and low levels of productivity and earnings in the cities are the consequence of demand and supply mechanisms in urban labour markets, which are often segmented into a formal and an informal sector. As discussed in Chapter 3, the demand for labour in the formal sector is constrained by the demand for output and the capital intensity of modern methods of production. During the recent economic crisis, the excess supply of labour in most Third-World cities led to increased open unemployment and/or expansion of the low-productivity informal sector, as noted above. Lower real wages in the formal sector, combined with declining incomes in the informal sector, have contributed to increased urban poverty. At the city level, budgetary constraints and structural adjustment programmes have forced authorities to cut down social service expenditures. Insofar as labour productivity, and hence wages, depend on the quality of health and nutrition of the workforce – an insight underlying the efficiency wage hypothesis – poverty and a lack of access to social services lead to greater poverty. The vicious cycle linking poor health and education with low productivity and earnings is thus reinforced.

As the economic crisis has forced a cut in subsidies, the real incomes of the lower-middle and poor income groups, who were the major beneficiaries of such subsidies, have declined. Evidence of this slide into poverty is to be found in Rio, where one notices some of the slums located on small hills in the city having a face-lift. Initially mystifying, particularly during a period of economic difficulties, the reason is to be found in the fact that the lower-middle income groups are moving in here, no longer able to afford their earlier rents. Drug traffickers, too, are buying land here because of the ease with which they can operate in such areas. The poor slum dwellers are thus being pushed out to the peripheries of the city, where municipalities have even fewer financial resources to cater for their needs (see Chapter 5).

Poor living conditions are made worse by high population densities. Bombay concentrates nearly 10 million people in a narrow land mass of 603 square kilometres, which means that each square kilometre contains over 16 000 people. Seven out of every ten families live in one room (see Chapter 5). Rocinha in Rio de Janeiro is the largest of the city's 300 slums, crowding 200 000 people in an area of six square kilometres. The density of population in the Mathare and Pumwani slums in Nairobi is as high as 70 000 per square kilometre.

As already mentioned, in most developing countries slum and squatter communities house from one-third to more than half of the city's population, while the formal housing sector rarely provides more than 20 per cent of new housing stock. In Cairo, between 250 000 and one million people rent above-ground burial vaults among the ancient cemeteries of the City of the Dead (United Nations, 1990a). The Cairo housing market shows a curious mismatch between demand and supply. Excess demand coexists with 250 000 housing units built since 1980 lying unoccupied, according to the latest 1986 census results. Many Egyptian migrants to the Gulf countries have built their houses in recent years and simply locked them up, fearing that land will not be available on their return to Cairo. Although the census results are disputed by many officials, the effective withdrawal of supply of houses for rent by private owners is largely due to a rent freeze and tenancy laws which make owners reluctant to risk renting their houses. Inappropriate land tenure systems thus often discourage private investment and hinder effective land use in most urban centres. India's Urban Land Ceiling Act of 1976, for example, illustrates how a government can sometimes unwittingly exacerbate the very problem it seeks to tackle. The Act expropriated vacant urban land for low-income settlement and in effect took some thousand square kilometres of vacant land off the market in 73 Indian cities. Partly as a result, land prices have risen by up to 100 per cent per annum in cities such as Bombay and Madras (World Bank, 1991).

Many health problems in mega-cities are linked to water – its quality, the quantity available, the ease with which it can be obtained, and the provisions made for its removal, once used (Cairncross, 1990). Approximately one-quarter of the urban population in most Third-World cities has no access to clean, piped water. In the case of Mexico City, over-exploitation of underground water reserves has irreversibly damaged the natural hydraulic system of the valley and caused the city to sink – by as much as nine metres in some areas (Schteingart, 1989). Maintaining water supplies now involves pumping water up more than 1000 metres, which has raised the cost of supplying water.

The glaring poverty in slums is accompanied by a high rate of crime. In India, the crime rate for cities is 2.5 times the national average. Rio is losing vast sums in tourism because of its soaring crime figures. In the Rocinha slum, drug trafficking is flourishing. The local drug lords provide help for emergencies, weddings and burials, partially fulfilling the role of the public sector, which is unable to provide such aid on a systematic basis. Such assistance ensures the people's support and protection against police action.

Rocinha's educational facilities are typical of poor urban areas. It has two elementary schools for approximately 15 000 children, catering thereby for just 5 per cent of the school-age population. Drop-out and failure rates are always high in such areas. Although urban facilities are certainly superior to those in rural areas, their lopsided distribution within cities does not necessarily leave the urban poor any better off than their rural counterparts, as will be discussed in Chapter 5.

Environmental degradation

High population densities and inadequate living conditions (poor housing, lack of waste disposal facilities, etc.) contribute to environmental problems, which in turn lead to a further deterioration in living standards. An estimated 30–50 per cent of solid wastes generated within urban centres remain uncollected (Cointreau, 1982). In 1987, less than 60 per cent of the world's urban population had access to adequate sanitation, and only one-third were connected to sewer systems (World Bank, 1991). These sewer systems typically serve the richer residential, government and commercial areas. The difficulties of providing satisfactory services for the poor are made more acute by the fact that they often live in far-flung areas or on inhospitable terrain. They often build on polluted sites beside open drains or sewers, or in industrial areas, or close to major highways or airports where rents are low, where they do not have to travel to work, or where the land has too little commercial value to make it likely that they will be evicted. In Manila, some 20,000 people live around a garbage dump known as Smokey Mountain, where the decomposition of organic wastes produces a permanent haze, and a powerful, rank smell pervades the whole area. Some of these people have lived there for 40 years or more, making a living scavenging on the dump (Hardoy and Satterthwaite, 1991).

In the Federal District of Mexico City in 1980, over two million people (25 per cent of the population) had no sewerage. With only two garbage deposits and one processing plant, the city is unable to deal with more than one-quarter of the 10 500 tons of garbage produced daily (Cointreau, 1982). Large piles of decomposing solid waste accumulate on urban backstreets and near clandestine taps, contributing to the presence of pathogenic micro-organisms in the human environment.

Industry in most Third-World countries is concentrated in a few locations, particularly in large cities, leading to serious problems with toxic waste and water and air pollution. Most toxic wastes are either disposed of untreated into rivers and streams or placed unprotected on land sites. Treatment plants, where they exist and when they are used, are often overwhelmed by the quantities of waste.

Inadequate garbage collection facilities also lead to much uncollected waste being washed into lakes and rivers. In India, the wastes of 114 cities go into the river Ganges alone, as well as those of a host of petrochemical, fertiliser and rubber industries. Shanghai alone produces 500 000 tons of industrial and domestic sewage every day, most of which is discharged untreated into the Huangpu river (Yeung, 1988). Water sources thus become contaminated, with rivers often becoming a chemical cocktail of industrial effluent, sewage, and urban and agricultural run-off (Lee, 1985).

In Mexico City, on more than 125 days in 1991, the air-quality index rose above 200, which is considered dangerous to health. During October 1991, the index hit 340, a record that forced the Urban

Development and Ecology Ministry to put into practice an emergency plan that cut industrial activity by half (*Financial Times*, 30 October 1991). If the index rises any higher, all of the city's 35 000 factories will be expected to close down.

Seoul's largest air pollution component, as with many other Third-World mega-cities, is sulphur dioxide. This contributes to the corrosion of suspended electric cables, which can lead to disruption and damage to the electrical railway system. But in Seoul the main cause of environmental degradation is the high concentration of population, and not industry. More than 90 per cent of all air pollutants come from residential and commercial buildings and motor vehicles (Kim *et al.*, 1991). Vehicles cause 30 per cent of the air pollution, but coal heating is the worst offender. Traffic itself is clogged and snarled: in 1988 the average speed was 13.5 kilometres per hour. The cost of delays and accidents in the same year amounted to US$1.25 billion. Cairo's provision of road space per person is one of the lowest in the world and leads to an accident rate which ranks among the highest – 80 fatalities and 600 injuries per 10 000 vehicles annually (United Nations, 1990a).

Motor vehicles cause over 75 per cent of the pollution in Mexico City. Only 10–40 per cent of sunlight filters through the suspended pollutants. The city authorities predict that by the year 2010, headlights will be needed during the day due to reduced visibility. Mexico City's annual vehicle growth rate in the 36 years between 1950 and 1986 averaged 11 per cent, more than double that of the metropolitan population. There are now roughly 2.6 million vehicles in circulation. The number of private cars rose most steeply, increasing 61 times. The number of buses went up only 2.8 times, despite the urgent need for more efficient and far-reaching public transport. This pattern of relatively slow growth in public transport compared with private transport is typical of most Third-World cities.

There are also environmental problems associated with the workplace. Among the more hazardous are dangerous concentrations of toxic chemicals and dust, inadequate lighting, ventilation and space, and inadequate protection of workers from machinery and noise. Environmental problems also arise from work in the home. A significant proportion of people in Third-World mega-cities, particularly in the informal sector, use their homes for the making, storing and selling of goods (see Chapter 5). Many formal sector (and often large) enterprises subcontract work to people (usually women) who work in their homes. Environmental problems for these home workers arise from the use of toxic or flammable chemicals which should be handled in carefully controlled conditions, in factories with special provisions to limit inhalation or skin contact and to guard against fire hazards. The advantages to the large enterprises of using home workers are obvious: low wages, no infrastructure costs, no social security costs and few problems with labour unrest, since the workforce is too scattered to allow them to be organised (Hardoy and Satterthwaite, 1991).

Fiscal constraints

Although GDP per capita is higher in most Third-World mega-cities than the national average, as noted above, this does not guarantee sufficient revenues to meet recurrent expenditures, let alone leave enough for capital investment and infrastructural development. Seoul is an exception in having a relatively sound financial base, with nearly half the revenue being raised by user charges (see Chapter 6). In Bombay, a significant source of municipal revenue is property tax, but although property values have been appreciating dramatically for some time, there has been no property revaluation for several years.

In Cairo, sanitary tax (for garbage collection) accounts for only 2 per cent of rental value. As rents have been controlled in nominal terms since 1963, there has been no significant increase in revenue although the per unit cost of garbage collection has increased several times. Water rates have risen slightly in recent years but not enough to cover the costs of providing water. This severely constrains the municipal authorities in their attempts to expand urban services.

Insufficient local resources often result in an over-reliance on central government transfers or large operating deficits with serious macro-economic consequences. A recent review of government finances for the period 1978–86 in 19 developing countries shows that provincial and municipal governments' deficits account for an average of 50 per cent of the consolidated government deficit, and thus a significant proportion of GDP (World Bank, 1991). The recent economic crisis has worsened the situation, especially in Latin America, where previously well-established municipal institutions have withered in the absence of central government transfers. Seoul, although not immune to these problems, does overcome them to a degree because of its special city status, which enables the mayor to report directly to the prime minister rather than to the minister of home Affairs or provincial governor. This undoubtedly facilitates central–local financial relations and helps maintain the city's stable and buoyant local financial base. This autonomy contrasts with that of Cairo, where even expenditures on basic social services are controlled by central government ministries.

The above-noted problems facing Third-World mega-cities cannot be attributed solely to rapid urban population growth. The slow pace of economic growth, government regulations (zoning and rent control laws, minimum wage legislation and so on) and macroeconomic policies (relating to industrial location, credit allocation, interest rates, public expenditure, etc.) also contribute to many of these problems. Since most of the problems afflicting Third-World mega-cities are similar in nature, city authorities and policy-makers can learn much from a sharing of their accumulated experience. The comparative analysis of the problems and policy experiences of mega-cities attempted in this volume is therefore designed to indicate the range of policy instruments available to deal with a specific problem, and the conditions under which these may or may not succeed. This, it is hoped, can help urban planners to avoid certain common mistakes and formulate more appropriate and cost-effective policies. It should be borne in mind, however, that the developed country model is unlikely to provide much help in this context since there are structural differences between large cities in the Third-World and those in the advanced countries (see Appendix 1, Table A1.1).

The essential difference between the two groups of cities lies in the fact that the Third-World cities are subject to what may be called 'expanding urbanisation' whilst those in the industrial countries are experiencing 'mature urbanisation'.[3] In the latter case, the large cities are often losing population to smaller cities rather than increasing in size. One important reason for this is that, unlike those in developing countries, the smaller cities in advanced countries already possess the necessary infrastructure for modern business activity. Thus, when the diseconomies due to congestion, higher rents or transportation inconveniences become too great in the big cities, there is a movement of people or businesses to smaller cities or suburbs. Thus, in mature urbanisation, city-to-city migration is the main factor affecting the system of cities. The determinants of city-to-city migration are rather different from those of rural–urban migration experienced by the Third-World cities.

Because of these differences, a policy framework which is appropriate for Paris or London is likely to prove only of limited help in coping with the problems of Bombay or Lagos. An analysis of the problems of Third-World mega-cities, the cities' responses to them, and the changes required in existing policies and programmes in order to deal with them more effectively, form the focus of the discussion in the subsequent chapters.

2 Urbanisation and Spatial Concentration

The role of rural–urban migration and spatial concentration in economic development depends on the nature and volume of migration, the level of urbanisation and the state of development of a country. This chapter examines the major trends in urbanisation in different regions and the relationship between urbanisation and economic development. It then examines the factors which contribute to urban growth and spatial concentration, structural differences between urbanisation in the Third World and in advanced countries, the conflict between decentralisation and economic efficiency, and the experience of national and city authorities in reducing urban growth, particularly in large cities in developing countries.

URBANISATION IN THE THIRD WORLD AND THE GROWTH OF LARGE CITIES[1]

The developing countries are rapidly becoming urbanised. As early as 1970, nearly one-quarter of the Third-World's population lived in urban areas (Table 2.1). Fifteen years later, this proportion had increased to nearly one-third. According to the latest UN projections, by the year 2000 urban dwellers will constitute more than 45 per

Table 2.1   Proportion of population living in urban areas, 1970–2025 (%)

Year	World	More developed regions	Less developed regions
1970	36.6	66.6	24.7
1980	39.5	70.3	28.9
1985	42.2	71.6	32.8
2000	51.1	74.9	45.1
2015	59.3	79.6	55.0
2025	64.6	82.5	61.2

Source: Adapted from United Nations, 1991, tables A.1 and A.2.

cent of the population of developing countries, and by 2025, over 60 per cent of the Third-World's population will be living in urban areas.[2]

Within the less developed regions there are notable differences in the levels of urbanisation. In the developing countries of Asia and Africa, about 34 per cent of the inhabitants lived in urban areas in 1990. Latin America, on the other hand, is nearly 72 per cent urban, reflecting that region's stage of development and the peculiarities of its urban structure and history. The Latin American countries had reached the current Asian and African levels of urbanisation as early as 1930, when 30 per cent of their 100 million inhabitants lived in towns. Fifty years later, the level of urbanisation had increased to two-thirds, with a population of 400 million. By the year 2000, the level of urbanisation in Latin American countries is expected to be similar to that of the advanced industrial nations.

Table 2.2 provides data on the rates of growth of the urban population in different regions. It shows that although the currently high level of urban population growth in developing countries is expected to decline over the next 40 years, Third-World cities will still be growing at an annual rate of 2.2 per cent by the year 2025. Urban population growth will be particularly fast in African countries as these countries have a much lower initial level of urbanisation and are also subject to high natural rates of population growth.

An outstanding feature of urbanisation in Third-World countries is the increasing concentration of urban population in the few large metropolitan cities. Recent data from the UN indicate that between 1970 and 1980, the proportion of developing countries' urban population

Table 2.2   Average annual rates of urban population growth in major regions, 1985–2025 (%)

Major area	1985–90	1995–2000	2020–25
World total	3.1	2.8	1.8
Less developed	4.5	3.7	2.2
More developed	0.8	0.8	0.5
Africa	5.0	4.7	3.1
Latin America	2.9	2.4	1.4
East Asia	5.0	3.5	1.2
South Asia	4.0	4.0	2.6

Source: Derived from United Nations, 1991, table A.5.

living in large cities (with a population of more than four million) rose from 13.2 per cent to 17.3 per cent; it is expected to increase further to 23.2 per cent by the year 2000. By contrast, the proportion of urban population in large cities in developed countries has been either stationary or falling. By 2025, about 28 per cent of the urban population in the developing regions will be living in cities of over four million, more than double the figure for the developed regions. In Africa, only a small proportion of the population currently lives in large cities, but by the year 2025 the figure could be the highest among the world regions (Table 2.3).

Table 2.3   Proportion of urban population living in large cities (four million or more), 1970-2025 (%)

Region	1970	1980	1990	2000	2025
World total	13.7	15.8	17.7	19.9	24.6
More developed regions	14.2	14.1	14.0	13.4	12.8
Less developed regions	13.2	17.3	20.2	23.2	28.2
Africa	6.6	5.3	9.0	19.8	33.9
Americas	20.8	20.8	23.6	24.0	26.6
Latin America	20.3	21.9	27.3	28.1	29.7
Northern America	21.2	19.4	17.8	16.5	19.6
Asia	14.6	19.5	21.1	22.7	25.1
East Asia	21.1	20.1	20.4	19.1	19.4
South Asia	7.4	18.9	21.6	25.1	28.4
Europe	11.1	11.4	13.0	12.1	10.0

Source: Adapted from United Nations, 1985a, table A.9.

URBANISATION, INDUSTRIALISATION AND ECONOMIC DEVELOPMENT

Urban centres play a strategic role in development; historically, the process of industrialisation and economic development has been associated with considerable migration to the growing urban centres of labour demand. Public-sector investment in infrastructure development (power generation, water treatment, transportation systems, etc.) is concentrated in these centres in order to exploit economies of scale. Industrial firms located in cities thus reap substantial cost benefits because of their access both to infrastructure and to large and diversified markets for labour and other inputs.

In the development scenario usually postulated by economists, an increase in industrial output leads to more high-wage industrial employment. Savings tend to increase as a result of the improvement in incomes, providing funds for investment in industrial capital. As incomes increase, the composition of domestic demand tends to shift from food to non-food goods, manufactured items, and modern health care and housing services, thereby stimulating growth of the modern sector. With continued changes in the composition of output and patterns of consumption, the agricultural share in employment declines, while the share of industry and services increases (Kuznets, 1971; Oberai, 1978).

Manufacturing industries play a particularly important role in economic development. As the income elasticity of demand for manufactured goods is considerably greater than that for food and agricultural products, growth of the manufacturing sector can be relatively fast. This growth usually leads to higher employment and to an increase in the pace of technological change, thus helping to improve the overall rate of productivity and growth in the economy (Singh, 1989).

In response to expanding modern sector employment, migration from rural areas in search of higher incomes continues. As urban population densities increase, however, the price of urban land rises, raising the cost of housing and other urban amenities. This narrows the real rural–urban income gap, thus slowing migration and the pace of urbanisation. As development proceeds, economic activity in the modern sector diversifies, and the urban sector diffuses into an integrated system of cities, with each tending to specialise in a particular economic area. In this highly stylised description, urbanisation contributes to overall development by attracting human resources to activities with greater economic returns. The movement of labour from relatively low-income rural activity to higher-income industrial and modern service sectors contributes to higher overall average income levels, further stimulating economic growth.

Real world conditions, however, do not always conform with the hypothetical framework of the economists' development scenario. Although contemporary rates of urbanisation in developing countries are comparable to those in the now developed countries at the end of the nineteenth century, there are significant differences in the urbanisation process, both in its antecedents and in its consequences. The proportion of the non-agricultural labour force engaged in the industrial sector, for example, is significantly lower in today's developing countries than in their historical counterparts – approximately 32 per cent in 1985–7 (Table 2.4) compared with 55 per cent in 1900 in the now-developed countries (Squire, 1981). One reason cited for the lower level of industrial employment in today's developing countries is the labour-saving bias in these countries, despite the abundance of labour. Moreover, in the now-developed countries, urbanisation was initially the product of increases in agricultural productivity which, on the one hand, provided capital accumulation and, on the other, created a rural labour surplus. Capital inputs were therefore available for urban development, including capital goods which made possible increased urban labour productivity and the expansion of industrialisation. The higher incomes which resulted served to pull surplus agricultural labour to urban areas, where the growing manufacturing sector provided job opportunities. The increase in the size of the urban workforce led to a greater division of labour, increased specialisation, easier application of technology, economies of scale and mass production. The significant result of these developments was increased productivity, higher wages and higher standards of living in urban areas, which further encouraged rural–urban migration. Urbanisation in the experience of the now-developed countries was thus both a cause and a consequence of higher standards of living.

While rural–urban migration in developed countries was a consequence of the pull or attraction of cities, that in developing countries has been more akin to a push of rural inhabitants to urban areas. After the Second World War, mortality declined at unprecedented rates in the developing countries, in both urban and rural areas. This was mainly due to modern public health measures and imported medicines

Table 2.4   Proportion of non-agricultural labour force in industrial sector, 1985–7 (%)

Country	%	Country	%
All developing countries	31.7	Kenya	35.8
Brazil	21.1	Republic of Korea	34.6
China	51.7	Mexico	19.0
Egypt	21.5	Nigeria	36.7
India	28.9	Philippines	17.1

* Includes mining, manufacturing and construction.
Source: Adapted from the United Nations Development Programme, 1990, table 15.

such as antibiotics, which led to plummeting death rates, while fertility rates remained high. The resulting increase in natural population growth had the dual effect of increasing both the growth of cities and the rate of urbanisation. The more rapid natural increase in rural areas led to an increase in the rural labour force which could not be absorbed by the agricultural sector. The pressure of population also meant declining incomes and increased poverty because of reduced agricultural holdings in many parts of the Third World, particularly in Asia. All these factors, combined with the diminished possibilities for international migration, contributed to the acceleration of rural–urban migration. Thus urban growth here, far from being a response to increased productivity and higher standards of living, has been largely influenced by the pressures of rural poverty. Its consequences, too, have been negative, bringing all the problems of labour absorption, proliferation of slums and all the squalor that accompanies urban poverty.

DETERMINANTS OF URBAN GROWTH AND SPATIAL CONCENTRATION

Since they have a different relationship to the development process, the growth of cities and increases in urbanisation must be carefully distinguished. While city growth rates represent the percentage change in the absolute number of people living in a given city or group of cities, increases in urbanisation refer to a growing proportion of the national population living in urban areas. It is also useful to differentiate between urbanisation patterns which exhibit a high degree of primacy, in which a large proportion of all urban residents live in the largest city, such as in Bangkok, Cairo and Mexico City, and more diffused patterns such as those in India and China. In 1990, for example, more than half of Thailand's urban population lived in Bangkok alone whereas the three mega-cities of India (Bombay, Calcutta, New Delhi) accounted for only 13.8 per cent of the urban population of India (Table 2.5). Among the developed countries, the populations of Japan and France are much more concentrated than those of the United States and the erstwhile Soviet Union.

In general, there are three major sources of urban population growth: net migration, natural increase and reclassification. The first two contribute the most, particularly natural increase. The relative contributions of migration and natural increase to urban growth do, of

Table 2.5   Proportion of urban population living in urban agglomerations in selected countries, 1990 (%)

Developing countries	%	Developed countries	%
Bangkok (Thailand)	56.8	Los Angeles (USA)	6.4
Bombay, Calcutta, Delhi (India)	13.8	Moscow (former USSR)	4.7
Cairo (Egypt)	37.0	Paris (France)	20.4
Lagos (Nigeria)	20.2	Tokyo (Japan)	19.1
Manila (Philippines)	31.9		
Mexico City (Mexico)	31.4		
Rio de Janeiro (Brazil)	9.5		
Seoul (Republic of Korea)	35.7		
Shanghai, Beijing, Tianjin (China)	8.8		

Source: Adapted from United Nations, 1991, table 13, p.27.

course, vary in different parts of the Third World. At an early stage of development, when levels of urbanisation are low and rates of both urban and rural natural increase moderately high, net migration generally contributes more to urban population growth than natural increase. At an intermediate stage of urbanisation, natural increase predominates. At a late stage, with high levels of urbanisation and low rates of natural increase, the relationship is likely to be reversed again in favour of net migration. A large number of developing countries are now in the intermediate stage. A study by the United Nations (1985b) found that between 1960 and 1970, in 26 large cities in developing countries, 37 per cent of population growth was due to migration and 63 per cent to natural increase. More recent data from the ILO mega-city survey, presented in Table 2.6, confirm that most large cities in developing countries are growing more through natural population increase than through migration. The contribution of migration to the growth of Cairo was negative during the period 1976–86 due to heavy out-migration to the Gulf region.

Although migration is not the major source of urban growth in many developing countries, the relatively young age of rural migrants to cities means a greater contribution to natural population increase through more birth and fewer deaths. This effect tends to offset the decline in fertility rates typically associated with urban residents (Stolnitz, 1984), with the result that urban rates of natural population increase often approximate to national population growth rates. The age selectivity of the migration process and the relatively higher fertility among migrants

Table 2.6 Net migration as a percentage of total population change in selected cities, 1960–85

City	1960–70	1970–80	1980–5
Bombay	48.8	47.7	–
Cairo	23.1	– 19.3	–
	(1960–76)	(1976–86)	–
Lagos	–	61.1	–
Manila	–	36.2	–
		(1975–80)	
Mexico City	–	45.8	28.4
Rio de Janeiro	26.5	39.5	–
Seoul	76.2	60.9	54.1
Shanghai	–	24.9	37.6
			(1981–8)

Source: ILO mega-city survey (1990).

than among urban natives also lead to a younger population in urban areas. In most cities in developed countries, the 0–19 age group comprises less than 30 per cent of the city population; for many cities in developing countries, the figure is over 40 per cent (Table 2.7). A relatively low figure for Shanghai (24.3 per cent) may be due to two reasons. First, migration to the city has been strictly controlled in recent years. Second, the natural population growth rate is very low in Shanghai (0.6 per cent) due to the effective implementation of a one-child policy, as noted earlier. In Brazil, although the proportion of population in the 0–19 age group in Rio de Janeiro is only 36.5, an examination of the data shows that the corresponding figure for the Rio metropolitan area is 40.5 per cent. This difference is largely due to the fact that in recent years there has been a greater concentration of urban poor, among whom fertility rates are usually relatively high, in the peripheries of the city (see Chapter 5). Nevertheless, the predominantly young urban population in most developing countries has enormous implications, particularly for the provision of social services such as education in urban areas.

In addition to altering the age distribution of the population, migration often changes the sex ratio in large cities. This, too, has important demographic and employment implications. Table 2.8 shows that in Bombay and Lagos the sex ratio is quite high. This is due to the fact that men often predominate in the migration flows in Asia and

Table 2.7   Proportion of population in 0–19 age group in selected cities (%)

Developed countries	%	Developing countries	%
Amsterdam (1980)	22.1	Bangkok (1981)	44.1
Birmingham (1980)	29.9	Bombay (1981)	41.5
Frankfurt (1981)	24.8	Cairo (1986)	44.4
London (1981)	27.6	Delhi (1980)	48.9
Los Angeles (1980)	28.8	Jakarta (1981)	52.9
Madrid (1980)	33.5	Lagos (1981)	45.7
Montreal (1980)	23.3	Mexico City (1985)	47.0
New York (1980)	28.1	Rio de Janeiro (1980)	36.5
Paris (1982)	18.7	São Paulo (1980)	40.0
Rome (1981)	29.6	Seoul (1980)	42.5
Tokyo (1981)	28.2	Shanghai (1988)	24.3

Sources: Adapted from Martin, Ness and Collins, 1986; ILO mega-city survey (1990); Institut d'Estudis Metropolitans de Barcelona: *Cities* (Barcelona, 1988), vol. v, table 13.

Table 2.8   Sex ratio (males per 100 females) in selected cities/countries, 1970–88

	City			National		
	1970	1980	1988	1970	1980	1988
Bombay	140.0	130.0	126.0	108.0	107.0	107.0
Cairo	104.9	104.7	104.7	101.1	103.7	104.4
	(1960)	(1976)	(1986)	(1960)	(1976)	(1986)
Lagos	131.2	–	–	102.0	–	–
Mexico City	96.1	96.9	95.2	100.9	100.6	100.4
Rio de Janeiro	91.7	91.6	92.5	98.9	98.7	99.6
Seoul	99.9	99.3	99.8	100.8	100.5	101.6
Shanghai	98.0	99.1	101.5	105.8	106.1	106.3

Source: ILO mega-city survey (1990).

Africa. The gradual decline in the sex ratio in Bombay is partly due to the diminishing contribution of migration to the city's growth, and partly due to the fact that more women are now joining their husbands or migrating to cities independently. In Latin American and South-East Asian cities such as Mexico City, Rio de Janeiro and Seoul, the sex ratio is low because most rural–urban migrants are women. The lower sex ratio in Shanghai is a consequence of restrictive migration policies and the rustication programmes used in China to settle mostly young urban males in the countryside. The rise in the sex ratio for 1988 reflects the recent relaxation of these policies.

Rapid population growth was once thought to be a major cause of rural–urban migration, with rural poverty aggravated by excess labour supply providing a 'push' to the cities (for example, Lewis, 1954). But rural out-migration now seems to be less strongly associated with rural population increase than with rates of overall economic growth (United Nations, 1980), changes in agricultural productivity, and land tenure systems which give rise to marked inequalities in landholdings and landlessness.

Migrants move to urban areas mainly in response to better employment and income opportunities. The true determinants of urbanisation and spatial concentration in developing countries are therefore to be found in the forces that determine the location of employment opportunities, such as the nature and pattern of industrialisation, the pace of agricultural development, and the growth of transportation and communications networks.

The pace and pattern of industrial development is, however, the most important of these. It has in fact given rise to a debate on a basic national settlement and development strategy issue: should the emphasis be on moving industrial investment to regions where current populations are located, or should population movements be allowed to become the principal means of adjustment, with labour moving to areas where industrial investment can be located most easily? As already noted, industries tend to locate themselves in urban areas, especially in the larger cities, because they can then benefit from ready access to capital and labour, and to specialised inputs such as financial, legal and technical support services. Cities offer markets for industrial products and provide convenient access to other domestic and international markets through already established transportation systems. The spatial concentration of economic activity and the emergence of large cities is therefore a necessary adjunct of a development process which relies predominantly on the growth of modern industry rather than on agriculture. In addition, public policies often bias this basic spatial development pattern towards even more rapid urbanisation and spatial concentration.

Foreign-exchange policies, tariffs and industrial incentives often encourage activities of the type located in major urban centres rather than in the economically less developed regions, as has been the case in Brazil and Nigeria. Governmental regulation of transport tariffs and energy prices also often favours large cities, as do public investment and subsidies for other urban services that influence the location of industries.

Urbanisation is also influenced by the pace of rural development. The ability of the agricultural sector to absorb a growing rural labour force depends on factors such as climate, the availability and distribution of land, the choice of agricultural technology, the demand for agricultural products, and the availability of credit, fertilisers and technical assistance. Climate and the availability of land are usually immutable constraints. The Sahel region of Africa, where recurrent droughts in recent years have spurred migration and urbanisation, provides an extreme example of the effect of climate. In some developing countries, particularly in Latin America and Africa, new land can still be brought into agricultural use, but in most countries there is little scope for increased agricultural employment and earnings based on newly cultivated land. The other factors impeding the expansion of agricultural employment can more readily be influenced by policy. Highly unequal distribution of land ownership, especially in Latin America, slow growth of agricultural production, premature mechanisation and market barriers in industrialised nations have all made it difficult for the agricultural sector to absorb the growing rural labour force in most developing countries. This in turn has increased the rate of rural–urban migration.

In view of the large rural populations, particularly in Asia and Africa, and the structural factors discussed above, there is still potential for further rural–urban migration. As noted earlier, the rural poor migrate to cities primarily because they offer more employment opportunities and higher incomes. The data presented in Table 2.9, although not corrected for rural–urban price differentials, show that the wage differential between rural and urban areas is quite large in many developing countries. In China and the Republic of Korea, the rural–urban wage differential is much smaller, which has perhaps contributed to the lower propensity to migrate in these countries. In most other countries, however, it has proved difficult to increase agricultural growth sufficiently to reduce urban-rural income differentials. This situation is unlikely to change because any extension of the area under cultivation, a major contributor to past growth in

Table 2.9   Ratio of industrial to agricultural wages in selected countries, 1980–5

Country	1980	1985
China	1.6	1.3
India	3.7	2.3
Kenya	2.9	3.0
Republic of Korea	1.0	1.2
Mexico	2.3	2.3
Philippines	2.0	2.1

Source: Estimated from ILO: *Year Book of Labour Statistics, 1989–90* (Geneva, 1990).

agricultural output, is becoming increasingly costly in many developing countries, or involves progressively less fertile soils. Moreover, if agricultural growth depends increasingly on intensification, the demand for urban–based inputs is likely to increase disproportionately. Rising rural incomes will also increase the demand for goods and services primarily produced in urban areas. This will not only affect the structure of urban output, but it will also stimulate urban incomes and expenditures. Raising rural per capita incomes relative to urban income levels is thus crucially dependent on lowering rural population growth, which itself depends on the rates of natural population growth and rural–urban migration. Population growth rates are now declining in many developing countries, while migration to urban areas leads to further reductions in rural population growth. Seen in this light, some observers argue that what is often considered 'excessive' migration, in that it multiplies problems of urban management, becomes a necessary and desirable contributor to raising relative rural per capita incomes.

Policies that protect domestic industries from foreign competition, give more favourable incentives to industry than to agriculture, neglect rural extension and training services, and provide agricultural credit that is biased towards machinery rather than labour, all tend to hamper rural development and employment. These policies therefore push the rural population to urban areas, and in effect favour the growth of large cities over that of small towns. During the 1950s many economists were involved in a long debate about the correct allocation of investment between agriculture and industry. Some favoured agricultural development, arguing that the agricultural sector must be made more productive in order to provide the necessary surplus for industrial and urban development. Without such a surplus adequate funds would not be available for industrial and urban growth, and a market for urban products and services would not develop.

Counterposed to this argument was the idea that industrial and urban growth are prerequisites for a more modern and productive agricultural sector. Surplus rural labour needs to be absorbed into more productive urban activities, thereby permitting the introduction of more modern and capital-intensive agricultural practices and encouraging the diffusion of modern ideas and institutions into traditional rural areas.

Throughout the world, both at an academic level and, more importantly, in major political circles, the debate continues.[3] The advocates of both the rural and the urban sectors remain convinced that most of the failures of the economy may be attributed to the excessive allocation of resources to the other sector. Thus, Jakobson and Prakash (1974) complain that the prevailing worldwide attitude among politicians of all persuasions is anti-urban and in particular anti-bigcity, while Lipton (1977) argues that the major development issue in the Third World is the need to stem 'urban bias'. He argues that power in most Third-World countries is held by urban groups who distort the allocation of resources in their own favour, thereby worsening inequality and slowing development.

Lipton's thesis covers most Third-World countries, including Latin America, Africa and Asia, even though most of his evidence is drawn from South Asia. Clearly, it is unlikely that any single generalisation of such importance will apply equally to all parts of the Third World. A particular danger with the urban bias thesis is that it portrays most power conflicts in Third-World countries as arising primarily from where people live (rural versus urban areas) rather than from the economic sector from which they derive their livelihood (industry versus agriculture) or from their position in the class hierarchy (Griffin, 1977). In fact much of the development literature has pointed out that many of the difficulties Lipton portrays stem not from urban bias but from policies that favour some rural groups at the expense of others. Thus, Lefeber (1978) points to a common situation in which rich agriculturalists support, or at least do not oppose, policies that keep agricultural prices down so as to reduce the cost of urban food. Such policies are less biased against rural areas than against the small and medium-sized farmer who is unable to benefit from other government policies such as export credit, loans and subsidies in the same way as the large farmer. The large farmer supports urban bias in one set of policies so as to benefit from rural bias in another area. The larger, commercial farmers usually prosper even in regions such as Asia, where the evidence suggests that conditions for large numbers of the rural poor are deteriorating (Griffin and Khan, 1978). Here lies the paradox of the green revolution: increasing agricultural production allied with increasing poverty. Large farmers who have access to credit and agricultural inputs increase their production, while small farmers suffer as a consequence of the fall in prices (due to increased agricultural production by the big farmers) and the rising cost of inputs. In such circumstances, it is more appropriate to analyse the problems of the poor farmer in class terms than in terms of urban bias. As Griffin (1978) has said, 'Lipton has tried to explain too much, indeed virtually everything, in terms of urban bias. In the end it becomes a brilliant obsession'.

The evidence as to whether the transfer of resources to urban areas at the expense of rural areas is always undesirable therefore seems to be mixed. The Chinese may have improved welfare through an anti-urban development path, but Brazil, despite having poured money into the Amazon region, has not achieved any significant benefits. Thus a policy which achieves higher productivity and greater welfare in urban areas through a relative concentration of resources cannot fairly be dismissed as mere urban bias. It is surely better, and certainly follows Lipton's meaning more closely, to apply the term only when an excessive allocation of resources to urban areas reduces economic growth and distorts the distribution of income. Thus, if agriculture is neglected because funds are being invested in urban areas, thereby fuelling land speculation and increasing government bureaucracy and the import of luxury consumption goods, we might legitimately conclude that urban bias is the problem. Unfortunately, while such a situation may appear to exist in many Third-World countries it is not easy to measure urban bias accurately. Although cost-benefit analysis and other forms of economic appraisal can approximate the returns on urban versus rural investment, great care needs to be taken because of the artificiality of prices and foreign exchange rates in so many Third-World countries.

There is little doubt, however, that many facts do point to urban bias in developing countries. Governments have often supported industry through special tax concessions, subsidised interest rates, tariffs and other forms of protection, while the rural sector is neglected and even burdened by these urban bias policies. In major urban areas, direct subsidies for food, along with the subsidised provision of infrastructure and health and education services, artificially lower living costs. The price of electricity in Mexico City, for example, is about the same as it is at the source some 1000 kilometres away. By increasing real rural–urban wage differentials beyond what results from differences in sectoral labour productivity, these subsidies encourage migration to cities (Squire, 1981). Trade and exchange rate policies also influence the spatial distribution of population. Large developing countries with significant primary resources have typically followed the import substitution strategy, using overvalued exchange rates and taxes on primary exports to subsidise imported capital goods, with quotas or protective tariffs on imported goods that are also manufactured domestically. The effect of such policies is to turn the terms of trade against agriculture, reduce rural output and increase rural–urban wage differentials, urban migration and the pace of urbanisation (Squire, 1981). A minimum wage law can also have a spatially differentiated impact, which could be reinforced when coupled with a system of transfer payments to support the unemployed. Such a law provides incentives which will stimulate the growth of large cities. This is due to the fact that in developing countries, the cost of living in large cities is often higher than that in smaller cities. Imposition of a minimum wage law which enforces a uniform wage rate for all cities will impose a higher real wage on industries located in smaller cities than on those located in large cities. If the demand for labour is elastic, there will be lay-offs in the smaller cities, which will give workers an incentive to migrate to the large cities, where the minimum wage rate is not yet effectively influencing industry.

Transportation and communications networks are also important determinants of the spatial pattern of development, since they influence the movement of people, commodities and information between regions. Public investment, taxation, pricing and regulation of a country's transport and communications system can easily bias spatial development in favour of certain locations. If domestic transport systems have only reached a rudimentary stage of development, industries will tend to locate themselves in cities, usually the large ports or capital cities, which have relatively good links with international and domestic markets. However, improvements in domestic transportation and communications, when unaccompanied by other measures, can actually accentuate the concentration of economic activity in the large cities by lowering the natural protection for industries located in small provincial centres and reducing the barriers to migration.

The main attraction for manufacturing industry, which flocks to urban areas, particularly the large cities, is, as noted earlier, the economies of agglomeration. These economies are important both analytically and from the policy perspective since they highlight the difficulties developing countries face with any programme to encourage a more balanced spatial distribution of population.[4] Since infrastructure, physical capital, developed land and management skills are not easily dispersed, only a few urban centres can be the focal points of expansion. Particularly important are the constraints imposed by the limited availability of infrastructure or social overhead capital. Communications, transport, universities, and harbour and port facilities are all extremely expensive; given the level of per capita income in developing countries, they are difficult to duplicate outside the large cities, at least initially. Business decisions to invest are also influenced by the availability of the specialised business services provided by brokers, banks, trade associations, consulting services, laboratories, equipment-leasing establishments, etc. Most of these facilities, which are so essential for modern industry and business, require a minimum population size for their profitable operation.

SPATIAL CONCENTRATION, ECONOMIC EFFICIENCY AND GROWTH

As discussed above, urban growth is often associated with economies of agglomeration. Industries benefit from the concentration of suppliers and consumers, which allows savings in communications and transportation costs. Large cities also provide big, differentiated labour markets, which often help to accelerate the pace of technological change. They also allow the exploitation of economies of scale as regards services such as water supply and electric power. The negative consequences of urban growth, however, include unemployment (which is generally higher in urban than rural areas), air pollution, congestion, social disturbances, crime and similar problems that are thought to increase disproportionately with growth in city size.

Most studies show that initially economies of scale increase rapidly as a city expands, but beyond a certain size the additional gains diminish rapidly (see, for example, Renaud, 1981). However, none of the studies has yet been able to pinpoint the city size at which the losses created by congestion and environmental deterioration equal or exceed the benefits of agglomeration, so that we cannot say, on these grounds, that three or six or ten million people in a metropolitan area are too many.

The judgement that major cities have become too large normally rests on the assumption that urban diseconomies – for example, pollution or traffic congestion – have become so severe that the only answer is to deconcentrate both population and economic activity. Such an argument has several failings. First, it does not recognise that diseconomies are only one side of the argument: if urban agglomerations generate still greater urban economies, then the balance of economic advantage still rests with spatial concentration. Second, even if diseconomies do exceed economies, the best policy may be to improve urban management rather than deconcentrate population and employment. To reduce traffic congestion, for example, the best policy may be to improve public transport, to cut the use of private cars, or to introduce parking meters. Air pollution can be reduced by the physical removal of polluting industries, but it can also be cut by fining errant companies. With regard to unemployment, as we shall discuss later, governments are sometimes themselves responsible for reducing the absorptive capacity of cities by intervening in labour markets (for instance, through licensing requirements and other restrictions on small businesses) and by pursuing inappropriate pricing policies for public services. National economic policies – for example, those providing fiscal incentives and low-interest loans to promote capital-intensive industry – may also exacerbate urban problems by encouraging rural–urban migration without creating enough new urban jobs.

In the interests of equity, it may be argued that industrial activities should be dispersed to smaller towns and rural areas throughout a developing country, but the efficiency costs of such a policy may well be prohibitive. Many economists believe that government intervention in the distribution of economic activity is likely to waste scarce capital resources and thereby slow the rate of economic growth. In the long term the country will thus be even less able to redistribute income and remedy the problems of poverty. Regional balance and urban deconcentration can therefore be attempted after a country has achieved a certain level of development. If a high rate of economic growth is to be achieved, further concentration of population into a few large metropolitan areas cannot be avoided.

This view is supported by the finding that large cities are often more efficient and innovative than other urban centres. 'In brief, there is no basis for the belief that primacy or over-urbanisation *per se* is detrimental to the efficiency goal of economic development. There are good grounds for believing in increasing returns to urban size' (Alonso, 1969). Several observers have sought to demonstrate that there is no 'optimum' size of city beyond which further growth is undesirable and that, in general, large cities are more efficient, and even more equitable, than smaller urban centres. A number of studies indicate that industrial productivity is relatively high in the largest cities even when allowance is made for differences in capital per worker and size of enterprise (Rocca, 1970; Richardson, 1973). The evidence also suggests that the per capita costs of social overhead capital tend to fall with increasing city size, or at least fail to rise (Richardson, 1973). These findings thus support the view that urban economies exceed urban diseconomies even in today's largest cities and that there is no prima facie case in favour of deconcentration.

Such a view is not uncontroversial, however, and the evidence on which it is based has been criticised on numerous grounds. Gilbert (1976) argues that evidence of higher productivity in large cities should not be attributed to agglomeration economies alone, for such 'economies' may derive from better urban infrastructure or higher-quality labour. In support of this case, it may be argued that higher productivity in large cities is to some extent achieved at the cost of lower productivity in smaller cities: if equivalent infrastructure or labour were available in small and medium-size cities then the productivity of these cities might well rise. In addition, productivity among private firms in large cities may appear high because private companies are often subsidised indirectly by the state. If firms had to bear their full costs, the higher productivity of large cities might well be less pronounced. Moreover, if firms were forced to pay some share of the diseconomies they created, they might well find the large cities less attractive and decide to move to smaller cities. This process would reduce the apparent differential in industrial productivity between small and large cities.

Even if urban economies do outweigh the diseconomies in large cities in developing countries, are the overall benefits equitably distributed? It can be argued that urban diseconomies most affect the lower-income groups, who are least able to escape them. The middle- and upper-income groups often have the resources and knowledge to move to different areas, command better public services and influence political decisions. Industrial zones are designated to keep pollution and lorries out of the high-income areas. Urban renewal schemes rarely displace the rich but often dislocate low-income communities. Public roads, telephones, water, electricity and other services are often superior in high-income areas, as is noted in Chapter 5, and when the public sector cannot provide adequate services, for example, in health or education, wealthy groups can resort to the private sector. The operation of the land and housing markets also guarantees that the wealthy gain most from uncontrolled speculation.

Those who support decentralisation thus argue that in the short run we may achieve the objectives of growth and efficiency by encouraging population concentration in a few urban centres, but in the long term the expected results are more likely to be mass starvation, greater economic and regional inequalities, urban discontent and social unrest. The state must therefore redistribute income and wealth between regions and between social classes, not only because extreme income inequality is morally wrong but also because it is impossible to achieve national unity and to prevent social unrest in the face of such glaring disparities.

DECENTRALISATION AND RESTRICTIVE URBAN GROWTH POLICIES

While the debate continues on whether large cities should be allowed to grow further, most city and national authorities have made some sort of policy intervention to restrict urban growth or to reduce the concentration of population in large cities. Policy instruments used to slow urban or large city growth vary widely in efficiency and cost-effectiveness.[5] In general, three kinds of policies have been adopted:

1. policies that aim at transforming the rural economy and thereby slowing the rate of urban expansion;
2. policies that aim at limiting the growth of large cities through migration control;
3. policies that try to slow the growth of large cities by stimulating the growth of intermediate cities or establishing new urban centres.

Rural-retention policies

As discussed earlier, any policy that transforms the rural economy affects the nature and pace of urban development. Policies such as the redistribution of land to the poor may reduce urban–rural income disparities and slow urban growth by raising agricultural incomes. Other rural programmes may, of course, have the opposite effect: the green revolution and other efforts towards the commercialisation of agriculture have accentuated landlessness and probably stimulated, rather than reduced, the flow of city-bound migrants (Griffin, 1977). In India, attempts to develop small-scale cottage industries in rural areas have tended to increase out-migration since these industries improve villagers' skills and make them more acceptable in urban labour markets. In general, agricultural and rural development activities which increase access to cities, commercialise agriculture, strengthen rural–urban integration, raise education and skill levels, or increase rural inequalities appear to accelerate rates of rural–urban migration.

Land-reform programmes have reduced inequalities and improved farmers' income and security only in a few countries such as China and the Republic of Korea. In most other countries (Egypt, India, Brazil, Pakistan, Peru, etc.) such programmes have been mainly cosmetic, and without technical and financial assistance have not significantly benefited small farmers. Moreover, rapid population growth has weakened the initial impact of land reforms in some areas. Nor have tenancy laws greatly improved the position of tenants, despite being designed to provide protection against eviction and rent increases. On the contrary, in many countries such as India, Peru, Colombia and Argentina they have actually worsened conditions, especially for small tenants. Land reforms have also encouraged landowners to mechanise production and shift to wage labour, with the result that many small peasants have lost even their previous meagre and often insecure incomes. For many, rural out-migration has been the only option.

Land-colonisation programmes have been implemented in several developing countries such as China, Malaysia, India, Brazil, Indonesia and Kenya. The main objective of these programmes has been to resettle residents from overpopulated rural areas to frontier regions or sparsely populated areas. The policy instruments commonly employed include infrastructure investments, transfer of land titles, and provision of social services, credit and other facilities to increase the productivity and income of the settlers. Despite substantial investment in land-settlement programmes, their performance has not been very encouraging. They are costly in relation to the number of people settled and frequently exhibit low productivity and high rates of desertion. In some cases they have also been known to create social tensions between the settlers and the local population (see Oberai, 1987).

Integrated rural development programmes have had some success in countries such as Sri Lanka and Malaysia, where they have been accompanied by radical changes in income distribution and the social relations of production. In most cases, however, the provision of credit and subsidies, and public investment in roads, schools and amenities, have merely helped the large farmers, increased class differentiation in agricultural areas and led to labour displacement through mechanisation. The slow pace of rural–urban migration in Sri Lanka, for example, is attributed to the retentive capacity of the rural sector due to social welfare measures introduced by the government, including free medical services and education, consumer subsidies and income support for poor farmers in the form of guaranteed prices for their produce. A major scheme aimed at providing better housing for the lower-income groups in rural and semi-rural areas was also introduced in 1973. These measures have reduced disparities between rural and urban living conditions. Another factor that seems to have played an important part in slowing migration in Sri Lanka is the subsidised transport which gives rural dwellers access to urban employment and amenities without their having to migrate permanently to the cities. A recent study shows that nearly 45 per cent of the workforce employed in Colombo commutes to work (Oberai, 1987). A similar policy has now been adopted in China.

In India, as part of rural anti-poverty programmes, the government of Maharashtra State has adopted the Employment Guarantee Scheme. The scheme was started in the early 1970s with the expenditure of Rs19 million, generating 4.5 million person days of rural employment in 1972–3. In 1988–9, Rs2.5 billion were spent to create 81.3 million person days of employment in rural areas. There have been several evaluations of the scheme but none has dealt with its contribution to reducing rural–urban migration. However, some recent studies suggest that the number of beneficiaries of the scheme has been small in relation to the number who migrate to cities annually. The fall in the rate of migration to Bombay in the 1970s has therefore been attributed more to the Industrial Location Policy than to the Employment Guarantee Scheme in the rural areas (Deshpande and Deshpande, 1991).

Policies to control the growth of large cities

Many city administrations in the Third World have felt the need to take direct measures to discourage rural–urban migration and even to reverse the flow of migration to urban areas. Such measures have usually included administrative and legal controls, police registration and direct rustication programmes to relocate urban inhabitants in the countryside.

In 1958, China instituted a permanent household registration system to prevent unauthorised movement from the countryside into the cities. The system classified the entire population into 'urban residents' and 'rural residents'. This system was reinforced by the requirement of registration for employment, housing and subsidised food rations (Kirkby, 1985). These measures were also complemented by rustication programmes referred to as *Shang Shan Xia Xiang* ('up to the mountains and down to the villages') and *Xia-fang* ('sending down'). According to Wu (1981), about 30 million urban residents (including 17 million urban youths) were sent to the countryside during the period 1966–76. From Shanghai alone, more than one million educated youths were relocated between 1969 and 1977 (Shanghai Planning Commission, 1991). However, the evidence suggests that most of them have since returned to the urban areas (Table 2.10).

The overall effect of migration controls through the registration system may be considered positive, for in their absence urban growth would have been greater. The rustication programme may also have served to reduce unemployment and stabilise population in the cities.

Table 2.10   Numbers of educated youths sent to the countryside and returned by Shang Shan Xia Xiang, 1962–79

Year	*Sent to countryside (millions)*	*Year*	*Returned (millions)*
1962–6	1.29	1962–73	4.01
1967–8	2.00		
1969	2.67		
1970	1.06		
1971	0.75		
1972	0.67		
1973	0.90		
1974	1.73	1974	0.60
1975	2.37	1975	1.40
1976	1.88	1976	1.35
1977	1.72	1977	1.03
1978	0.48	1978	2.55
1979	0.25	1979	3.95
1962–79	17.77	1962–79	14.89

Source: Adapted from Kim Won Bae, 1990, table 4.

Rural areas, too, may have benefited from the transfer of human resources. But some recent studies indicate that strict controls on rural–urban migration did not promote rural development to the degree intended by the government. Instead, the controls temporarily bottled up the pressure in the rural areas, which eventually led to increased migration in recent years. These studies also suggest that the rustication programme did not really solve the problems of urban unemployment and food shortages but simply transferred them to the rural areas. Moreover, most urban youths did not make good farmers, and they were hardly welcomed by the peasants (Kim Won Bae, 1990).

Since 1978 there have been major changes in China's economy. The most important was the introduction in 1979 of the responsibility system in rural areas, which places a premium on individual initiative and more efficient production. Insofar as this has led to rationalisation of labour use, there has been a substantial increase in rural surplus labour. The problem has been compounded by the entrance into the labour force of youths born during earlier periods of high fertility (Goldstein, 1987). Chinese sources estimate this surplus labour to be 40 per cent of the total agricultural labour force, amounting to 100 million people in 1985 (Chen and Hu, 1989).

The surplus labour has been partially absorbed into rapidly growing rural enterprises and non-farm activities. Chinese policy-makers also advocate the absorption of rural surplus labour in small towns. *Li tu bu li xiang* ('leaving the land but not leaving the village') has been a popular slogan since the early 1980s: many peasants are expected to continue to live in their villages while commuting to nearby small towns and cities to work in private, collective or state-owned commercial and industrial enterprises. In 1984 a new policy was proclaimed that permitted peasants to move to officially designated towns for permanent settlement and to engage in non-agricultural activities, but they were not granted food rations. In 1985, the state further relaxed its control of migration to cities and towns by permitting migrants to become 'temporary' urban residents. According to a recent survey, the 'floating population' accounts for about 10–20 per cent of the total population of major cities in China (Zhao, 1989). Shanghai alone has more than 1.5 million 'temporary' residents.

Direct migration control policies have also had some success in Cuba and Poland. In Cuba, the overall system of ration, residence and worker identification cards, although not directly monitored for migration purposes, has probably made it easier to enforce restrictions on moving to Havana. In Poland also, after the Second World War, administrative restrictions were imposed on entry into large cities and it was obligatory to register every change in residence. A recent study suggests that internal migration, and particularly rural–urban migration, would have been substantially greater in Poland in the absence of administrative restrictions (Frankel, 1983). In other countries such as Indonesia, the Philippines, Tanzania and Kenya, attempts to control migration through residence permits have been largely unsuccessful because legal restrictions are difficult to enforce, licences are easily forged, monitoring entire cities is costly and people who are evicted can return (Oberai, 1987). By restricting access to education and housing in Manila, for example, the government of the Philippines hoped to deter migrants, but these measures were administratively difficult to enforce and only encouraged corruption. In some cities, such as Nairobi, repeated demolitions of squatter settlements may have influenced the pattern of urban growth, but there is little evidence that they have substantially discouraged urban in-migration. In Lima and Jakarta, street vendors have been forcibly removed from the city. There have also been periodic expulsions of unemployed migrants from cities, a practice that has been attempted in parts of Africa, notably the Congo, Niger, United Republic of Tanzania and Republic of Zaire. These measures have had little visible impact on urban growth, but have undoubtedly caused much anguish and resentment.

Among the reasons for migration into big cities, the education of children has been one of the most important in some countries. One-quarter of the migrants to Seoul during the 1960s, for example, moved in order to give their children access to the better educational facilities which were heavily concentrated in Seoul.

Recognising the importance of creating widespread educational facilities to encourage population dispersal from Seoul, the government has devised various programmes since 1970. These include:

1. restricting the transfer of high-school students into Seoul from the rest of the country;
2. imposing different education fees according to city size;
3. restricting both new establishments and the expansion of existing college departments in Seoul;
4. initiating a programme of faculty exchange between the national universities in Seoul and those in other regions;
5. supporting colleges in local cities in the expansion of their facilities and departments;

6. allocating scholarships and research grants in favour of provincial students and professors.

Table 2.11 shows changes in the degree of concentration of various aspects of socio-economic infrastructure in Seoul from the 1970s to the 1980s. It shows an increased concentration of managerial jobs, private cars, employment in finance and insurance, annual sales in retail and wholesale trading, business telephone subscribers, and gross regional product (GRP).

In contrast, certain indicators show a decreased share in Seoul relative to the country as a whole, including college, university and graduate school enrolments, which registered a drastic decline from 66.6 per cent in 1970 to 35 per cent in 1985, and value added in manufacturing, which exhibited a similar drastic decline from 34.7 per cent in 1971 to 15.5 per cent in 1985.

As already discussed, the pricing of urban services is merely one instance of the many price distortions that result from government interventions. The net effect of these price distortions is, more often than not, to shift the internal terms of trade in favour of the cities and against the rural areas. Common examples include controls which keep the prices of food, water, electricity, transport and refuse collection far below cost. The result is to make metropolitan living costs low compared with those in other areas and to make urban–rural and big

Table 2.11   Degree of concentration of various aspects of socio-economic infrastructure in Seoul (%)

Selected indicators	Degree of concentration			
	1970s	(year)	1980s	(year)
Managerial jobs	77.0	(1975)	81.0	(1979)
Bank deposits	63.4	(1970)	60.9	(1985)
Private cars	49.9	(1970)	53.2	(1985)
Employment in finance and insurance	46.6	(1976)	52.0	(1980)
Annual sales in retail and wholesale trade	32.3	(1971)	41.5	(1982)
College, university and graduate school students	66.6	(1971)	35.0	(1985)
Telephone subscribers	42.9	(1970)	34.9	(1985)
Business telephone subscribers	31.8	(1970)	36.6	(1985)
Gross regional product (GRP)	26.5	(1970)	30.7	(1980)
Value added in manufacturing	34.7	(1971)	15.5	(1985)

Source: Adapted from Jin-Ho Choi, 1990, table 8.

city–small town income gaps wider than they would otherwise have been. In Egypt, subsidies for food, especially bread, were, until the mid-1970s, concentrated in the urban rather than the rural areas. In India, Bombay, with 14 per cent of the population of Maharashtra State in 1989, accounted for 40 per cent and 31 per cent of the state's share of rice and wheat distribution respectively through fair price shops. For the poor, who spend two-thirds of their incomes on food, the assured availability of subsidised food grains in urban areas could be one of the many factors influencing their decision to migrate to these areas. One method of correcting these spatial biases, short of eliminating price distortions altogether, would be to impose high taxes on mega-city living, in the form of metropolitan residential taxes, urban wage taxes or property taxes. In the Republic of Korea, resident tax was introduced in 1973 as a control measure to reduce the influx of people into Seoul. This tax was initially applied only to Seoul residents, but it was subsequently adopted in other cities, thus defeating its original purpose. This happened because the Ministry of Home Affairs recognised its value as a source of revenue for local government. Even though the tax rate is higher in Seoul, the difference is not big enough to affect individual household location decisions (Kim *et al.*, 1991).[6]

In some countries, the establishment of green-belts around major urban areas has been used as a strategy to restrict urban sprawl and to preserve open land for agricultural or recreational use. In the Republic of Korea, for example, a green-belt of 166.8 square kilometres was established around Seoul in 1971 (Kim *et al.*, 1991). This policy has been strictly enforced and no development has taken place in green-belt areas. In Egypt, too, a law has been enacted to ban construction on agricultural land, but it has been difficult to enforce. The green-belt policy has, however, been criticised for its negative effects such as increasing land and housing prices by limiting the supply of land for urban development.

Dispersed urbanisation and secondary city strategies

Some countries have attempted administrative decentralisation in order to reduce population pressure in large cities. In Egypt, for example, such an attempt was made in 1979 by granting autonomy to different governments. However, it did not prove very effective because of the heavy concentration of infrastructure and industrial projects in the capital city. Moreover, rent controls and subsidised food and urban services, which kept the cost of living artificially low in Cairo, to some extent neutralised the effect of administrative decentralisation, as noted earlier. In the Republic of Korea, the government announced a package of programmes in 1977 to relocate secondary government offices and public enterprise headquarters outside Seoul. Altogether 60 public agencies (36 government agencies and 24 state-run firms) were earmarked for transfer from Seoul, but only 29 (12 government agencies and 17 state-run firms) have actually been moved out.

Concern about the education of children and the shortage of basic amenities seems to be the prime reason behind the reluctance to move. In fact, a recent survey revealed that only 46.4 per cent of the employees of relocated establishments from Seoul brought their families to the local cities with them (Jin-Ho Choi, 1990). Programmes for relocating public agencies have thus had only a limited effect on population dispersal.

Another policy for slowing metropolitan growth is to decentralise economic activity by relocating it outside the primary city in the surrounding hinterland, usually through the adoption of a metropolitan regional plan. The result is the creation of a polycentric metropolitan region with satellite subcentres. This may be efficient in terms of spatial organisation but it usually tends to accelerate rather than retard primary city growth, although over a broader geographical area. In India, for example, attempts to create satellite towns near Delhi and Hyderabad have ended in failure. The evidence suggests that these satellite towns tend to grow towards the metropolitan centres and therefore defeat the very purpose for which they are established. The same has been true in Mexico and Venezuela. In Egypt, there is a plan to construct a ring road around Cairo and to set up ten satellite towns along it. The target is to absorb 2.5 million people in these towns. This has, however, created some fears among urban economists that these satellite towns will draw more people from other areas and grow towards Cairo, thus leading to more problems. Many of them therefore consider a policy of regional development and of strengthening infrastructure in small and medium size cities away from Cairo to be more rational. In China, industrial parks and satellite towns set up near Shanghai have failed to attract people away from the city centre because of the lack of social infrastructure in such towns.

Sometimes governments have established new towns and cities to stimulate migration to a different area. Governments have encouraged businesses to relocate to these new urban centres by providing the necessary infrastructure and services and by subsidising interest rates.

In Egypt, for example, the government has created several new communities or towns, but the available evidence suggests that although these new cities (6th of October, 10th of Ramadan, 15th of May, Sadaat City), have had some success in attracting industry, they have drained away huge investment resources without attracting many people because of the lack of social infrastructure in such cities. In 1986, Sadaat City and 10th of Ramadan, for example, had a population of only 1927 and 8500 respectively. The government aims to settle four million people in new communities by the year 2000, but during this period the population of Cairo alone will increase by four million. Many observers therefore feel that the creation of new towns, which is an expensive strategy requiring a large commitment of administrative and financial resources, may not be an appropriate strategy for capital poor countries such as Egypt.

In China and Cuba, however, the policy of small-town development has met with some success. According to China's 1987 census results, the proportion of the urban population in small towns increased rapidly from 24.3 per cent in 1982 to 47.9 per cent in 1987[7] (Table 2.12).

In Cuba, more than 300 new small towns have been set up since 1964 in an attempt to make the country a web of small, interconnected urban communities comprising a predominantly agricultural population. In the past two decades, no country in Latin America has experienced such balanced growth in its rural and urban populations or such low rates of urban population growth.

Table 2.12 Number and population of small towns, and their share of the urban population in China, 1982–7

Year	Number of small towns	Population of small towns (millions)	Proportion of urban population (%)
1982	2 664	61.91	24.30
1983	2 786	62.34	25.81
1984	6 211	134.47	40.58
1985	7 511	166.22	43.23
1986	–	207.88	47.14
1987	11 103	241.31	47.92

Source: Adapted from Ebanks and Cheng, 1990, table 4.

The relocation of the national capital is a strategy which is becoming popular in Africa (Nigeria, United Republic of Tanzania, Côte d'Ivoire, Cameroon, Malawi, Lesotho), with two striking examples elsewhere (Brazilia and Islamabad in Brazil and Pakistan). But even when the new capital reaches a substantial size (Brazilia and Islamabad had populations of 1.57 million and 1.23 million respectively in 1990), its impact on national population distribution is small. The resource costs meanwhile are massive.

By far the most common response to rural–urban and regional imbalances has been a programme to stimulate the economies of small and medium-size cities. The prime candidate for inclusion in such a programme is often the industrial sector. Existing or new companies are persuaded to locate their plants in peripheral regions through a combination of tax incentives, the provision of infrastructure, the construction of industrial estates and, occasionally, compulsion. In general, however, the stick has been used much less than the carrot: most governments have feared that too strong a programme of deconcentration would dissuade foreign companies from investing in the country, lower efficiency in the industrial sector or run counter to important national business interests.

Various incentives have been used to attract industries to new locations. In Brazil, major tax incentives have drawn numerous companies to the principal cities of the poverty-stricken north-east. Experience shows, however, that unless the incentives to do otherwise are appropriate and sufficiently attractive to overcome the risks and uncertainties involved, manufacturing companies have a tendency to locate themselves in the areas that are closest to their preferred locations.[8] Thus in north-east Brazil, new industry was located only in the three largest cities, and in Peru, new industrial estates attracted companies only to the most prosperous and attractive city, Arequipa (Gilbert, 1974). In India, the Second and Third Development Plans led to the establishment of 486 industrial estates throughout the country, but only those close to the large cities prospered.

In the state of Maharashtra in India, as discussed in Deshpande and Deshpande (1991), the government offered a package of incentives in 1964 to encourage industry to regions other than the Bombay–Thane–Pune belt. The package has been modified many times since, the latest being in 1988. It divides the state into five regions identified as A, B, C, D and No Industry regions. The more backward the region industrially, the higher the incentive offered to the new unit locating in the region. The Bombay–Thane–Pune belt, being region A, attracts no incentives, region B attracts the minimum incentives, while the No Industry region attracts the maximum.[9] The success of this dispersal policy is reflected most clearly in the change in the regional distribution of factory employment. Bombay accounted for 65 per cent of the state's employment in factories in 1961 when there were no restrictions on the location of industries. During the period 1961–74, when some restrictions were in force, Bombay's share dropped to 57 per cent. In the following ten years, when a fully enunciated locational policy became effective, Bombay's share declined to 47 per cent. Bombay accounted for barely 6 per cent of the state's increase in factory employment between 1961 and 1984. These 23 years saw factory employment grow at a compound rate of 1.2 per cent a year in the state as a whole and 0.2 per cent a year in Bombay (Deshpande and Deshpande, 1991).

The main policy instruments used to encourage a dispersal of population away from Seoul have been the promotion of industrial relocation and the creation of satellite cities. These cities were, however, too close to Seoul and were eventually engulfed by it as its boundaries continued to expand. They also attracted more migrants from the rural regions than from Seoul itself. However, the industrial decentralisation strategies have encouraged the relocation of industries from Seoul to other industrial centres. The large industrial estates in the south-eastern coastal zones have succeeded in directing firms and labour away from the capital region. The annual population-growth rate in Seoul declined from 9.8 per cent during the period 1966–70 to 2.8 per cent in 1980–5, while for other cities the corresponding rates were 4.9 and 5.9 per cent (Table 2.13).

Table 2.13 Annual growth rate of population, Republic of Korea, 1960–85 (%)

	1960–6	1966–70	1970–5	1975–80	1980–5	1960–85
Seoul	7.9	9.8	4.5	3.9	2.8	5.5
Pusan	3.6	7.0	5.5	5.1	2.1	4.4
Other cities	5.3	4.9	6.2	5.7	5.9	5.5
Rural	1.3	−1.2	−0.7	−2.3	−2.7	−1.0
Total	2.7	1.9	2.0	1.5	1.6	1.9

Source: Adapted from Kim *et al.*, 1991, table 1.3.

To restrict industrial development in Seoul, the government enacted the Industrial Redistribution Law in 1977. The law divided the capital region into three zones: dispersal zone, status quo zone and inducement zone. In the dispersal zone, the government strictly controlled the establishment and expansion of firms and ordered the relocation of undesirable plants such as those violating municipal zoning laws and those which generated excessive pollution. On the other hand, the government provided positive incentives such as a reduction in corporate income tax of up to 10 per cent of building costs for firms locating in inducement zones, with accelerated depreciation rates and exemption from capital gains tax on the sale of land and buildings for firms relocating away from dispersal zones. Under these policy guidelines, 2112 out of 11 724 factories in Seoul were required to relocate. Of these, 890 actually moved from Seoul between 1977 and 1982 (Jin-Ho Choi, 1990). In addition, the government created or helped to create three different types of industrial estate (national industrial estates, local industrial estates and full export zones) in 28 locations with a view to achieving balanced regional development. In order to attract industries to them, a package of tax incentives was offered including exemption from local taxes (property tax, registration tax, acquisition tax, etc.) for five years, exemption from all corporate income taxes for three years, and a 50 per cent exemption for an additional two years. On the other hand, newly established industries in the Seoul Metropolitan Area (SMA) faced registration, acquisition and property taxes at rates which were five times higher than normal.

As a result of these policies, Seoul's share in national manufacturing employment decreased to 17.9 per cent in 1987 from 33.9 per cent in 1970 (Table 2.14). Seoul's decreasing share appears to have been made up largely by Kyonggi Province, which has witnessed a rapid increase in manufacturing employment.

This trend is a result of the strict land-use regulations imposed in Seoul since the mid-1970s and the high prices for factory sites. Unable to find suitable sites in the city, large highly visible establishments have had to locate themselves in areas surrounding the city or in industrial estates far from it. On the other hand, small establishments which do not require large land and capital inputs have been able to exploit the locational advantages offered by the city, such as easy access to raw materials, markets, skilled labour, information, and financial and administrative services, even though their location is not legal. It is estimated that over half of all factories in Seoul are at present not officially registered.

Table 2.14   Regional distribution of manufacturing employment, Republic of Korea, 1970–87 (%)

Province	1970	1980	1987
Seoul	33.9	22.1	17.9
Pusan	16.0	15.8	13.9
Kyonggi	12.1	23.8	29.2
Kangwon	2.2	1.1	2.5
Chungbuk	2.3	2.0	2.3
Chungnam	5.3	4.4	3.9
Chunbuk	4.2	2.7	2.5
Chunnam	4.9	3.3	3.3
Kyungbuk	11.5	13.1	12.3
Kyungnam	7.0	11.5	12.0
Cheju	0.6	0.2	0.1
Total	100.0	100.0	100.0
(No.)	861 041	2 014 751	3 095 652

Source: Adapted from Kim *et al.*, 1991, table 4.2.

The reluctance of firms to forgo the business opportunities offered by Seoul is best illustrated by the flourishing manufacturing activity in the areas surrounding the city. Not subject to strict land use regulations and with land prices lower than Seoul's, the city of Inchon and Kyonggi Province, with their easy access to Seoul, have attracted a large number of manufacturing establishments, especially during the 1980s. During the period 1970–87, the number of manufacturing establishments, employment and value added in the capital region, which includes Seoul, Inchon and Kyonggi Province, grew at annual rates of 8.4, 8.0 and 15.8 per cent respectively, exceeding the corresponding rates for both Seoul and the country as a whole (Table 2.15). However, the number of establishments in Seoul itself increased at an annual rate of 6.2 per cent, exceeding the national rate of 4.9 per cent. The increasing attractiveness of the areas around Seoul meant that Seoul's own share in manufacturing employment and value added declined from about one-third of the national total to 18.5 and 13.9 per cent respectively, while its share in the number of establishments increased from 23.7 to 29.2 per cent. Thus, Seoul now has a greater number of relatively small manufacturing establishments.

In China, industrial decentralisation and the transfer of skilled labour from coastal to inland areas have contributed to a more balanced distribution of industry between coastal and inland regions.

Table 2.15   Manufacturing activity in Seoul and the capital region, 1970–87*

	Establishments		Employment		Value added	
	(No.)	*(%)*	*(1,000 persons)*	*(%)*	*(billion won)*	*(%)*
1970						
Nation	24 114	(100.0)	861	(100.0)	3 481	(100.0)
Capital region	7 916	(32.8)	396	(46.0)	1 544	(44.4)
Seoul	5 708	(23.7)	292	(33.9)	1 158	(33.3)
1980						
Nation	30 823	(100.0)	2 015	(100.0)	11 857	(100.0)
Capital region	13 512	(43.8)	924	(45.9)	4 964	(41.9)
Seoul	7 652	(24.8)	445	(22.1)	2 193	(18.5)
1987						
Nation	54 389	(100.0)	3 001	(100.0)	40 569	(100.0)
Capital region	31 285	(57.5)	1 459	(48.6)	18 566	(45.8)
Seoul	15 859	(29.2)	554	(18.5)	5 631	(13.9)
Average annual rate of growth, 1970–87 (%)						
Nation	4.9		7.6		15.5	
Capital region	8.4		8.0		15.8	
Seoul	6.2		3.8		9.7	

* The data only cover etablishments with five or more employees.
Source: Adapted from Kim *et al.*, 1991, table 2.10.

Foremost among the exporters of labour have been Shanghai and Tianjin. However, the industries relocated from coastal to inland areas turned out to be less efficient in their new locations and imposed a severe loss of efficiency on the national economy (Kirkby, 1985).

The Chinese experience therefore suggests that the issue of economic efficiency is extremely important when considering industrial dispersal policies. A related issue is whether the decentralisation of industry will have a positive effect on the poorer regions. The available evidence suggests that in many countries industrial dispersal has increased regional output but created few jobs. Indeed, deconcentration programmes have tended to suffer from the same weakness as national industrialisation programmes: the capital-intensive nature of the technology has not created many local jobs or much demand for local inputs in the way envisaged by growth centre theory. Studies of the regions around Kuala Lumpur (Robinson and Salih, 1971) have found that as a result of weak 'spread' effects and/or substantial 'backwash' effects, the regions beyond the immediate vicinity of the growth centres receive little by way of positive economic or social benefits. Large-scale industrialisation within a growth centre seems to be a poor means of developing a poor region in the absence of fundamental changes in the agricultural economy, the marketing system, and the pattern of landholdings. Industrial deconcentration may serve to reduce pressure on the metropolitan areas, but unless accompanied by other, often more radical, programmes it brings little benefit to the poorer regions.

The problem is that while the poor regions may benefit from regional policies, the poor within those regions do not benefit sufficiently. Too often the benefits go to the industrial and large-scale agricultural groups in the region. A reduction in interregional disparities is then accompanied by an increase in intraregional disparities and interpersonal inequalities.

Another important issue in need of attention is that of selective deindustrialisation. A common tendency among city planners is to discourage the growth of manufacturing activities, which thwarts employment generation, as has happened in Seoul, Bombay and in many other Third-World mega-cities. Open unemployment in Seoul in 1986 was 5.9 per cent as against the national unemployment rate of 3.4 per cent (Kim *et al.*, 1991). As Rakesh Mohan (1990) has argued:

a determining factor in the pattern of industrial location within a city is the relative magnitudes of capital and land elasticities of substitution inherent in the technologies underlying different industries. Batch production processes are more susceptible to substitution between capital and land than process industries. Garment production, much of electronics production, printing and other such industries can be conducted in multi-storey factories as well as in spread out factory layouts. This, however, cannot be done in most chemical or metallurgical industries.

As land prices get bid up in the central city, such land intensive activities move out to the periphery, yielding to higher value uses, usually for commercial or trading activities. These activities use land more intensively and also use more labour per unit of land. Alternatively, batch production industries replace continuous assembly line type industries in the central city. Thus, planners must understand that not all industries are inappropriate for a large city and moreover, they tend to sort themselves out if permitted to (p. 16).

There is also the question of premature decentralisation of trading activities from the city centre. The optimal distribution of employment location varies between different sectors such as trading, manufacturing and services. In most cities in developing countries trading activities are typically highly concentrated as compared with cities of smaller size in developed countries. The reason is that a typical household in a city in a poor country has a low purchasing power. Thus, even a large population gives rise only to limited demand; this can be met by a limited number of shops and service establishments, which therefore tend to concentrate in the centre of the city.

As a city and the income of its residents grow, such activities start decentralising. City planners therefore have to understand the nature of this decentralising trend and its determinants. In the absence of such understanding, it has been observed that city planners, who typically see urban congestion as a menace, tend to plan for decentralisation of shopping centres far in advance of the appropriate time. Premature decentralisation of trading activities can have a number of adverse effects on employment. First, expenditure on new infrastructure could be more efficiently utilised for the maintenance and upgrading of existing infrastructure. Second, enterprise overhead costs are typically higher in new green-belt locations. Thus, capital–labour ratios in new enterprises are higher than would otherwise be the case. Third, the lack of appropriate transportation to such new sites also inhibits employment generation (Mohan, 1990).

While major regional and industrial decentralisation programmes – and indeed programmes for planning major cities – may be essential, they are not in themselves sufficient. What is critical is the type of development strategy followed. When urban and regional policy goals have come into conflict with national economic growth, the latter has usually been the winner. Many governments have established regional programmes with a view to attaining greater equity and regional balance. Almost invariably these policies have been counteracted by national programmes that have tended to accentuate regional disparities and encourage the growth of major urban areas. Of course, the introduction of regional programmes may have reduced the level of spatial concentration that would have resulted from the national programmes alone. But, in general, the weakness of regional and decentralisation programmes suggests that they are never given priority nor intended to achieve a real balance. Take the case of Lagos, which demonstrates well how macro-policies can submerge decentralisation efforts. More than 90 per cent of total net subsidies granted to industries in Nigeria benefit those located in Lagos. This could not be expected to have a positive impact on industrial decentralisation. In India, too, decentralisation policies have come into conflict with macro-objectives. The Indian government instituted a policy of not licensing any new industrial activities in its five large urban centres. At the same time, however, export promotion has also been a declared policy, and three of the large urban centres, the ports of Calcutta, Bombay and Madras, happen to be prime locations for export-oriented industries.

Although major differences of opinion exist as to the desirability of spatial deconcentration and the possibility of good metropolitan planning, most urban experts agree on certain points. First, although the concept of an optimum size of city is useful as an analytical tool it cannot be assigned a single numerical value. Since city organisation is at least as critical as size, and the nature of metropolitan economies varies considerably across the globe, no single size of city can be deemed optimal. If a case is to be made in favour of deconcentration it has to be made on the basis that certain goals such as equity and national unity can be better achieved with a less concentrated settlement system. Second, there is a trade-off between efficiency and equity: an emphasis on one requires some sacrifice of the other. Third, whether or not deconcentration is favoured, more effective and fairer urban planning is a necessity in large cities because there is no sign, even in China, that metropolitan growth can be restrained for long. Such planning requires the implementation of policies and programmes to improve the conditions of the urban poor. Fourth, more should be done to compensate those who suffer from noise, pollution and congestion. If large cities do indeed generate vital urban economies, companies will remain there even if they are forced to pay the costs they impose on other city dwellers. Fifth, increasing urbanisation is unavoidable in rapidly industrialising societies because rural areas, given their weak economic base, cannot absorb rapid population growth. Unless this push factor from the rural areas is properly dealt with, population dispersal away from large cities is unlikely to occur. Finally, rather than directly intervening in population distribution, governments should try to correct the biases of national development policies which have implications not only for industrial location patterns but also for the regional distribution of purchasing power. Industrialisation policies should be consistent with overall macroeconomic policies and concentrate on improving people's welfare regardless of where they live.

3 Urban Growth, Employment and Poverty

Rapid population and labour force growth in developing countries, and the prospect that these trends will continue, has aroused great concern about the ensuing economic and social consequences, particularly since many urban areas, especially the large cities, have serious employment and poverty problems. The purpose of this chapter is twofold. First, to examine the effects of urban population and labour-force growth on urban labour market structure and labour absorption. Second, to assess the implications of changes in urban labour-market structure for urban employment and poverty.

LABOUR FORCE GROWTH, LABOUR-MARKET STRUCTURE AND LABOUR-ABSORPTION

Labour force growth and employment

The size and distribution of a city's labour supply are determined by the natural population growth in the city, the net migration to (or from) the city, the participation rate of the labour force, and the human capital embodied in the labour force (that is, the availability of skills and health, both of which affect the composition and quality of the urban labour force).

The data presented in Table 3.1 show that the rate of population growth in most cities has declined during the 1980s compared with the 1970s. However, this does not imply that the population pressure, or the contribution of population growth to labour supply, has diminished in absolute terms. Both the supply of labour and population size continue to increase in most cities, making labour absorption more difficult. In Latin American cities such as Mexico City and Rio, the size of the labour force more than doubled between 1970 and 1987–8. In Asia, Bombay's labour force continues to grow rapidly while employment is growing relatively slowly, resulting in increasing unemployment. Unemployment in Bombay grew at an annual rate of 8.3 per cent during 1971–81 as compared with 3.9 per cent in the period 1961–71. In

Table 3.1 Labour force and employment growth in selected cities, 1970–88

City	Millions		Period	Annual rates of growth (%)			
	Population	Labour force		Population	Labour force	Employment	Unemployment
Bombay							
1970	5.9	2.3	1961–71	3.6	2.7	2.6	3.9
1981	8.2	3.1	1971–81	3.2	3.0	2.6	8.3
Cairo							
1976	5.0	1.4	1960–76	2.6	3.1	3.0	4.8
1984	6.0	1.8	1976–86	1.7	1.7	2.4	10.1
Mexico City							
1970	9.2	2.6	1970–79	4.5	6.9	6.9	6.2
1987	16.7	6.0	1979–87	3.0	2.3	2.4	0.0
Rio de Janeiro							
1970	7.0	1.6	1970–80	2.4	8.0	7.9	10.7
1988	10.9	4.8	1980–88	2.5	4.2	4.0	9.4
Seoul							
1970	5.5	1.7	1970–80	4.1	5.1	7.2	−5.2
1988	10.3	3.6	1980–88	2.6	3.0	3.5	−3.7
Shanghai							
1971	11.6	5.6	1971–81	0.9	2.9	2.9	–
1988	12.6	7.7	1981–88	1.2	0.5	0.5	–

Source: ILO mega-city survey (1990).

Shanghai, on the other hand, although the size of the labour force increased from 5.6 million in 1971 to 7.7 million in 1988, the rate of growth of the labour force declined substantially during the 1980s (0.5 per cent per annum) compared with the 1970s (2.9 per cent), largely because of the restrictive population growth policies pursued in earlier periods. In the case of Seoul, the rate of growth of both population and labour force declined significantly during the period 1981–8 compared with 1971–81, partly due to the decline in natural population growth and partly due to the success of decentralisation policies. Moreover, employment in Seoul has grown faster than the labour force due to rapid economic growth in recent years, causing unemployment to fall. But it is interesting to note that in Cairo, despite considerable growth in GDP as noted below, unemployment grew faster during the period 1976–86 than in 1960–76. This is largely because of the adoption of more capital-intensive technology.

Table 3.2 provides data on rates of unemployment in mega-cities. The data presented here, together with the data included in Table 3.1, show that in spite of a growth in employment, rapid growth of the labour force has contributed to an increase in unemployment in most large cities. Although rates of unemployment declined somewhat between 1980 and 1988, around 5 per cent of the labour force

Table 3.2   Rates of unemployment in selected cities, 1970–88 (%)

City	1970			1980			1988		
	M	F	T	M	F	T	M	F	T
Bombay[1]	4.9	7.7	5.1	8.4	10.9	8.7	–	–	–
Cairo[2]	3.5	11.6	4.3	4.2	15.0	5.7	10.8	18.9	12.2
Mexico City[3]	4.0	6.6	4.8	5.4	7.5	6.1	4.5	5.9	4.9
Rio de Janeiro	2.6	1.5	2.2	–	–	2.9[4]	4.0	5.0	4.3
Seoul	12.2	17.7	13.4	8.2	11.2	9.4	6.3	3.8	5.3
Shanghai	–	–	–	–	–	1.5[5]	–	–	–

Notes: [1] 1971, 1981.
             [2] 1960, 1976, 1986.
             [3] 1970, 1979, 1987.
             [4] 1981: 6.6 per cent.
             [5] 1982: unemployment defined as 'people waiting for jobs'.
             M = Males; F = Females; T = Total.
Source: ILO mega-city survey (1990).

remained unemployed, the situation being more grave for the female labour force. In the case of Seoul, despite the growth in employment, rates of unemployment continued to be higher than in the rest of the country. The rates of unemployment for the Republic of Korea as a whole were 4.4 per cent in 1970, 5.2 per cent in 1980 and 2.5 per cent in 1988 (Kim *et al.*, 1991). The relatively high unemployment rates in Seoul were due to the declining employment opportunities in manufacturing. In the case of Latin American cities, the unemployment situation deterioriated in the early 1980s with the rate of unemployment reaching 6.6 per cent in Rio in 1981. In subsequent years, however, open unemployment fell. The fall was largely due to the fact that an increasing number of people were forced by the difficult economic situation to accept low-productivity jobs in the urban informal sector. The decline in unemployment was thus accompanied by an increase in underemployment and a rapid expansion of the informal sector, as noted below.

Table 3.3 shows that an increase in labour-force participation rates has been partly responsible for the rapid growth of the labour force in most Third-World mega-cities. The data also show that although female labour-force participation rates are generally low (except in China), these have been rising in recent years, especially in the Latin American cities. In Mexico City, Rio and also Seoul, between one-third and one-half of women in the working age group (15–59 years) participate in the labour force. In cities such as Bombay and Cairo, however, less than 20 per cent of women in this age group participate in the labour force, for cultural reasons. Great variations in female participation rates therefore exist among cities in different regions. In the Asian cities such as Seoul and Bombay, the slight increase in female participation rates has been accompanied by a slight decline in male participation rates.

The data in Table 3.3 suggest that there is no child labour in Seoul or Shanghai. Labour-force participation rates among minors (the 0–14 age group) have also been declining in Bombay and Cairo. In Cairo, in particular, the participation of children in the labour force declined from 4.6 per cent during the 1970s to 0.9 per cent in the 1980s. But in Latin American cities, there has been a slight increase in the incidence of child labour because of the different economic situation.

With regard to elderly persons (60 +), the data suggest that labour-force participation rates, particularly among men, have been declining in many cities. In Cairo, for example, labour-force participation among men in this age group declined from 41.3 per cent in 1976 to 29.2 per

Population Growth, Employment and Poverty

Table 3.3   Labour-force participation rates by age group in selected cities, 1970–88 (%)

City/age group	1970			1988		
	Male	Female	Total	Male	Female	Total
Bombay[1]						
0–14	2.4	1.0	1.7	1.8	0.8	1.3
15–59	82.2	12.5	55.6	79.2	13.6	52.3
60+	47.9	4.9	27.2	39.8	4.6	22.8
Cairo[2]						
0–14	6.3	2.8	4.6	1.6	0.2	0.9
15–59	75.6	13.9	46.1	77.1	19.0	49.4
60+	41.3	2.3	22.6	29.2	3.2	16.7
Mexico City[3]						
0–14	1.2	1.3	1.2	1.6	1.4	1.5
15–59	74.5	30.1	51.7	78.1	38.2	64.4
60+[4]	69.5	15.4	37.2	72.1	20.4	42.0
Rio de Janeiro						
0–14	0.8	1.3	1.0	1.8	0.9	1.7
15–59	79.5	33.0	54.7	91.5	51.9	70.7
60+	29.3	7.9	20.1	30.8	11.5	20.4
Seoul						
0–14	1.3	2.1	1.7	–	–	–
15–59	73.5	26.2	49.6	68.3	30.3	49.5
60+	31.8	3.5	13.7	29.0	5.0	14.4
Shanghai[5]						
0–14	–	–	–	–	–	–
15–59	89.9	82.1	86.0	90.0	86.0	87.4
60+	15.7	8.8	11.0	29.8	11.8	20.0

Notes: [1] 1971 and 1981, respectively.
             [2] 1976 and 1986, respectively.
             [3] 1970 and 1979, respectively.
             [4] 55 and above.
             [5] 1982 and 1987, respectively.
Source: ILO mega-city survey (1990).

cent in 1986. This is because of the increase in open unemployment, particularly among educated youth, which is making it difficult for older people to find employment. A similar trend is noticeable in Bombay. In the case of Shanghai, however, it is interesting to note that the participation rate among the elderly has increased from 11.0 per cent in 1970 to 20.0 per cent in 1988. In Latin American cities, labour force participation among this age group has been more or less stable, although a slight increase can be noticed in the case of Mexico City. In Rio, one in every five people aged over 60 is still economically active. The relatively high proportion of elderly people working in Mexico City is due to the fact that the available data relate to the age group 55 and over.

Increasing labour-force participation rates, particularly among women, are reflected in the rapid growth of the female labour force and female employment (Table 3.4). The data indicate that in Bombay, the female labour force and female employment grew more dramatically during the 1970s than in the 1960s. As a result, the employment situation is worsening relatively more for men than for women. In Cairo, employment growth is lower than labour-force growth for both men and women, resulting in increased unemployment for both sexes, although the increase is again much faster in the case of men. In the case of Seoul, employment is growing faster than the labour force. As a result, unemployment is declining among both sexes but the decline is more rapid among women. In Mexico City, the decline in the rate of growth of the labour force from the 1970s to the 1980s is much larger

Table 3.4   Labour force and employment growth by sex in selected cities, 1970-88 (%)

City	Rate of growth of labour force		Employment growth rate		Unemployment growth rate	
	M	F	M	F	M	F
Bombay						
1961–71	2.6	3.3	2.6	2.8	3.2	11.6
1971–81	2.8	5.0	2.4	4.7	8.2	8.7
Cairo						
1960–76	2.8	5.5	2.7	5.3	3.9	7.1
1976–86	1.9	4.9	1.2	4.5	11.3	7.3
Mexico City						
1970–79	6.3	3.5	6.1	8.3	9.5	9.8
1979–87	2.4	3.0	2.6	3.2	0.1	0.0
Rio de Janeiro						
1970–88	5.8	7.4	5.7	7.2	8.2	14.3
Seoul						
1970–80	4.5	6.4	5.7	11.5	−3.3	−7.8
1980–88	3.0	2.9	3.4	3.9	−1.0	−10.6

Source: ILO mega-city survey (1990).

for men (from 6.3 to 2.4 per cent) than for women (from 3.5 to 3.0 per cent). This is because the economic recession and debt crisis of the 1980s have led to increased underemployment and a fall in wages, as noted earlier, forcing women to participate in the labour force to complement the family income.

How is the process of labour absorption affected by the segmentation of the urban labour market into a formal and an informal sector? To examine this issue, it is necessary to consider the implications of this segmentation for the demand for labour in urban areas. The formal sector is generally characterised by protected wage work, advanced technology and high labour productivity. The informal sector retains the features of low capital–labour ratio, lack of protection, dominance of self-employment, easy entry and low productivity. The differences in the adjustment mechanisms in the two sectors are crucial with regard to the process of labour absorption. While the informal sector behaves in a classical manner, with employment and earnings determined simultaneously by supply and demand conditions, market imperfections often limit modern sector wage flexibility (for example, earnings being determined by the bargaining position of unions in the wage-setting process). Employment in the formal sector is thus mainly demand-determined, the level of output itself being demand-constrained. Consequently, the excess supply of labour in the modern sector spills over into the informal sector, bringing about underemployment together with open unemployment.

Apart from union pressure, there are several other possible sources of labour-market imperfections in the modern sector. The large-scale production firms may pay a wage premium in order to encourage worker productivity and ensure stability, given the relative scarcity of skilled workers and the costs of training. Another imperfection may arise from discrimination based on race, ethnicity and sex, which may restrict access to high-wage employment (Knight and Sabot, 1982). It is also important to highlight the role of rural–urban migration as one of the factors which lie behind the progressive growth of the informal sector, and which contribute towards widening the gap in inter-sectoral productivity, thereby generating the dualistic economic structure.

In the Lewis model with unlimited labour supply, migrant workers from low-productivity rural jobs are absorbed into high-productivity urban industrial jobs, which implies a one-stage process of labour transfer. However, Todaro (1969) emphasises a two-stage migration process: in the first stage, the migrants enter the 'urban traditional sector' (informal sector) due to their limited access to the 'modern sector' (formal sector). Workers in the urban traditional sector are likely to acquire skills and eventually graduate to the formal sector, which Todaro calls the second stage, 'the eventual attainment of a more permanent modern sector job'. But his model is essentially based on the assumption of free entry of labour from the urban traditional sector into the urban modern sector, which seems unrealistic. Alternatively, what one may find in actual labour market conditions is that many unskilled rural labourers are not in a position to meet the skill requirements of the urban modern sector, nor can they afford to remain unemployed for long. Second, even if they possess the requisite skills, their absorption into the industrial sector may not take place on a large scale either because of the limited spread of this sector or because of the sluggish growth of employment resulting from the sluggish growth of output and/or the adoption of capital-intensive technology. Consequently, they may continue to work in the unorganised sector of the urban labour market permanently or for a long time. Thus, when the employment-generating capacity of the formal sector lags behind the growth of the urban labour force, the informal sector is burdened with the excess labour supply. The concentration of employment in low-productivity activities or marginal jobs leads to increased dualism.

But while there is evidence of labour-market imperfections, it would be a mistake to conclude that supply factors have no impact on modern-sector wage levels. Indeed, there is evidence that, as theory would predict, rapid increases in labour supply result in slower wage growth, in both manufacturing and non-manufacturing modern-sector activities (Squire, 1981). It should be noted, however, that often the presence of increasing returns in the modern sector implies that, while formal sector wages do not necessarily have to fall as employment increases, earnings in the informal sector may decline with employment growth. Thus productivity factors, rather than supply pressure, may contribute to the deterioration in earnings which tends to accompany expansions in informal sector employment. But the relatively free play of supply and demand factors in the informal sector means that labour-force growth does influence wage levels and earnings in this sector.

But how does the urban labour-market adjust to the substantial and growing imbalances in labour demand and supply? The response of the labour market to increasing excess supply can take the form either of adjustments tending to reduce the imbalance between demand and supply, or of reactions which do not contribute to moving the market towards equilibrium. The adjustment can take five principal forms:

1. a reduction in rural–urban migration;
2. a rise in open unemployment;
3. a decline or stagnation in formal-sector employment;
4. a fall in formal-sector wages;
5. an expansion of informal-sector employment, often accompanied by a decline in wages and earnings.

The response of labour markets in mega-cities in different regions of the developing world during the economic crisis of the 1980s took the form of different combinations of these adjustment mechanisms. However, the shift of employment from the formal to the informal sector, which substitutes the worsening of underemployment and disguised unemployment for increases in open unemployment, was a basic element in the response of labour markets to labour-supply pressures. Table 3.5 shows that informal-sector employment grew two to five times as fast as formal-sector employment during the 1980s. The high growth rate of informal-sector employment (relative to the formal sector) in Mexico City and Rio points to the severe cost in terms of employment conditions of the adjustment process undergone by Latin America. Even in Bombay, the modern sector has been severely

Table 3.5 Structure and growth of employment in selected cities, 1970-88 (%)

City	Share in employment			Annual rates of employment growth			
	Year	Formal sector	Public sector	Period	Formal sector	Informal sector	Public sector
Bombay	1979	50.1	21.5	1961–71	–	–	–
	1981	44.5	25.5	1971–81	1.4	3.8	3.1
Cairo	1976	69.4	52.1	1960–76	3.8	1.8	–
	1986	66.3	45.9	1976–86	1.2	4.2	0.4
Mexico City	1970	–	–	1970–79	4.0	–	–
	1987	70.5	–	1979–87	2.2	6.0	–
Rio de Janeiro	1970	72.0	11.8	1970–80	–	–	6.8
	1988	68.8	7.8	1980–88	1.4	8.9	0.5
Seoul	1970	76.7	1.5	1970–80	6.0	10.3	7.2
	1988	64.1	1.7	1980–88	2.8	5.1	4.7
Shanghai	1971	–	–	1971–81	–	–	2.8
	1988	–	–		–	–	0.3

Source: ILO mega-city survey (1990).

constrained in absorbing the available labour supply. The particularly high proportion of employment in the informal sector in Bombay (55.5 per cent in 1981) makes apparent the extent to which the city's huge slum population is denied access to the modern sector. Similarly, the excessively high proportion of employment in the public sector in Cairo (45.9 per cent in 1986) reveals the extent to which the state is forced to substitute for a private sector unable to fulfil its labour-absorption role. In Bombay, too, the public sector has become increasingly involved as a buffer accounting for a growing proportion of total employment (25.5 per cent in 1981). During the period 1971–81, public-sector employment in Bombay grew at an annual rate of 3.1 per cent. The case of Bombay also illustrates two pervasive characteristics of the adjustment process. First, the link between the declining weight of formal-sector employment and the deterioration of manufacturing vis-à-vis services and construction (as discussed later), and, second, the relationship between the stagnation of modern vis-à-vis informal-sector employment and the restructuring process undertaken by manufacturing firms, shifting labour from stable to casual arrangements.

Although the crisis of the early 1980s affected the growth of the formal sector, especially manufacturing, in all the regions of the developing world, the heavy burden imposed by the debt crisis on the Latin American and African economies was particularly detrimental for modern-sector employment in these regions.

A recent study of several African countries based on data on growth in the non-agricultural labour force during the periods 1970–80 and 1980–5 concludes:

There has been a steady deterioration in the employment situation in most sub-Saharan African countries in the seventies with a marked accentuation in the eighties. This is the result of a continuing deceleration in economic growth accompanied by a rise in the growth of labour supply.

The brunt of the crisis had to be borne by the urban sector. Reduction in rural–urban migration and rise in open unemployment have been of limited importance in most countries as means of adjustment to the pressures in the urban labour markets. The predominant way in which the labour markets have adjusted to the economic crisis of the past decade has been through sharp reductions in real wages which have helped sustain employment in the formal sector, and a rapid expansion of the informal sector with falling real wages and earnings, resulting in work-sharing and increasing underemployment (see Table 3.6; Ghai, 1987).

In sub-Saharan Africa, informal-sector employment increased by 6.7 per cent per annum between 1980 and 1985, which is higher than the urban labour-force growth rate (5.3 per cent) and the growth rate of modern-sector employment (1 per cent) (Table 3.7).

Table 3.6   Growth of non-agricultural employment and real wages in selected African countries (% per annum)

Country	Employment		Real wages	
	Period	*Growth*	*Period*	*Growth*
Burundi	1972–79	4.7	1977–82	−4.9
	1981–85	0.7	1980–85	3.8
Cameroon	1969–81	8.5	1976–81	0.0
Ghana	1969–79	1.7	1975–80	−24.2
Kenya	1972–85	5.1	1976–85	3.3
Malawi	1969–84	4.4	1969–83	−2.1
	1977–84	2.7	1980–84	−6.4
Mauritius	1969–85	5.2	1982–85	−0.8
Nigeria	−	−	1975–80	−7.5
Sierra Leone	1974–81	2.2	1969–81	−4.2
Tanzania	1970–81	5.4	1971–81	−6.5
Zambia	1969–84	0.3	1972–84	−3.9

Source: Adapted from Ghai, 1987, table 10.

Table 3.7   Structure of employment in sub-Saharan Africa, 1980–5 (millions)

Indicator	1980	1985	Annual change (%)
Urban labour force	28.1	36.3	5.3
Urban unemployment	2.8	4.5	10.0
Urban wage employment* (formal sector)	9.6	10.1	1.0
Urban informal sector employment	15.7	21.7	6.7

* Wage employment is considered as a proxy for modern sector employment.
Source: Adapted from ILO/JASPA, 1989, table 1.11.

A similar process took place in Latin America, where both rising urban unemployment (Tokman, 1987) and erosion of real wages (Singh, 1989) were among the costs imposed upon workers by the recession of the early 1980s (see Table 3.8). Furthermore, in the case of Mexico City and Rio, the rise in underemployment revealed in the increasing weight of informal-sector employment appears to have played a more important role than rising open unemployment.

Even though rapid growth in the labour force typically results in lower wages than would otherwise prevail in urban labour markets, in both the modern and the informal sectors, it is important to note that most urban workers are probably at least as well off as they would be in rural areas. Recent research suggests that migrants to cities are often able to increase their incomes relative to rural levels and, over time, achieve earnings comparable with those of non-migrant urban residents (Yap, 1977; Squire, 1981; Oberai and Singh, 1983; Oberai, 1987). The evidence does not support the notion that migrants flock to cities and swell the ranks of the unemployed. They are not much more likely to be unemployed than urban residents of longer standing.

Table 3.8   Informal-sector employment as a proportion of the non-agricultural labour force in selected Latin American countries, 1980–5 (%)

Country	1980	1985
All	26.1	30.7
Argentina	26.3	28.9
Brazil	24.1	30.1
Colombia	32.0	35.4
Mexico	24.2	29.5
Venezuela	25.6	26.2

Source: Adapted from ILO/PREALC, 1986b.

Labour-market structure and labour absorption

Table 3.9 presents data on the evolution of the structure of employment and GDP by major economic sector. The data show that the services sector accounts for 50–70 per cent of total employment in most mega-cities, except in Shanghai where this sector has remained relatively neglected (28 per cent in 1988). Manufacturing accounts

Table 3.9 Structure and growth of employment and GDP by sector in selected cities, 1970–88 (%)

City/Sector	Employment				GDP			
	Share[1] (%)		Annual rate of growth		Share[1,3]		Annual rate of growth	
	1970	1988	1970–80	1980–8	1970	1988	1970–80	1980–8
Bombay[2]								
Manufacturing	41.6	40.0	2.1	–	41.0	37.3	3.2	–
Construction	3.1	3.4	3.6	–	6.0	14.8	5.0	–
Services	54.3	55.4	2.3	–	51.6	47.5	3.3	–
Cairo[4]								
Manufacturing	27.2	23.2	4.1	–0.2	34.8	23.4	4.9	2.3
Construction	8.4	11.9	6.2	4.9	8.5	17.9	5.1	6.6
Services	62.8	59.7	2.0	2.7	56.0	56.3	3.2	7.3
Mexico City								
Manufacturing	31.0	22.7	6.4	–0.3	38.3[5]	31.4	4.7	–
Construction	5.9	4.4	6.1	0.1	–	–	6.6	–1.3
Services	59.6	70.5	8.0	3.3	61.2[5]	68.3	7.0	3.9
Rio de Janeiro								
Manufacturing	23.6	27.3	11.4	–1.0	19.2[6]	24.0	9.0	–0.1
Construction	–	7.3	–	2.1	11.0[6]	9.8	8.2	–0.4
Services	75.4	64.2	7.4	5.0	69.2[6]	65.7	6.4	–0.4
Seoul								
Manufacturing	22.8	30.7	10.6	2.9	26.6	19.1	6.4	8.7
Construction	7.2	9.1	9.3	3.8	3.6	19.0	8.7	12.8
Services	67.7	59.8	5.6	4.0	68.4	61.2	9.0	8.3

Shanghai								
Manufacturing	45.7	53.5	3.0	3.3	76.9[7]	61.7	5.2	1.2
Construction	4.5	5.6	4.3	5.0	0.6[7]	5.1	5.5	1.9
Services	23.3	28.0	3.6	3.3	17.6	29.2	7.8	8.0

Notes: [1] Totals do not add up to 100 because of the exclusion of agriculture.
[2] 1971, 1981.
[3] Construction = Industry − Manufacturing.
[4] 1976, 1986.
[5] 1970, 1985.
[6] 1971, 1987.
[7] 1971, 1987.

Source: ILO mega-city survey (1990).

for less than one-third of total employment in most cities except Bombay and Shanghai. Its share has also been declining in many cities, Seoul, Shanghai and Rio being the exceptions. The increase in Rio is, however, largely due to changes in the area covered, which now includes manufacturing activity located in the periphery. It is interesting to note that the rate of growth of manufacturing employment not only fell from the 1970s to the 1980s in all cities except Shanghai but in many cities, particularly in Latin America, it actually became negative. Similarly, although the rate of growth of employment in services also declined in most cities, its fall was less marked than in the case of manufacturing. In Mexico City, the relative decline in manufacturing employment vis-à-vis services was so severe that, despite the fall in the rate of employment growth in the services sector, the share of services in total employment increased (from 59.6 per cent in 1970 to 70.5 per cent in 1988). As for construction, its share in total employment is relatively small, accounting for 3–7 per cent in most cities. In Seoul and Cairo it is somewhat higher (9-12 per cent). Agriculture has not been included in the table due to its low weight in all cities except Shanghai, where it declined from 26.5 per cent in 1970 to 12.9 per cent in 1988.

Looking at the demand side in terms of the evolution of the structure of GDP, the first point to emphasise is the relatively low labour-absorption capacity of the manufacturing sector. The manufacturing sector share in aggregate GDP is substantially higher than the percentage contribution of the sector to total employment (Table 3.9) in many cities because of the use of capital-intensive technology in this sector. Furthermore, the decline in the share of manufacturing in employment in most cities (recall Rio's methodological problem) was a result of the decline in the manufacturing sector's share in GDP. Thus, a high elasticity of employment to the level of output is indicated by the fact that the fall in the rate of growth of manufacturing employment was more acute than the decline in the rate of growth of manufacturing GDP. This illustrates the crucial role of demand in the determination of the level of employment, which was mentioned above as one of the basic characteristics of the formal sector of the urban labour market.

The exceptional character of Seoul, where growth in manufacturing GDP increased from 6.4 per cent during the 1970s to 8.7 per cent during the 1980s while employment growth in the same sector declined (from 10.6 per cent to 2.9 per cent), forcefully illustrates the capital-intensive nature of the production process in the manufacturing sector. The active process of incorporation of more productive technologies in the manufacturing sector in Seoul is indicated by the fact that although the rate of growth of capital stock in manufacturing fell from 14.2 per cent to 5.6 per cent (at the national level), that of real value added per worker increased from 2.2 per cent to 5.7 per cent (ILO mega-city survey, 1990). With regard to employment and GDP in Seoul's manufacturing sector, it is important to note that, consistent with the high rate of growth of employment during the 1970s (10.6 per cent), the observed growth in the share of employment between 1970 and 1988 (from 22.8 per cent to 30.7 per cent) mostly occurred during the 1970s. In fact, during the 1980s this share declined from a high point of 32.1 per cent, reached by 1980, to 30.7 per cent in 1988. Similarly, the bulk of the fall in the manufacturing sector's share in GDP between 1970 and 1988 (from 26.6 per cent to 19.1 per cent) had already taken place by 1980 (when it had dropped to 20.8 per cent). Both these facts (and the enormous growth in construction GDP during the 1980s) explain why, in spite of faster growth in manufacturing GDP compared with employment in manufacturing during the 1980s (8.7 per cent and 2.9 per cent, respectively), the 1988 share of the manufacturing sector in total employment continued to be higher than that of 1970, while the 1988 share in GDP was lower than that of 1970.

In general, the tendency of services to account for a higher share in GDP has been largely due to the fact that the fall in the rate of GDP growth in manufacturing has been greater than that in services. In Seoul, where both sectors continued to grow at substantial rates, the fall in the manufacturing share of GDP was more acute (in relative terms) than the fall in the services share. The shift of employment away from manufacturing had two special features in the case of Seoul: first, industrial decentralisation policies which moved manufacturing activity away from Seoul led to the worsening of unemployment in the city in comparison with the rest of the country; second, these policies shifted the demand for labour from unskilled and semi-skilled to the skilled labour required by the services sector (Kim *et al.*, 1991). In Table 3.10, the consequences of the decentralisation process for the structure of employment in terms of firm size are illustrated for both Bombay and Seoul. In the case of Bombay, the share in employment of firms with less than 100 workers increased from 1970 to 1980 vis-à-vis that of bigger firms. In Seoul the share of firms with 10–99 workers increased from 48.5 per cent to 59 per cent and their share in employment from 21.6 per cent to 46.1 per cent between 1973 and 1987. If the structure of employment had not shifted towards the small labour-intensive firms, the growth of employment would have been slower. In other words, the relative growth in the number of smaller

Table 3.10   Percentage distribution of establishments and employment in manufacturing in Bombay and Seoul, 1970–87

Number of workers	Share of establishments		Share of employment	
	1970	*1980*	*1970*	*1980*
Bombay				
0–9	84.3	84.8	16.7	25.5
10–99	14.1	14.2	20.1	23.8
100–499	1.2	0.8	17.7	14.3
500 +	0.4	0.2	45.5	36.4
Seoul				
	(1973)	(1987)	(1973)	(1987)
0–9	39.5	35.7	3.9	7.1
10–99	48.5	59.0	21.6	46.1
100–499	9.4	4.5	29.9	24.3
500 +	2.6	0.7	44.8	22.5

Sources: Adapted from Deshpande and Deshpande, 1991, table III.2; Kim *et al.*, 1991, table 2.13.

firms with 10–99 workers and in their share of employment compensated (although only partially in the 1980s) for the reduced labour absorption of the bigger firms as a result of the introduction of more capital-intensive technologies, as noted earlier. It should be noted, however, that although the growth in the relative number of smaller firms in Third-World mega-cities may have helped the process of labour absorption, it also has important implications for the revenue base of cities, particularly since the smallest firms (with less than 10 workers) do not generally have the capacity to pay for urban services and infrastructure development.

Looking at the sectoral distribution of employment by sex, the data presented in Table 3.11 show that the share in employment in the services sector is higher for women than for men. In most mega-cities, at least 70–80 per cent of female workers are employed in the services sector. This structural capacity of the services sector to absorb the female labour force contrasts with that of manufacturing, where the share in employment is higher for men than for women in all cities except Seoul. In the case of Seoul, there has been a significant decline in the proportion of women in the services sector, from 73.2 per cent in 1970 to 64.2 per cent in 1988, with a corresponding increase in the manufacturing sector (from 24.0 per cent to 33.4 per cent) during the same period. In terms of annual growth rates, the data indicate that the contribution of female employment to the growth of manufacturing employment during the 1970s was more important than that of male employment (in Seoul, 15.5 per cent for women as against 8.8 per cent for men), and the fall in the growth of manufacturing employment from the 1970s to the 1980s was more severe for male than for female employment, particularly in Cairo and Latin American cities such as Rio and Mexico City. Similarly, the observed fall in the growth of services-sector employment over the same period was more severe for female than for male employment (especially in the case of Rio, Mexico City and Seoul).

With regard to employment status, the contribution of self-employment to the observed growth in manufacturing employment in Seoul during the 1970s was important both for male and female employment (Table 3.11). In the case of Bombay, self-employment in manufacturing grew faster (4.6 per cent) than wage employment (since total employment grew at 2.1 per cent, see Table 3.9) during the 1970s. The figures here indicate the importance of the role of the informal segment of manufacturing in female labour absorption. In turn, the importance of self-employment for labour absorption in the construction sector is illustrated by its dynamism during the 1970s in both Seoul and Cairo (growth rates of 19.8 per cent and 7.8 per cent per annum, respectively). Similarly, the significant contribution of self-employment to the observed growth of employment in services during the 1970s is apparent in Seoul, Mexico City and Rio. In keeping with the crucial role of the informal segment of the services sector for absorption of the female labour force in Latin America, the female segment was particularly dynamic in Rio and Mexico City, with annual growth rates of 22.9 per cent and 7.8 per cent, respectively.

The fact that the fall in the growth rate of wage as well as total employment in manufacturing from the 1970s to the 1980s was more severe than the fall in self-employment points to the shifting of the labour force from the formal to the informal sector of the labour market in periods of recession (see Tables 3.9 and 3.11). Nevertheless, this tendency is not necessarily the same for the other sectors. In the case of construction the impact of the demand constraint on smaller productive units is shown by the sharp fall in the growth of self-employment in Seoul and Mexico City (even worse for female

Table 3.11 Structure and growth of employment and self-employment by sex and major economic sector in selected cities, 1970–88 (%)

	Employment								Self-employment					
	Share				Annual rates of growth				Annual rates of growth					
	1970		1988		1970–80		1980–88		1970–80			1980–88		
City/sector	M	F	M	F	M	F	M	F	M	F	T	M	F	T
Bombay														
Manufacturing	43.3	23.9	42.2	21.4	2.0	3.5	–	–	4.5	5.4	4.6	–	–	–
Construction	3.1	3.1	3.4	3.6	3.3	6.0	–	–	1.4	8.1	3.4	–	–	–
Services	52.6	72.5	53.2	74.0	1.9	4.6	–	–	1.7	5.6	1.9	–	–	–
Cairo														
Manufacturing	28.7	17.1	25.1	13.7	3.7	11.7	−0.3	1.7	2.7	16.3	3.1	0.4	−5.1	0.1
Construction	9.9	1.8	13.9	1.9	6.0	21.9	4.9	4.6	7.8	–	7.8	8.8	–	8.8
Services	60.3	79.7	55.0	82.7	2.0	2.6	2.7	2.6	1.2	−0.6	1.1	1.1	3.4	1.2
Mexico City														
Manufacturing	39.7	22.6	25.0	18.2	6.0	7.4	−0.9	1.2	0.1	3.2	0.7	−0.9	−0.4	−0.7
Construction	8.1	0.8	6.4	0.7	6.1	5.8	−0.1	2.8	4.5	–	4.1	4.1	–	−2.0
Services	52.7	74.8	65.4	80.3	7.4	8.9	3.6	2.9	4.5	7.8	5.6	5.6	2.7	3.9

Rio de Janeiro																
Manufacturing	30.6	10.2	17.8	11.8	10.6	15.8	−1.5	0.4	7.4	12.2	8.1	–	–	3.5		
Construction	–	–	11.4	0.5	–	–	–	–	–	–	–	–	–	5.0		
Services	68.0	89.7	69.0	87.5	6.6	9.4	5.3	4.6	10.8	22.9	12.1	–	–	6.4		
Seoul																
Manufacturing	22.5	24.0	29.4	33.4	8.8	15.5	2.9	3.1	10.6	–	12.2	4.6	14.8	6.8		
Construction	8.7	1.2	12.2	2.1	8.4	21.2	4.3	−1.6	20.6	6.9	19.8	−3.9	−8.7	−4.1		
Services	66.3	73.2	57.9	64.2	4.2	9.6	4.3	4.7	7.1	7.6	7.2	2.8	3.8	3.2		

Source: ILO mega-city survey (1990).

employment in the former case). With regard to services, the more severe fall in the growth of wage employment in Mexico City, where the growth in male self-employment actually accelerated from the 1970s to the 1980s, once again illustrates the shifting of the labour force from the formal to the informal sector. Although in the case of Seoul a sharper decline took place in the rate of growth of self-employment (from 7.2 per cent to 3.2 per cent per annum), the fact that the fall was worse for male (from 7.1 per cent to 2.8 per cent) than for female self-employment (from 7.6 to 3.8 per cent) points to the buffer role of the informal sector for the female labour force.

FRAGMENTED URBAN LABOUR MARKETS AND ACCESS OF THE POOR TO EMPLOYMENT OPPORTUNITIES

Segmentation in urban labour markets can persist only if there are forces controlling and differentiating access to jobs in the different segments. Rodgers (1989) argues that in a smoothly functioning market economy, access to jobs and rewards would depend on the leisure preferences and productivities of individuals, so there would be no need to study the problem of access as such: it would be sufficient to analyse the characteristics of labour supply and demand, and the processes by which they are brought into equilibrium. But he suggests that the interaction between poverty and labour markets can indeed be posed as essentially one of access: as discussed above, labour markets are in general highly stratified, with mobility between segments impeded by institutional barriers and dependent on characteristics, credentials and resources to which access is unequally distributed. Rodgers further argues that the access routes to different parts of the labour market can vary greatly but in general depend on:

1. interpersonal networks in terms of kin, caste, community or ethnic origin;
2. formal education;
3. skills and experience acquired through apprenticeship or on-the-job training;
4. personal characteristics likely to appeal to employers, which may – depending on the job – include age, sex, migrant status, docility and initiative;
5. access to capital and product markets needed for self-employment.

There are also negative characteristics which may well be important in job access, such as:

1. experience of unemployment, or irregular employment history;
2. personal appearance or accent;
3. inadequate health or nutritional status.

Differentiation in access to employment opportunities thus amounts to differences in the characteristics noted above. Lack of access to jobs and poverty are closely associated with lack of schooling above the primary level; it is mainly secondary level qualifications which facilitate access to the more desirable employment opportunities. This is one reason why the studies reviewed in Rodgers (1989) showed that in urban areas in the Philippines and Panama, the lack of access to secondary education was a key variable in explaining poverty. In Panama, for instance, 35 per cent of workers with primary education fall below the poverty line, compared with only 11 per cent of those with secondary education. A survey in Calcutta found that consumption levels were closely correlated with all measures of post-primary education. Taken at face value, such evidence would suggest that urban wage differentials may be due less to market imperfections than to differences in productivity levels (the human capital approach). However, studies reviewed by Rodgers also indicate that education is more likely to be used as a screening device by employers than as an accurate reflection of the relative productivity levels of workers. It discriminates against the poor since they are less likely to have access to secondary education.

The gender-based discrimination in employment opportunities is also often attributed to pre-entry discrimination against women as regards access to education. Table 3.12 shows that in Bombay in 1981 a greater proportion of women (39.3 per cent) than men (26.1 per cent) were illiterate.

Table 3.13 shows that female attendance at educational institutions in Bombay falls perceptibly after the age of 15, since females in the 15–19 age group are expected to share the housework with the other women. In the 20–24 age group, marriage further reduces female attendance at educational institutions and therefore also the share of women holding higher qualifications compared to men. The reluctance of parents to educate their daughters thus confines them to housework and low-paid occupations.

Table 3.12   Percentage distribution of population by education and sex, Bombay, 1981

Education level	Males	Females
Illiterate	26.1	39.3
Literate*	12.5	12.9
Primary	16.1	14.8
Middle	16.3	13.7
Secondary	17.7	11.7
Higher secondary	4.3	2.9
Diploma not equal to degree	0.8	0.4
Graduate and above	6.2	4.3
	100.0	100.0
Literacy rate	73.9	60.7

* Can read but no formal schooling.
Source: Adapted from *Census of India, 1981, Series 12, Social and Cultural Tables*, table C.II.

Table 3.13   Proportion attending school/college by age and sex, Bombay, 1981 (%)

Age group	Proportion attending			Index of inequality (proportion females/ proportion males)
	Males	Females	Total	
0–4	3.4	2.9	3.1	0.85
5–9	75.5	71.6	73.6	0.95
10–14	87.7	81.8	84.9	0.93
15–19	51.0	44.4	48.1	0.87
20–24	13.8	8.7	11.7	0.63

Source: Deshpande and Deshpande, 1991, table II.41.

While education is important, it is not necessarily the dominant factor in all labour-market situations. In Calcutta, for instance, Bardhan found that wages vary much less according to level of education in casual jobs than they do in regular jobs (Bardhan, 1989). Perhaps the most important way in which education interacts with poverty is at the intergenerational level: poverty and low levels of education of parents are associated with high drop-out rates from school and the earlier entry of children into the labour market, as discussed in more detail in Chapter 4. This limits the possibilities of acquiring educational qualifications or vocational training, and perpetuates the existence of an unskilled lower stratum of the labour force.

There is evidence of discrimination in earnings as well as job access on the basis of sex (see, for example, Anker and Hein, 1985). In Bombay, it was found that the earnings of female regular workers were lower than those of men with similar qualifications. Female earnings were lower by 11–59 per cent, depending on the level of education (Table 3.14).

Migrants to urban areas may be expected to face greater difficulties in job access than urban natives. This may be for several reasons. First, migrants may be discriminated against because of ethnic, religious or tribal differences from urban natives. Second, migrants are often considered to have a lower degree of commitment to work than natives, and may therefore be less favoured by employers. Third,

Table 3.14   Average earnings per day by sex, age and education, Bombay, 1983 (Rupees)

Age/education	Males (A)		Females (B)		Index of female earnings (B/A) × 100	
	Casual workers	Regular wage or salary workers	Casual workers	Regular wage or salary workers	Casual workers	Regular wage or salary workers
Age						
5–14	3.89	6.91	–	5.00	–	75
15–19	14.98	28.31	8.43	20.47	56	72
60 +	17.84	22.71	2.80	15.70	16	69
Completed years of education						
0–2	–	18.59	–	7.70	–	41
3–9	–	21.47	–	11.34	–	53
10–11	–	30.92	–	27.49	–	89
12	–	37.18	–	23.55	–	63
13–16	–	48.40	–	31.96	–	66
17 +	–	65.70	–	37.72	–	57

Source: Adapted from Deshpande and Deshpande, 1991, tables II.30 and II.31.

migrants are not likely to have as many contacts as natives, and this may reduce their chances of finding suitable employment. For these reasons there has long been an assumption in the development literature that rural–urban migrants form a relatively low-wage, easily exploited urban stratum. But while some empirical work supports this view, and there is widespread evidence of low-income points of entry for migrants such as domestic service or construction work, on balance the evidence that migrants systematically do badly in urban labour markets is unconvincing. Moreover, a large proportion of migration seems to occur after a job has been found, usually through a network of contacts. Such networks, built up on kin, community, caste or similar lines, often appear to dominate the process of job access for the poor.

Harriss (1989), on the basis of several studies in India, argues that access to urban jobs for migrants does not involve entry at the bottom of the urban labour market, but rather a horizontal shift in which the level of entry reflects position in the rural hierarchy, with the result that migrants are distributed throughout the urban employment structure. The rigidity of the rural hierarchy is then reflected in low levels of mobility within urban labour markets, with such mobility as does exist being mainly between jobs of similar status. However, the evidence on intersectoral mobility among migrants is mixed in the literature (Oberai, 1987).

Segmented labour markets should not, however, be seen purely as a cause of increasing poverty. By reducing competition, they may make it more difficult for employers to push wages down; they also appear to generate a sense of solidarity which provides support in times of particular hardship. But at the same time they inhibit access to work, thus swelling the ranks of casual workers in those sectors where entry is unconstrained.

LABOUR MARKET STRUCTURE, PRODUCTIVITY AND POVERTY

Urban poverty poses a major challenge to policy-makers and urban planners because of its negative impact on productivity and the working environment. A recent study of Rio notes that

> contrary to the poor in rural areas and smaller cities, the metropolitan poor live in a very competitive environment and cannot turn to small production for self-consumption as a means to supplement

their real income. Moreover, in the large metropolis, family ties become loose and income in kind is virtually non-existent. This set of conditions usually gives birth to negative attitudes towards work and self-improvement. By the same token, these conditions encourage criminality and other forms of illegal activities. Hence, unless the so-called *metropolisation of poverty* process is reversed, or at least controlled, it is likely to create hindrance to economic development and political participation in large Brazilian cities. (Tolosa *et al.*, 1991, p. 102)

No matter how poverty is defined, it always implies a state of deprivation or dispossession. The individual's judgement on poverty depends on (a) how deprived or dispossessed he feels according to some absolute measure, and (b) his own situation or condition relative to others in society. The former refers to the concept of absolute poverty, which implies the existence of some socially acceptable norm for subsistence or survival, while the latter refers to relative poverty, focusing on income (or asset) distribution. A commonly used indicator to describe inequality is the Gini coefficient, which measures the area between the Lorenz Curve (accumulated inequality) and the diagonal (perfect equality). This indicator is, however, susceptible to criticism, *inter alia*, of insensitivity to inequalities in the lower tail of the distribution.

Most of the measures of absolute poverty are related to the level of income (purchasing power) necessary to provide a biologically and/or socially acceptable living standard. Such an income level is used to define the so-called 'poverty line'. The group of individuals or families below such a line are thus characterised as 'poor' and constitute the main target of redistribution policies. In India, the Sixth Five Year Plan (1980–5) defined the poverty line as 'the mid-point of the monthly per capita expenditure class having a daily calorie intake of 2,100 in urban areas'.[1] In the case of Brazil, the poverty line is often set as a fixed proportion of the minimum wage.

The head-count approach has certain serious limitations. Average nutritional intake, for example, ignores the variations required for different age and occupational groups. Moreover, various food baskets, each perhaps requiring a different purchasing power, can produce the same level of nutrition. If a fixed proportion of the minimum wage is used as a measure, the erosion of purchasing power in the course of the inflationary process is often missed unless the minimum wage is revised upwards more frequently than usually occurs in most developing countries. There is also the problem of the distribution of the poor below the poverty line. How close they are to the poverty line will determine the impact of incremental incomes or consumption on the alleviation of poverty.

Notwithstanding these limitations and the variations in the definitions used, which make comparisons across cities difficult, the data presented in Table 3.15 on the incidence of poverty do suggest that in general about one-third of the population in most cities, particularly in Latin America, is living in absolute poverty. The comparison of city-level and national figures also shows that despite relatively high productivity and growth rates in mega-cities, as noted earlier, the incidence of poverty in most such cities is at least as high as in the countries as a whole. This may indicate that the pattern of economic development in large cities is characterised by high income inequality. In terms of policy, it implies that economic growth may not necessarily solve the problem of urban poverty without the active implementation of direct anti-poverty programmes.

Table 3.15 Proportion of population below the poverty line in selected cities, 1970–88 (%)

	City			National		
	1970	1980	1988	1970	1980	1988
Bombay	–	15.7	–	48.1	37.4	–
Cairo	–	30.4	34.0	–	30.0	33.8
Lagos	–	–	22.2	–	.	17.9
Mexico City	47.1	–	30.8	22.9	–	–
Rio de Janeiro	–	27.2	32.5	54.1	34.8	32.5
Seoul	7.0	15.1	7.8	4.8	13.3	7.7

Source: ILO mega-city survey (1990).

An equally worrying picture emerges from a consideration of the figures on relative poverty. The data in Table 3.16 on Brazilian cities point to a pattern which illustrates the impact of the economic crisis in Latin America, that is, a worsening of the inequality in income distribution, which is especially severe in large cities such as Rio. Between 1981 and 1989, the Gini coefficient for Rio increased by 16.2 per cent as compared with 9.7 per cent for São Paulo during the same period.

Table 3.16   Relative poverty in Brazilian metropolitan areas, 1981–9

Metropolitan areas	Gini index	
	1981	*1989*
Rio de Janeiro	0.579	0.673
Belem	0.551	0.636
Fortaleza	0.597	0.654
Recife	0.602	0.652
Salvador	0.595	0.641
Belo Horizonte	0.566	0.621
São Paulo	0.516	0.566
Curitiba	0.535	0.582
Porto Alegre	0.518	0.571

Source: S. Rocha: 'Pobreza Metropolitana e Ciclos de Curto Prazo', *Boletim Conjuntural do IPEA* (Rio de Janeiro, Jan. 1991), quoted in Tolosa *et al.*, 1991, table 3.12.

The figures for the Asian mega-cities show a more severe relative inequality in the cities than in the countries as a whole (Table 3.17). While income distribution in Bombay became slightly less skewed between 1970 and 1988, there was no perceptible change at the national level. In the case of Seoul, however, income distribution worsened

Table 3.17   Income distribution in selected Asian cities, 1970–88

	Percentage share of household income					
	City			National		
	1970	*1980*	*1988*	*1970*	*1980*	*1988*
Bombay						
Bottom 30%	9.0	–	11.6	14.6	14.5	–
Middle 40%	24.2	–	26.3	33.8	34.3	–
Top 30%	66.8	–	62.1	51.6	51.2	–
Seoul						
Bottom 30%	14.3	9.4	12.7	13.7	9.9	13.0
Middle 40%	34.4	31.5	32.0	33.1	32.3	32.9
Top 30%	51.3	59.1	55.3	53.8	57.8	54.1

Source: ILO mega-city survey (1990).

during the same period (the bottom 30 per cent had only 12.7 per cent of income in 1988 compared with 14.3 per cent in 1970, while the top 30 per cent increased their share to 55.3 per cent in 1988 from 51.3 per cent in 1970). Although there was an improvement in 1988 compared with 1980, it was not enough to compensate for the severe deterioration of the 1970s. This illustrates the plausibility of such deterioriation in income distribution occurring in the course of rapid economic growth.

There is a great deal of controversy about the role of open urban unemployment in generating poverty in developing countries. Some observers regard growing open unemployment as the main cause of urban poverty, while others argue that it is not the primary cause. According to this alternative view, the urban poor cannot afford to remain without some form of employment, since they do not have any alternative source of subsistence. In most cities, as mentioned earlier, open unemployment can be found among the relatively well-educated younger members of the urban middle- and higher-income groups, who can rely on family support while they search for jobs commensurate with their qualifications and wage expectations. In accordance with this view, most open unemployment is voluntary and the main problem then is not unemployment but low productivity and low earnings. Neither this view nor that citing open unemployment as the main cause of poverty finds much support from empirical evidence.

Tokman (1987) notes that between 1980 and 1985 the number of unemployed in urban areas in Latin American countries increased by 48 per cent as a consequence of the economic recession. This he regards as a new phenomenon since historically underemployment has been the main problem, with open unemployment being low and stable, except for short cyclical fluctuations. In addition, the unemployed used to belong mainly to the secondary labour force (mostly women and young adults), since heads of households could not afford to be without incomes while searching for jobs. The expansion in the rate of open unemployment during the 1980s was accompanied by changes in the structure of unemployment. Heads of households, men in the most active age groups, and workers with previous experience and more education were all more likely to become unemployed. Many other empirical studies conducted in Latin America and Asia confirm that unemployment is indeed associated with poverty and not confined to the relatively better-off sections of the community. Although the poor are not simply the unemployed, and many unemployed are not poor, there is on the whole a positive relationship between poverty and unemployment.

Rodgers (1989) shows higher rates of unemployment among the poor in some Latin American cities (Table 3.18).

Table 3.18   Unemployment and poverty in selected Latin American cities

	Poverty or income group*		
	Very poor	*Poor*	*Middle/high*
Urban Costa Rica, 1982			
Unemployment rate	11.0	6.0	2.0
Metropolitan Panama, 1983			
Unemployment rate	14.8	11.1	3.8
Santiago de Chile, 1982			
Unemployment rate, heads	50.0	18.3	5.3
Unemployment rate, spouses	25.5	19.4	6.8
Unemployment rate, children	63.6	45.4	23.7
Santiago de Chile, 1985			
Unemployment rate, heads	23.7	9.1	3.1
Unemployment rate, spouses	23.4	14.6	4.5
Unemployment rate, children	30.1	16.5	12.7

* The subgroups are not strictly comparable from country to country, because of varying definitions of poverty. They should therefore be interpreted as conveying relative positions. Unemployment rates are also not strictly comparable between countries because of varying definitions and reference periods.
Source: Adapted from Rodgers, 1989, table 1.2.

While open unemployment was rising in the 1980s, real wages were also generally falling in most Latin American countries (Singh, 1989). Thus poverty can be expected to increase not only as a consequence of rising unemployment and underemployment but also as a result of falling real wages. The available evidence suggests that during the initial years of the economic crisis, the number of families below the poverty line increased from 12 per cent to 16 per cent between 1981 and 1982 in Chile and from 17 per cent to 29 per cent in Costa Rica. In Brazil, the number of individuals below the poverty line in urban areas increased from 31 per cent in 1980 to 36.6 per cent in 1982.[2]

Several recent research studies also suggest that urban poverty is not simply a preserve of the informal sector but occurs in many parts of the formal sector as well. The principal income earners of poor urban households are found in virtually all types of employment – in large, medium and small firms; in wage employment and self-employment; in government service as well as in the private sector. Furthermore, the poor are not necessarily those who have most recently migrated to a city, and, as already noted, migrants do not tend to enter into what are considered typical informal-sector activities such as street vending, shoe shining, etc., in disproportionate numbers. Nevertheless, the evidence does suggest that the proportion of poor tends to be higher in the informal sector than in the formal sector (Rodgers, 1989). In Brazilian large cities in 1983, 16 per cent of protected workers were poor (that is, had earnings below the minimum wage) compared with 52 per cent of unprotected workers; 11 per cent of organised-sector workers were poor compared with 66 per cent of unorganised-sector workers. Similarly in urban Costa Rica, 75 per cent of the destitute household heads and 54 per cent of the other poor household heads worked in the informal sector, where 68 per cent of households were poor. In Bombay, 40 per cent of casual workers were below the poverty line compared with 10 per cent and 12 per cent of regular workers in small and large firms, respectively. The existence of poor and vulnerable groups in urban areas is therefore related to labour-market segmentation in that both unemployment and underemployment stem from the weak labour-absorption capacity of the modern sector. The labour force then spills over into the informal sector, where wages are generally low. The unequal distribution of technical progress between modern and traditional sectors, mentioned above as leading to highly differentiated growth in productivity, thus leaves the traditional-sector labour force in a situation of underemployment, low productivity and poverty. Table 3.19 illustrates the higher rate of productivity growth in the capital-intensive manufacturing sector. In the case of Bombay, for example, value added per worker in manufacturing grew at a rate of 8.2 per cent per annum between 1981 and 1985, while GDP per worker as a whole contracted at an annual rate of 1.5 per cent.

The existence of poor and vulnerable groups in urban areas thus raises doubts about the efficiency and equity of the way urban labour markets function. Some studies argue that labour-market segmentation keeps the urban poor locked within a 'poverty trap'. But, as noted above, the empirical basis for this view is flimsy. Poverty and poorly paid and precarious work certainly exist, but it is by no means clear that it is the structure of labour markets, as opposed to overall development and employment policies, that is the main cause. In many low-income countries labour-market vulnerability is only one aspect of the overall poverty and income distribution issue. A large proportion of the poor are to be found in low-productivity self-

Table 3.19   Average annual rate of growth of real GDP and value added per worker in manufacturing in selected cities, 1970–88 (%)

	City				National			
	GDP	GDP per capita	GDP per worker	Value added per worker in manufacturing	GDP	GDP per capita	GDP per worker	Value added per worker in manufacturing
Bombay								
1971–81	4.2	0.9	1.5	3.8	3.2	1.3	0.9	3.3
1981–85	2.0	−0.9	−1.5	8.2	4.8	2.0	2.0	6.0
Cairo								
1960–76	3.9	1.3	1.1	–	4.5	2.4	2.2	2.0
1976–86	7.2	5.0	10.0	–	7.9	4.8	6.1	4.5
Lagos								
1971–81	7.1	−0.7	–	–	5.8	3.1	–	–
1981–88	1.8	−4.5	–	–	1.0	1.8	–	–
Mexico City								
1970–80	6.9	2.5	1.2	4.7	6.2	3.1	1.0	6.1
1980–85	2.1	−5.2	–	–	1.9	−1.1	–	2.2
Rio de Janeiro								
1971–80	7.0	4.7	3.0	–	8.3	5.5	4.4	–
1980–87	−0.7	−3.5	−3.9	–	2.2	0.1	−1.4	–
Seoul								
1970–80	8.9	4.7	1.7	2.2	11.1	7.1	3.6	3.8
1980–88	7.9	7.2	6.3	5.7	10.4	7.8	8.4	4.8
Shanghai								
1971–81	5.8	4.9	2.8	2.9*	1.9	0.3	−0.2	–
1981–88	4.2	2.8	3.8	3.0*	9.9	8.4	6.8	–

* Growth rate of labour productivity in industries.
Source: ILO mega-city survey (1990).

employment activities, which are largely outside the reach of traditional labour-market regulation and intervention. It can be argued that it is the pace and pattern of economic growth rather than labour-market interventions which will potentially have the greatest impact on poverty alleviation.

The importance of economic stagnation in generating poverty, particularly in relation to the impact of the crisis in Latin America, has already been noted above. Table 3.20 complements Table 3.19 in substantiating the role of the pace and pattern of economic growth in generating urban poverty by showing the impact of a decline in growth upon earnings. The most severe falls in earnings per worker from the

1970s to the 1980s took place in Latin American and African countries (that is, Brazil, Mexico and Nigeria), where the crisis of the early 1980s brought about a sharp decline in the growth of per capita GDP.

Referring back to Table 3.19, the following points concerning the evolution of GDP and value added per worker in manufacturing are worth noting. First, in all cases (except Cairo, where the data relate to a different time period) the fall in GDP growth was more severe for the cities than for the countries as a whole; this indicates that manufacturing activities largely located in urban areas were relatively more affected by the economic crisis of the early 1980s. Second, per capita GDP fell in most countries but the decline in Latin America and Africa (Lagos, Mexico City and Rio) was more severe and reached alarming proportions. Third, the fall in per capita GDP and per worker in Bombay compared with the increase for India as a whole illustrates the negative effect of labour supply pressure resulting from the rapid growth of the city's population. Conversely, the increase in the growth of GDP per capita and per worker compared with the overall decline in GDP growth in Seoul reveals the consequences of decentralisation and capital-intensification processes operating in the city. Fourth, between the 1970s and the 1980s, a fall in GDP per worker can be observed in Bombay (where its rate of growth fell to 1.5 per cent), Rio (where its rate of growth declined to −3.9 per cent) and Mexico City. Conversely, a substantial increase in the rate of growth of value added per worker

Table 3.20   Annual growth rate of earnings per employee and GDP per capita in selected countries, 1970–88 (%)

Country	Earnings per employee		GDP per capita	
	1970–80	*1980–7*	*1965–80*	*1980–8*
Brazil	4.0	−1.1	6.3	1.2
China	–	4.2	4.1	9.2
Egypt	4.1	1.6	2.8	2.8
India	0.5	4.9	1.5	3.3
Kenya	−3.4	−2.3	3.1	−0.2
Korea, Rep. of	10.0	5.6	7.3	7.7
Mexico	3.8	−0.6	2.3	−2.4
Nigeria	–	−9.6	4.2	−4.3

Source: Adapted from *Human Development Report 1991*, table 16, pp. 151–2; table 23, pp. 164–5.

in manufacturing took place in the case of both Bombay and Seoul. The case of Bombay, where a large increase in productivity growth in manufacturing between the 1970s and the 1980s contrasts with the fall in the rate of growth of overall productivity (GDP per worker), suggests that there is a pervasive segmentation of productive activity in developing countries between a small number of highly productive capital-intensive firms and a large number of less productive labour-intensive firms. In particular, the process of capital intensification in the technologically advanced segment seems to have been accompanied by the previously noted movement of labour towards the less productive segment.

With regard to the implications of the pace and pattern of economic growth for poverty conditions, the case of the Republic of Korea provides some interesting insights. The data presented in Table 3.19 show that during the 1980s, GDP grew in Seoul at a rate of 7.9 per cent while it declined by 0.7 per cent per annum in Rio. The incidence of poverty fell in Seoul and increased in Rio (Table 3.15). This may indicate that rapid economic growth leads to an improvement in poverty conditions. But it is interesting to note that no such improvement took place in Seoul during the 1970s, although the rate of economic growth was even faster during this period (8.9 per cent) than during the 1980s. This suggests, therefore, that economic growth alone may not help alleviate poverty, since much also depends on the nature of the growth process and on other conditions being met. In Seoul during the 1980s, for example, rapid economic growth was accompanied by an increase in real earnings which was made possible by increases in productivity. This therefore led to a reduction in poverty. During the 1970s, however, the government was more concerned with establishing international competitiveness in export markets. As a result, a policy of wage restraint was adopted, leading to a worsening of poverty. The experience of Seoul thus suggests that the objective of poverty alleviation may be deferred until the attainment of a certain level of economic growth. It is only when economic growth has been sustained that redistribution mechanisms may be allowed to operate. Sri Lanka provides an interesting contrast of a growth process where competitiveness in export markets has been achieved through exploitation of a cheap (mainly female) labour force rather than through an increase in productivity. This has therefore created a situation where economic growth is accompanied by a fall in living standards.

While economic growth may be necessary to reduce poverty, most observers agree that there is also a need for protective action to alleviate the worst manifestations of labour-market vulnerability. Protection of workers would help particular groups such as domestic servants and wage workers in small-scale businesses. Moreover, it is suggested that the growth of GDP in recent years, although not sufficient to generate the number of new jobs required, has been concentrated mainly in the modern sector of the economy. As already noted, an unequal distribution of technical progress between modern and traditional-sectors has led to highly differentiated rates of productivity growth, leaving the traditional sector labour force in a permanent situation of underemployment, low productivity and poverty. This process is reflected in the segmentation of the labour market: on the one hand there is the modern sector, responsible for a large proportion of total production but only a small proportion of total employment; on the other hand there are activities of a traditional type, employing the majority of the labour force, but making only a limited contribution to total production. This leads to a situation in which workers with equal abilities obtain different incomes, depending on the production stratum of the enterprises in which they are employed.

4 Scope for Employment Promotion and Poverty Alleviation in Third-World Mega-Cities

Employment creation and improving the earning capacity of the poor in urban areas are two major challenges facing city and national authorities in developing countries. This chapter identifies institutional and other constraints on increasing employment and productivity. It also examines the role of macroeconomic policies, labour-market interventions and targeted anti-poverty programmes in employment generation and poverty alleviation. Chapter 5 will examine the way in which increasing the access of the urban poor to social services can contribute to employment promotion and poverty alleviation.

INSTITUTIONAL AND OTHER CONSTRAINTS ON INCREASING EMPLOYMENT, OUTPUT AND PRODUCTIVITY

In relation to employment policy for urban areas there are, as noted earlier, two rather different schools of thought. According to one, creating more jobs is the central issue for Third-World cities; tackling this represents the best way of dealing with poverty and most of the other ills of urban society. The alternative view, which has gained more prominence in recent years, regards productivity rather than employment as the main policy issue in relation to the urban poor.

Whatever the merits of this latter thesis during periods of 'normal economic growth', open unemployment and underemployment greatly increased in the towns and cities of developing countries, particularly in Latin America and Africa, during the economic crisis of the 1980s, as already noted. Such unemployment and underemployment can only be significantly reduced by national governments adopting overall macroeconomic policies, which can bring about a resumption of economic growth.

Singh (1989) suggests that the most important channels through which the world economic crisis has adversely affected economic growth and the balance of payments position in developing countries are the following:

1. a reduction in the demand for Third-World products, particularly commodity and mineral exports;
2. a fall in commodity prices as a consequence of (1), and hence adverse movements in the terms of trade;
3. an increase in the real burden of interest and debt-service payments, partly due to (1) and (2) and partly due to an enormous increase in interest rates;
4. a reduction in the quantum of aid and other capital flows.

The balance of payments crisis has been particularly severe in Latin America and Africa where it has adversely affected economic growth. Only countries in South and East Asia (including India and China) continued to register an increase in per capita income.

Empirical research shows that more often than not it is the urban areas that have been the most affected by the economic crisis. As noted earlier, per capita GDP has declined in most mega-cities, particularly in Latin America and Africa. Singh (1989) argues that the main reason for this is that in many countries the balance of payments constraint has forced imports of industrial raw materials, spare parts, etc., to be curtailed, which in turn has led to low levels of industrial production

Table 4.1   Average annual growth rate of GDP per capita in selected developing countries, 1965–88 (%)

Country	1965–80	1980–8
Brazil	6.3	1.2
China	4.1	9.2
Egypt	2.8	2.8
India	1.5	3.3
Kenya	3.1	−0.2
Korea, Rep. of	7.3	7.7
Mexico	3.6	−1.4
Nigeria	4.2	−4.3

Source: Adapted from *Human Development Report* (1991) table 23.

and capacity utilisation. Although this "import strangulation" has adverse effects on both agricultural and industrial production, the latter has usually been more affected since it requires more inputs from abroad. Because of the worsening economic situation and resource constraints in urban areas, the real rate of growth of per capita expenditure on health and education became negative during the 1980s in most Third-World mega-cities (as discussed in more detail in Chapter 5; see Tables 5.11 and 5.13).

Research findings therefore suggest that in general overall growth of the economy is a powerful determinant of labour demand. Output–employment conflicts are, however, possible. Whether this conflict actually arises in practice depends on two key questions:

1. whether factor prices in an economy are market-determined or whether 'factor price distortions' render capital artificially cheap and labour artificially expensive;
2. whether technologies are of the neo-classical type with smooth substitution possibilities between capital and labour or whether technological possibilities are limited to one or a few fixed proportions.

Economic growth alone, therefore, may not guarantee a higher level of employment nor a better distribution of income. Moreover, the balance of payments deficit associated with reduced economic growth may also adversely affect employment and poverty through other important channels. First, the balance of payments constraint and reduced economic growth together may lead to inflation, which often has very unfavourable effects on disadvantaged groups in a society. Second and equally important, all countries, developing as well as developed, often respond to an economic crisis by instituting changes in monetary, fiscal, exchange rate or commercial policies. These adjustment measures may have important implications for income distribution and poverty. More specifically, during the 1980s most countries in Latin America and Africa, as well as many in Asia and elsewhere in the Third World, had to accept IMF-approved adjustment programmes. The economic policy measures (large-scale devaluations, reductions in public expenditure, etc.) which invariably constitute these programmes have had adverse effects, particularly for the poor. Stabilisation and structural adjustment measures have led to increasing retrenchments in organised-sector employment and a corresponding rise in casual and precarious forms of employment in the informal sector, as noted earlier.

In recent years many developing countries have also followed an import-substitution strategy. The paradox of the import-substitution type of development strategy is that, while it discriminates severely against the agricultural sector and appears to be partly responsible for the fast growth of large urban centres, it has led to excessive dualism within the urban sector and has made the absorption of labour more difficult. Import substitution often results in capital-intensive projects with high capital costs which make heavy demands on foreign exchange and affect real savings in the economy. By implication the demand for labour, especially for unskilled or semi-skilled labour, falls, and low wages and underemployment continue to be the lot of such workers.

Some developing countries, especially in Asia, have relied on a labour-intensive, export-led industrialisation and growth strategy. Much concern has, however, been expressed about the quality of employment generated by this strategy. A specific issue has been that of low-wage, 'dead-end' jobs, with harsh and demanding labour conditions, which have proliferated in industries such as clothing and electronics. The labour force for such industries has been drawn almost exclusively from young women, and the issue of exploitative wage and employment relationships has been heightened by sex discrimination, as already noted in the case of Seoul. The debate on this issue has been polarised between the view that prevailing wage and employment conditions are determined by market factors (the supply price of labour and considerations of international competitiveness) and the view that they reflect the exploitative use of market power by multinational enterprises with the connivance of governments eager to attract foreign investment at any cost. According to the former view, the 'bad jobs' created are better than the alternative of 'no jobs', whereas the latter view emphasises that less exploitative employment-creation alternatives exist. Another difference relates to the benefits to be derived from a process of industrialisation that is based on a heavy reliance on foreign capital. The critics of the exploitative methods used also maintain that the suffering of the workers is futile since the process in fact yields no long-term benefits in terms of the enhancement of indigenous industrialisation capacity.

These opposing viewpoints remain unresolved, given the political and ideological differences involved. The advocates of export-led industrialisation point to rising real wages in the newly industrialised countries (NICs) and the growth in the industrial and technological capacity of these countries as refutation of the strong radical views about the impossibility of industrial progress through the process of 'dependent industrialisation'. Against this, however, the critics point to the continuing problems of political liberalisation in the NICs, the continuing limitations on workers' rights, and the severe retrenchment of labour and sharp fall in wages in export-oriented industries in countries such as the Philippines and Malaysia, as manifestations of the precarious and uncaring nature of dependent industrialisation.

Economic growth policies alone will clearly not solve the general employment problem of developing countries, nor specifically the problems encountered in the absorption of urban labour supply. As noted earlier, institutional practices such as minimum wage legislation, public employment restrictions, educational requirements unrelated to productivity criteria, ethnic and caste barriers to job access, and labour registration requirements often contribute to labour-market imperfections. Some recent studies of workers' earnings in developing countries have found that the standard human capital variables such as age, education, experience and sex fail to account fully for earning differentials between different segments of the labour market. Labour market imperfections, it is argued, account for some of the unexplained variation in earnings. Other elements of labour market imperfections relate to the lack of adequate information about jobs and, more importantly, to commuting costs (both in time and money), which essentially act as transaction costs in the labour market. The importance of these transaction costs in reducing employment and earnings is vividly demonstrated by the extreme political sensitivity of raising fares for public transport in cities, and by the impact of commuting costs on the employment patterns of low-income households, which are often located in areas far from the city centre (as in Rio de Janeiro; see Perlman, 1986).

Regulatory measures such as zoning laws and laws relating to land use also affect the functioning of urban labour markets. All too often, the use of residential premises for business purposes is prohibited. This has serious consequences, particularly for microenterprises in poor neighbourhoods where people cannot afford to have business premises separate from their homes. Apart from the extra investment or leasing costs, such regulations can add to time and travel costs, thereby making it difficult if not impossible for family members to contribute to the running of the business.

Minimum wage legislation, if it succeeds in raising the average wage level or the wages of certain categories of workers above the market-clearing wage, is also likely to introduce distortions with negative effects on employment. Many governments have also promulgated protective labour legislation aimed at regulating wages and other conditions of employment. While in some countries there are virtually no legal barriers to the dismissal of workers, for example, the Republic of Korea and Sri Lanka, others make workers' dismissal difficult and costly (for example, Brazil, India, Sudan). In the context of developing countries, however, it is not clear whether such legislation in fact affords workers much protection. A common response to protective legislation has been a greater reliance on casual labour and a shift to more capital-intensive technology. In Bombay, the decline in the use of labour per unit of output between 1975–7 and 1985–7 can be seen from the fact that value added in manufacturing increased at 2.2 per cent a year in real terms while employment of production process workers declined by 3.2 per cent (Deshpande and Deshpande, 1991). Several studies also show that if wages are artificially pushed too high too fast, the goal of improved earning opportunities may not be achieved. In the case of Jamaica, for example, with wages several times as high in the unionised manufacturing sector as in the rest of the economy, but with no other obvious production advantages, attempts at export-led growth have failed. This has led to real wages among the Jamaican labour force becoming lower and unemployment higher (Fields, 1987).

The extent to which minimum wage legislation can restrict the growth of employment depends on the ease with which it can be evaded. In the case of Bombay, for example, Deshpande and Deshpande (1991) note that 85 per cent of small-scale units (employing less than ten workers) do not pay the minimum wage. On the other hand, many employers have stopped employing young boys, whom they used to pay about half the minimum wage. These boys were mostly migrants and primary school drop-outs who worked as apprentices to learn the necessary skills before being absorbed. The minimum wage legislation has thus hit teenagers most because they have lost the opportunity to acquire skills. They do not want to carry on formal schooling and are condemned by parents and society for idling. The authors also note that by and large the minimum wage fixed by the government has followed rather than led the market wage. Once fixed, the minimum wage is not revised regularly, and unless it is indexed, it falls in real value when prices rise. The implementation of the Minimum Wage Act is also difficult because there are so many units to be policed and corruption is widespread. There is thus no evidence that minimum wage legislation in Bombay has restricted employment growth substantially.

On the other hand, several studies argue that urban labour-market imperfections are not an important determinant of urban poverty. Mazumdar's (1979) study on urban labour markets in Malaysia shows that labour-market segmentation is, at most, only a relatively minor factor in earnings differentials and the persistence of low earnings. Job mobility within the labour market was found to be fairly high – a finding which is at variance with the view that workers entering the low-wage sector in segmented labour markets in developing countries remain trapped there. A number of other studies on urban labour markets in South-East Asian countries also assign labour-market distortions a minor role amongst the causes of urban unemployment. Indeed, they support the prevailing view that labour markets in the ASEAN (Association of South-East Asian Nations) countries and in the NICs function competitively and that this has been a major factor behind their relative success in export-led industrial growth.

While labour-market imperfections may not be a major cause of urban unemployment and poverty, distortions that affect the demand for labour and investment in human capital do constrain the growth of urban employment and productivity. According to Linn (1983) such constraints can be roughly grouped into three types:

1. those that inhibit human capital accumulation, for example insufficient or unequal access to education, training, health, and managerial and entrepreneurial know-how;
2. those that distort access to or prices of complementary inputs, such as imperfections in the markets for investment and working capital, land and other material inputs, or inadequate availability of public utilities and services such as telecommunications, water, electricity and transport;
3. those that impose unnecessary cash and time costs on business transactions, such as those caused by inappropriate land use, business permits and licensing requirements.

Distortions in the capital market that affect urban employment and labour productivity are widespread and can be traced to a number of national policies (relating to interest rates, taxes, subsidies, tariffs, etc.), to the perception or actual existence of high levels of risk, and to various institutional biases. A common instrument used for the promotion of any activity is the provision of cheaper credit for that activity. For example, the main instrument for the promotion of industrial dispersal in India, the Republic of Korea and other countries is to provide interest-rate concessions, credit subsidies or investment subsidies. Each of these actions results in lowering the price of capital relative to labour, thereby providing an incentive to use more capital-intensive modes of production. Similarly, a significant portion of labour legislation has the net effect of increasing the price of labour, as noted above. This is not to argue that all labour-welfare legislation is undesirable. However, as Mohan (1990) has argued, such measures for the protection of labour should be taken with an awareness and understanding of their effect on potential employment generation. The distortion of factor prices, lowering the price of capital and increasing the effective price of labour, typically reduces the demand for organised manufacturing labour. Since much of organised manufacturing is found in urban areas, this is a very important issue in urban employment generation.

Frequently, special support programmes for small and medium-size businesses provide only investment capital, whereas it is now established that working capital is often much more important for the regular operation and growth of small businesses. Sometimes they cater only to manufacturing enterprises, excluding businesses in construction and tertiary activities, although such exclusion is unwarranted given the importance of these sectors for urban employment, income generation and growth. Finally, such programmes often offer subsidised interest rates on the mistaken assumption that smaller enterprises cannot pay the same rates as larger ones. The capital base of these programmes is eroded because of inadequate returns, and they create a set of 'privileged' businesses which are often tempted to move into more capital-intensive activities and technologies, thus diminishing the potential for employment creation.

Distortions of product prices, usually resulting from the structure of indirect taxation, can also have unintended negative effects on the demand for labour. If the excise rates on different commodities are such that they are higher, on balance, for products which are relatively labour-intensive, the effect on employment generation will be negative. In general, agro-based and metal-based industries are more labour-oriented than chemical-based industries. An excise structure which reflects this reality would thus be more desirable in countries with an abundant supply of labour and which are going through a rapid phase of urbanisation.

It is therefore expected that removing such distortions will in many cases produce positive pay-offs, even if labour markets are more severely segmented into high- and low-wage sectors than is currently the case. But to the extent that product and factor price distortions are introduced by national economic policies, there is little that local-level planners can do to mitigate their harmful effects on employment generation.

What then is the scope for city-level action to encourage employment generation? There are essentially three kinds of activity which city planners can undertake to promote employment.[1] First, an overall understanding of the effect of national policies on urban employment generation should lead to a review of local-level policies which lead to similar product and factor price distortions. There are usually a number of local taxes, regulations and restrictions which have similar effects on prices, leading to low levels of employment generation. Second, an understanding of the employment structure of the city, including its spatial aspects, should lead to more appropriate land use, planning and zoning regulations which will have a more favourable effect on employment generation. Urban planning must be based much more closely on residential and employment location patterns and on the resulting commuting needs. Premature attempts to decentralise trading and other activities should also be avoided, as entrepreneurs who are forced to set up activities in distant locations incur higher capital costs and have to provide for higher fixed costs in the absence of agglomeration economies. Since location in a distant area makes it difficult to attract labour except at a higher price, these businesses may also turn to more capital-intensive techniques. Successful decentralisation also requires the provision of infrastructural support. City planning agencies therefore need to monitor city expansion carefully so as to provide timely help in the provision of services and infrastructure. Third, city-level planners can promote specific activities which are employment-generating. By providing training, credit and workspaces they can encourage the growth of microenterprises and self-employment opportunities. Local development authorities can also promote employment by accelerating programmes for the provision and upgrading of basic services in low-income/slum areas.

TARGETED ANTI-POVERTY PROGRAMMES

As already discussed, at the root of the problem of urban poverty lies the inability of the poor to increase their earnings through gainful employment. The key to poverty alleviation is thus the creation of conditions in which a labour force can be absorbed at decent wages.

Rapid economic growth, involving increased earnings led by a growth in productivity in the modern sector, plays a crucial role in poverty alleviation, particularly if it is accompanied by specific policies geared to spill demand and productivity gains into the informal sector. Although economic growth is a necessary condition for reducing poverty, the benefits of growth may not accrue to certain groups of the population. Some sections of the population such as recent migrants, unskilled workers and retired people may even become marginalised during the process of economic growth. This is particularly true during a period of structural adjustment, which inflicts heavy burdens on the urban poor. Targeted anti-poverty programmes are therefore necessary to improve the economic conditions of the poorer groups in major urban centres.

The cases of Cairo, Mexico City and Rio illustrate the type of process which has been taking place in Africa and Latin America. On the one hand, both Mexico and Egypt have seen the collapse of populist projects which emphasised the provision of subsidised food and public services for urban workers as part of a policy designed to favour the import substitution industrialisation process. On the other hand, in both Mexico and Brazil, programmes have been implemented to protect the poorer groups which have suffered a decline in real incomes due to the curtailment of subsidised social services and increases in the price of such services. Mexico has invested substantial resources in social welfare programmes such as the new National Solidarity Programme (PRANASOL). In Rio, the emphasis on education has shifted from the preparation for obtaining a better job or going on to university to a broader-based system of elementary education accompanied by a school feeding programme targeting lower-income groups (Tolosa *et al.*, 1991).

With regard to direct employment generation and poverty alleviation policies and programmes, a number of initiatives have been taken by national and city authorities. However, the distinction between these two types of effort must not lead us to overlook their complementary character. As already discussed, the lack of social services reinforces the vicious cycle linking poor health and educational standards with low productivity and earnings. Consequently, expenditure on improving the standards of living of the poor enhances their ability to engage in productive employment.

Indian labour legislation, including minimum wage and labour contract regulations, social security and protection from retrenchment and business closure, represents a typical form of intervention in labour markets. In this respect it is interesting to reiterate the limitations of minimum wage policies, in that they do not lead the market wage (as in Bombay) and are eroded by inflation (as in Mexico City or Rio) to the point of dropping to one-quarter of the income needed to keep a household above the poverty line (as in Cairo). The difficulties involved in business closure often hinder the process of industrial restructuring and produce a notable decline in new employment generation. This has been the case for a large number of sick textile industries in Bombay. In the interests of renewed employment generation, it should be the objective of city planning agencies to anticipate such problems and to coordinate the activities required to break the impasse that is often encountered in such a situation. This involves bringing together representatives of employers, workers, financial institutions and city administrators. Amendments may need to be made to the existing zoning and land regulations in cases where a substantial amount of land released from the industry that is closing needs to be put to some alternative use. Workers can be given compensation as well as the assurance of appropriate retraining and employment in order to persuade them to be redeployed. Employers may need to be helped with the disposal of their physical and land assets and to be allowed to appropriate some of the gains from capital appreciation.

Although public-sector wage and employment policy has been an important instrument in employment generation in the urban areas of many developing countries (for example, the Republic of Korea, Nigeria, India), Egypt's use of public employment as a means of poverty alleviation has been the most ambitious outside the socialist world (recall that the public sector still accounts for half the Egyptian workforce). However, several problems beset this policy from the early 1970s. Government guarantees of employment for school-leaving graduates had harmful effects on labour productivity in the public sector, and the attempt to sustain labour absorption through the promotion of public-sector employment became increasingly difficult. The policy of guaranteed employment was therefore abandoned in 1978.

Seoul has implemented a number of specific schemes which include wage employment in public works projects, a self-employment fund providing loans to the poor, job-placement centres offering employment counselling and job referrals, vocational training centres run in cooperation with businesses and a special aid programme for street vendors displaced by city regulations.

As shown in Table 4.2, about 40 per cent of the funding for public-works projects in Seoul comes from the central government. The wages paid out under this programme were approximately four billion won in 1977 and 10 billion won in 1988. The level of employment in terms of the number of person-days exceeded 1.1 million in 1977, and continued to increase to over two million by 1982, before declining to around one million in 1985. In 1987 and 1988, the figure recovered to around two million. The average number of days worked per participating household declined from 27 days in 1977 to 16 days in 1985 but increased to 27 days in 1988.

The role of local governments in employment programmes has generally been limited to acting as the local agent of the central government, selecting project sites, organising labour and accounting for expenses. Since the early 1980s, however, the role of local governments has grown. The Seoul Municipal Government, for example, uses funds from the central government to operate the Saemaul Self-Employment Financing Fund, which makes loans to members of urban households from the lowest income groups who have the desire and ability to work for themselves. Such individuals can borrow up to five million won; repayment is deferred for three years, after which the loan is repaid in instalments over two years without interest. In 1989, this fund provided 4078 million won in loans to a total of 2700 households (Kim *et al.*, 1991).

Table 4.2   Public works projects in Seoul, 1977–88

Year	Financial resources (million won)			Households	employed (thousands)	Income per Person-days (thousand won)	household Person-days per household
	Total	National	Local				
1977	4005	1870	2135	43 673	1175	91	26.9
1978	4803	1559	3244	52 610	925	91	17.6
1979	6970	2787	4183	50 154	1300	136	25.9
1980	8450	3450	5000	65 000	2000	130	30.8
1981	7893	3610	4283	91 097	1960	87	21.5
1982	11060	8060	3000	111 985	2230	99	19.9
1983	6821	1321	5500	83 999	1476	81	17.6
1984	4998	1834	3164	67 035	1300	75	19.4
1985	5819	2759	3060	63 021	1014	92	16.1
1986	6016	1946	4070	36 352	1105	167	30.4
1987	10 338	4268	6070	67 039	1920	154	28.6
1988	10 003	4339	5664	65 277	1788	154	27.4

Source: Kim *et al.*, 1991, table 4.4.

Job placement for the poor is another important component of the anti-poverty programme. The Ministry of Labour has established 37 job-placement bureaux, and the municipalities have organised another seven in Seoul. The job-placement bureaux have been established at the *Ku* (ward) and *Dong* (neighbourhood) levels, which have frequent contact with local residents. These offices provide employment counselling as well as referrals for daily labourers. In 1989, job placement services were provided for 18 000 people.

Seoul City Government operates nine municipal vocational training centres and 26 training centres in cooperation with business. In 1990, about 15 000 low-income people in the 14–55 age group received training (Table 4.3). Although the training period varies depending on occupation, on average it lasts one year.

Seoul has a special aid programme for street vendors. In April 1989, a total of 20 305 street stalls were operating throughout the city. Since these street stalls obstruct traffic and cause other problems for the city, the authorities are taking steps to register and resettle a large number of them in approved kiosks. The remaining unapproved stalls will be cleared away. The displaced street vendors will receive livelihood assistance as well as job transfer assistance. More than two billion won is budgeted by the city authorities to expand temporary employment programmes to ease the job transition process. Under these programmes, the wage level has been set at 6500 won per day, and up

Table 4.3   Vocational training in Seoul, 1985–90

Year	Total	Men	Women
1985	5761 (100.0)	1747 (30.3)	4014 (69.7)
1986	5695 (100.0)	1759 (30.9)	3936 (69.1)
1987	7191 (100.0)	1202 (16.7)	5989 (83.3)
1988	8775 (100.0)	1398 (15.9)	7377 (84.1)
1989	10 642 (100.0)	3342 (31.4)	7300 (68.6)
1990	15 000 (100.0)	4500 (30.0)	10 500 (70.0)

Note: Figures in brackets are percentages.
Source: Adapted from Kim *et al.*, 1991, table 4.5.

to two persons per household may work. The programme can thus support 5000 households at a monthly income level of about 400 000 won per household.

The city authorities are also providing free job training to about 9000 people for such occupations as driver, security guard and sanitary worker. During training they receive financial assistance of 400 000 won per household per month. Former vendors who wish to relocate outside Seoul receive 700 000 won for moving expenses and one million won for living expenses as well as an additional one million won in special assistance.

As far as direct poverty-alleviation strategies are concerned, it is important to consider target-group-oriented welfare programmes and expenditures on social services as redistribution devices. It is through the provision of public services such as shelter, urban infrastructure, education and health care that city governments can attempt to eliminate, or at least reduce, the incidence of poverty. Careful design of public expenditure programmes is, however, necessary to ensure that the benefits from public expenditure actually accrue to the poor. Although the effects of public expenditure on social services are discussed in Chapter 5, some aspects deserve consideration here. The devastating effect of structural adjustments on housing programmes is apparent in Cairo and Rio. In Egypt the provision of low-cost housing has slowly withered since the 1973 Arab–Israeli war; the National Housing Bank was finally dismantled in 1986 (the increase in expenditure on housing in Mexico reflects the reconstruction programme after the 1985 earthquake). Consequently, the housing shortage has worsened and the standards of housing for low-income groups have deteriorated in these two cities. Similarly, in Bombay a fall in the share of expenditure on housing was accompanied by a rise in that on electricity (see Table 4.4). In Seoul, various initiatives designed to upgrade squatter settlements have been succeeded by a less ambitious cooperative redevelopment programme.

Another widely used redistribution device which has been undermined by structural adjustment programmes is the provision of subsidised services, and in particular the provision of staple food at below market prices. This type of scheme has been particularly important in Egypt, Mexico and India. In Egypt, the subsidised food programme, which was initiated by Nasser and strengthened after the 1973 war, is being dismantled as a result of agreements with the IMF. In Mexico, programmes initiated in the 1950s were weakened as a result of the implementation of the 1977 Co-ordination of National

Table 4.4   Percentage distribution of revenue expenditure and per capita real revenue expenditure by heads of expenditure, Bombay, 1970–87

Heads of expenditure	Share in revenue expenditure (%)			Per capita real revenue expenditure in Rs (at 1970–72 prices)		
	1970–2	1980–2	1985–7	1970–2	1980–2	1985–7
General administration	4.5	2.8	2.8	7.8	6.1	6.2
Shelter						
Housing	1.1	0.7	0.4	1.9	1.4	1.0
Slums and squatter upgrading	5.2	3.9	3.5	9.0	8.6	7.9
Primary infrastructure						
Electricity	12.5	20.8	24.1	21.7	45.2	53.9
Water supply	9.5	6.7	6.6	16.5	14.5	14.7
Roads	7.0	6.0	6.1	12.2	13.1	13.6
Sewerage and drainage	3.5	4.2	3.7	6.0	9.1	8.2
Transport	16.4	18.3	16.0	28.4	39.8	35.8
Other	2.1	1.5	1.4	3.6	3.2	3.1
Social services and amenities						
Health	12.5	11.6	9.5	21.7	25.3	21.3
Education	16.3	14.6	14.0	28.3	31.7	31.3
Solid waste management	3.8	4.0	3.9	6.5	8.7	8.8
Parks, markets, etc.	1.8	2.1	2.0	3.0	4.7	4.4
Environmental hygiene	–	0.1	0.1	–	0.2	0.2
Other	3.8	2.7	5.9	6.6	5.9	13.1
Total revenue	100.0	100.0	100.0	100.0	217.6	223.6

Source: Deshpande and Deshpande, 1991, table IV.2.

Plan for Deprived Areas and Marginalised Groups (COPLAMAR) and the recent National Solidarity Programme (PRANASOL). In India, the Public Distribution System (PDS) provides subsidised commodities to protect the urban population against inflation. Each adult is entitled to 10 kilograms of subsidised food grains, 425 grams of sugar and 20 litres of kerosene oil per month – the last item only if the ration-card holder does not use liquified petroleum gas for cooking. The PDS has not been scaled down over time even though it has been criticised on various grounds: quantities available fall short of entitlements and are often of poor quality; the very poor rarely earn enough to buy the monthly quota, and the system is abused by shopkeepers who sell unclaimed stocks to hoteliers. The system is also criticised on the grounds that it is open to all. Since the state government does not bear the cost of the subsidy, it is considered bad electoral politics for the state politicians to try and restrict coverage to the poor alone. Both the central government which bears the cost of the subsidy, and the state government which does not, probably stand to gain by the extended coverage. The prices that go into the construction of the cost-of-living index are a weighted average of the prices in the open market and those charged by the fair-price shops. The depressed index saves both governments millions in the cost-of-living allowances they would have to pay to their employees if the index were based wholly on market prices. Nevertheless, the PDS is credited with protecting lower-income groups from the impact of inflation (Deshpande and Deshpande, 1991).

A variety of experiences are observed with regard to social-welfare programmes in Third-World mega-cities. Seoul's medical assistance programme, which provides free medical services for those below the poverty line, constitutes the core of the city's welfare policies (Kim *et al.*, 1991). Another major welfare programme in Seoul is the livelihood-protection programme. This programme provides low-income and/or disabled poor families with subsidies in cash or kind. The allowance per person is equivalent to US$20–32 per month, which is lower than the US$40 per month minimum required in urban areas. Almost half of the expense is met by the central government. Table 4.5 shows the number

Table 4.5   Livelihood protection programme, Seoul, 1981–8

Year	Persons protected at home (A)	Low-income persons (B)	Population (C)	$\frac{A+B}{C}$ (%)
1981	14 202	202 783	8 676 037	2.5
1982	12 600	443 069	8 916 481	5.0
1983	13 010	298 804	9 204 344	3.4
1984	11 565	240 878	9 501 413	2.7
1985	11 946	213 267	9 639 110	2.3
1986	12 992	191 469	9 798 542	2.1
1987	14 556	196 818	9 991 089	2.1
1988	15 390	191 578	10 286 503	2.0
Average annual growth rate (1981–8)	1.2	−0.8	2.5	

Source: Kim *et al.*, 1991, table 4.6.

of people receiving livelihood assistance from the city government. During the period 1981–8, the number of persons classified as the 'Protected at Home' (those unable to work, but not residing in institutions) increased slightly, by 1.2 per cent per annum, while the number of beneficiaries of the 'Low-Income Persons' programme declined by 0.8 per cent per annum. Two per cent of Seoul's total population was receiving assistance in 1988.

The Bombay Municipal Corporation (BMC) provides free medical services and free maternal and child health care. However, much more is needed than is available. The mass immunisation programme launched by the BMC could not achieve even 50 per cent of its target. The infant mortality rate continues to be unduly high in the city (mortality rates are even higher in the slums).

In Mexico City and Rio, where health services are provided mainly within the framework of the social security system, there is a heavy concentration of services in the city centre as opposed to the peripheral municipalities, as discussed more fully in Chapter 5. However, this concentration has been reduced in Mexico City as a result of the reconstruction effort after the 1985 earthquake, given that the bulk of the hospital facilities were located in the central area and suffered a great deal of damage in the earthquake.

With regard to education, viewed as part of social-welfare policy, a major proportion of the public expenditure of the Governorate of Cairo is allocated to the maintenance of the school system and the provision of higher education. Although the proportion is overstated by the figures in Table 4.6 (due to the fact that expenditure on social

Table 4.6   Percentage distribution of planned public expenditures, Cairo, 1981–89

Sector	1981–2	1985–6	1988–9
Administration	23.80	40.30	39.00
Housing	0.84	0.73	0.59
Roads	1.34	0.69	0.59
Health	15.42	11.48	11.52
Schools	52.30	41.00	42.60
Other	6.30	5.80	5.70
Total	100.00	100.00	100.00

Source: Farah, 1991.

infrastructure is mostly carried out by central-government ministries), the emphasis on education is very marked.

In the case of Mexico City and Rio, important efforts towards upgrading the educational system are illustrated by the shift of emphasis from primary to secondary schools during the 1970s. In Rio, however, such efforts received a setback during the economic crisis of the 1980s. There, as in Bombay, awareness of the fact that many of the children attending municipal schools are ill-fed has led to the strengthening of school feeding programmes.

NATURE AND ROLE OF THE INFORMAL SECTOR IN EMPLOYMENT GENERATION AND POVERTY ALLEVIATION[2]

It is often alleged, as already noted, that informal-sector activities, requiring little skill or capital and yielding very low and irregular incomes, are only marginally productive. Additional entrants share the same activities and add little to the total output of the sector. Income per worker is therefore low and close to subsistence level. The popular impression is that the informal sector is composed primarily of small-scale units producing goods and 'marginal activities' such as hawking, shoe shining or domestic service.

This somewhat negative view of the informal sector has been challenged in recent years. Many informal-sector activities, far from being marginally productive, are now considered economically efficient. Although low incomes are common in the informal sector, all informal-sector workers are not necessarily poor.

One thing informal-sector units do have in common, however, is their vulnerability. These units are for the most part unregistered and unregulated by the government. They are thus compelled by circumstances to operate outside the framework of law and social protection.

For analytical purposes it is now considered more useful to divide the informal sector into two broad subsectors based on organisational structure, behavioural patterns and related characteristics: (a) the individual-enterprise sector or irregular sector; and (b) the family-enterprise sector. The irregular sector corresponds to the popular image of informal sector activities described above. The family-enterprise sector involves a higher degree of organisation and is more productive. The enterprises in this sector generally have a fixed place of work and utilise a larger amount of capital per worker. The enterprise may be operated individually, or with the help of family members or hired workers. This sector thus includes both non-wage earners – consisting of own-account workers, employers and unpaid family workers – and wage earners. Because capital is required to set up and operate an enterprise, and it cannot generally be obtained from formal credit institutions, entry into the family-enterprise sector as an own-account worker or employer is more difficult than entry into the irregular sector, and is restricted to those who have the necessary financial resources or can afford to borrow from private moneylenders. Lack of skill can also be a barrier to entry into certain activities, particularly in manufacturing, as an own-account worker.

The tendency to regard the informal sector as synonymous with self-employment, and the controversy over whether this sector is unproductive or a potential dynamic growth point for employment-led development, have resulted in relative neglect in the development literature of wage employees in the family-enterprise sector. Jobs within the family-enterprise sector often require few specific skills. Employers therefore have little incentive to provide on-the-job training, or to be selective in their recruitment. This reduces the fixed costs of hiring new workers and, consequently, the concern about labour turnover. Employers are therefore not motivated to pay premium wages, to develop internal labour markets, or to enter into long contractual relationships with their workers. These limitations from the point of view of the workers, along with the limited possibilities for career advancement, reduce the incentive of workers to remain on the job or to perform exceptionally well. Hence it is argued that wage employment in the informal sector is characterised by high rates of labour turnover. This favours ease of entry.

Tokman (1987) thus observes that even when there are support programmes for family enterprises, their first impact is an increase in the incomes of entrepreneurs. The increase is not necessarily transferred to the wages of their employees, given the abundance of labour, the job instability, the low skill requirements and the lack of labour contracts or organisation. A second-round effect is an increased demand for labour, which could mean either new jobs or longer periods of work for those who are already employed, both of which have a beneficial effect on (potential) employees.

There has recently been a noticeable revival of interest in the role of the informal sector in labour absorption in many developing countries, particularly in Latin America. Tokman suggests that the main economic reasons for the increased appeal of policies for the informal sector have been:

1. the failure of the trickle-down strategy to reduce significantly the share of the informal sector in urban employment;
2. the over-expansion of the informal sector as a result of the crisis of the 1980s;
3. the strong correlation between poverty and informal-sector employment;
4. the gloomy prospects for rapid growth in the next decade;
5. increased evidence of the low resource requirements for the implementation of informal sector policies.

This, however, presents a dilemma for policy-makers. Should the sector be allowed to continue to expand outside the framework of laws and institutions governing social and economic life, and thus to provide a convenient, low-cost way of absorbing labour that cannot be employed elsewhere? Or should attempts be made to bring it into the legal and institutional framework, with the risk of impairing its capacity to absorb labour? Most observers believe that these two objectives of labour absorption and regulation could only be reconciled if measures were taken simultaneously to enhance the employment-generating capacity of the informal sector, to increase the productivity, incomes and welfare of informal-sector producers and workers, and to find practical and realistic ways of progressively improving the legal and social protection of informal-sector workers. Repressive measures aimed at making the sector disappear by force, or law-enforcement measures aimed at applying laws and regulations with which informal sector enterprises and workers could not comply, would only serve to increase the vulnerability and the poverty of those engaged in informal-sector activities.

Policy approach towards the informal sector

It is now often implicitly assumed that the informal sector makes an invaluable contribution to development and the policy issue is reduced to that of finding ways to promote its growth. The issue cannot, however, be prejudged in this way. We need to begin by asking what exactly it is that we seek to influence through development policies. Put this way, we face the fundamental issue of the optimal size of the informal sector. If the informal sector is too large in relation to this optimum, promotional policies would not be warranted. There seems to be no a priori way of determining the desirable size of the informal sector; it is an empirical question to be resolved in each specific context. The optimal size of the informal sector can be defined, for instance, by reference to efficiency criteria in the allocation of capital and labour. It might be considered too large in terms of the labour-allocation criterion if labour has flowed into it beyond the point where marginal returns have become lower than in alternative sectors. Excessive rural–urban migration tends to suggest an informal sector which is too large. Conversely, an informal sector may be considered too small if there is evidence of misallocation of capital, such as is the case where capital–labour ratios are very high in the modern sector, and an excessive proportion of total capital resources of the economy is concentrated in this sector.

It should be noted, however, that the optimal-size issue cannot be settled simply by static, cross-sectional analysis. Ideally, we also need to build upon analyses of the dynamics of the growth of the informal sector, which provide information on why and how the informal sector has grown. Such analyses will not only provide answers to the optimal size issue, but, more importantly, will yield insights into the specific form that overall policies towards the informal sector need to take.

There has been a basic divide as regards interpretation of the growth of the informal sector between those who see such growth as the manifestation of an involutionary process and those who see the process as evolutionary. According to the involutionary view, the growth of the informal sector is seen as essentially pathological, fuelled by the influx of migrants pushed out of the rural areas by lack of employment and income opportunities, highly unequal agrarian structures, and labour-saving technical change in agricultural production. As noted earlier, this process is usually exacerbated by barriers to entry into the modern sector arising from the structure of production, oligopolistic industrial structures, capital-market distortions, labour-market segmentation, and exploitative employment practices on the part of employers. Informal-sector growth does not therefore reflect any normal response to economic incentives but is merely symptomatic of a deep malaise in the economic structure and growth process. The way forward would not be to try to ameliorate production conditions in the informal sector, since this does not represent a productive growth strategy. Rather, the best solution would be to tackle the problem at its roots, that is, to reduce the excessive movement of labour from the rural sector and to remove barriers to labour absorption in the modern sector. Such a strategy would raise growth rates in the economy as well as to reduce inequality in the distribution of income.

A topical illustration of involutionary growth of the informal sector is to be found in the wake of the severe recession which has recently been experienced by many developing countries, particularly in Latin America and Africa. As noted earlier, modern-sector employment in many Latin American countries has fallen in absolute terms (or the rate of growth of demand for labour in it has declined substantially). This has led to a movement into informal-sector employment by redundant workers, since this is the only survival strategy available in situations where no effective social-security system exists. Apart from those actually made redundant, the ranks of the informal sector have also been swelled by those who have lost the opportunity of being absorbed into the formal sector as a result of the fall in the rate of growth of that sector. The data presented in Table 4.7 show that in sub-Saharan Africa and Latin America, urban informal sector employment has increased by 6.7 per cent and 6.8 per cent per annum respectively between 1980 and 1985, which is higher than the rate of growth of the urban labour force (5.3 per cent in sub-Saharan Africa and 3.4 per cent in Latin America) or of the urban formal sector (1.0 per cent in sub-Saharan Africa and 2.0 per cent in Latin America). With such a conjuncture of events it would be difficult to put any positive interpretation on the growth of the informal sector, apart from noting that it serves as some buffer against destitution. The policy stance towards the informal sector might still be to assist it, but this would be

Table 4.7   The structure of employment in sub-Saharan Africa and Latin America, 1980–5

Indicator	*Annual rate of growth (%)*	
	Sub-Saharan Africa	*Latin America*
Urban labour force	5.3	3.4
Urban unemployment	10.0	8.1
Urban formal sector	1.0*	2.0
Urban informal sector	6.7	6.8

Wage employment is considered as a proxy for modern sector employment.
Sources: Adapted from ILO/JASPA, 1989, table I.11; ILO/PREALC, 1986a,b, table 2; ILO/PREALC, 1991, table 4.

motivated more by welfare considerations and social pressures than by considerations of growth potential. In terms of overall policy, the priorities would be structural adjustment and economic recovery which, if successful, would result in a relative shrinking of the temporarily swollen informal sector.

The opposite view of the informal sector would tend to see it as being at or below its optimum size. This evolutionary view focuses on the economic virtues of the informal sector. It is depicted as a system of production which is appropriate to the factor and resource endowments of labour-surplus, low-income countries. It is also seen as a reservoir of entrepreneurship and innovativeness which uses resources efficiently and competitively and which would grow, given the right institutional and policy environment. According to this view, the growth of the informal sector can be promoted through a combination of policies such as the forging of regulatory linkages between it and the formal sector and the removal of regulatory restrictions and disincentives. These regulations either forbid particular activities (for example street trading) or impose onerous regulatory conditions which increase start-up and operating costs (for example standards of construction, environmental regulations, licence fees, taxes, etc.).

These two opposing views have been presented in order to illustrate the complexities involved in deciding overall policies towards the informal sector. There is no basis for assuming that one or the other view must necessarily prevail. Given the heterogeneity and complexity of the informal sector, elements of both views will be correct, but it is nonetheless important to have some calibration of the relative proportions involved. This is important not only to avoid the error of basing policies on an assumption that the informal sector conforms entirely to one or the other view, but also to emphasise the need to search for a differentiated set of policies to deal with different facets of the informal sector.

One can think of a basic division in types of policy on the basis of whether we are dealing with the 'growth potential' or involutionary aspects of the informal sector. The former would be directed at promoting the growth of potentially viable micro- and small enterprises through the removal of unwarranted market and institutional handicaps as well as through subsidies justified on the basis of infant industry-type arguments. In contrast, policies designed to deal with the informal sector as a symptom of involutionary growth would not look for solutions within the sector, but in economy-wide structural changes which could reduce the pressures resulting in the expansion of the informal sector. These would be directed at issues relating to equitable growth in agriculture and the possibilities for rapid, labour-intensive industrialisation.

It should be noted that these two types of policy approach towards the informal sector are not mutually exclusive. They can be deployed simultaneously, each being directed at different facets of the sector. But there is an important difference in the scope of their potential impact. Policies based on the involutionary view of the informal sector will deal with issues of far-reaching structural change whereas the others will be more narrowly focused. While success with the latter type of policy will benefit the better-endowed producers in the informal sector (sometimes referred to as the 'intermediate' sector), this will not, of itself, do much to tackle the malaise identified by the involutionary view. While the growth of the 'intermediate' sector will yield benefits in terms of increased labour demand and some redressing of the biases against micro- and small enterprises, the overall magnitude of these effects is unlikely to be large enough to offset the effects of deeper structural malaise where these are present.

Specific policy instruments to enhance the role of the informal sector in urban development

The most common of the specific interventions recommended and applied are those directed at providing credit and extension services to micro- and small enterprises in the informal sector. A related set of measures sometimes deals with start-up assistance and entrepreneurship training to induce the setting up of new enterprises and other forms of self-employment. It is more unusual, however, to see this sort of small-industry promotion measure being supported by wider policies aimed at changing the overall institutional and policy environment affecting the growth potential of small enterprises. There are few attempts, for instance, to redress the fiscal and other policy biases in favour of large modern-sector enterprises, to shift the pattern of income distribution so as to increase the demand for products from the small enterprise sector, or to forge greater linkages between small and large industries. In consequence, these small industry-oriented interventions tend to have only a limited and localised impact, the benefits being confined to those enterprises actually reached by a particular project. Moreover, this type of intervention is invariably carried out in isolation from the larger issues of structural change. For these reasons, such interventions have been dismissed as a 'reformist package' by radical economists.

It will be noticed, however, that the proponents of such a policy package for the informal sector have implicitly assumed an answer to the question of the optimal size of the informal sector. The thrust of these interventions is obviously to encourage an expansion of the sector by fostering enterprise growth. However, unless the issues relating to the optimal size of the informal sector are in fact addressed, there is no basis for deciding whether or not this policy package represents the best use of development resources.

Apart from this general objection, serious questions have also been raised about the feasibility of attaining growth in informal-sector production through this route. A basic objection relates to the limited capacity for accumulation in micro- and small enterprises and their ability to compete with the modern sector. A second objection springs from the low earnings and onerous working conditions that are typical of employment in the informal sector. The promotion of informal-sector growth, even if successful, will lead to the expansion of arduous, poorly paid, unstable and precarious employment. This goes against the major social objective of improving living and working conditions through the development process. Finally, it has been pointed out that a typical small-industry promotion package will benefit only the better endowed enterprises within the informal sector while leaving the majority of the poor untouched. Inequalities are thus likely to be exacerbated.

Thus, instead of proceeding from the assumption that informal-sector activities across the board are worthy of promotion, it would be more effective to carry out assessments of the competitive and growth potential of specific activities, and to concentrate promotional resources on those with the highest likelihood of survival and success.

All this points to the additional measures which need to be adopted in order to ensure that effectiveness is increased and negative effects minimised. One such set of measures must obviously involve structural reforms aimed at slowing down excessive expansion of the informal sector. As noted earlier, the persistence and growth of an informal sector, particularly in Africa and Latin America, has often been due to an unbalanced approach to development which has bypassed large masses of the population, as well as to a generally unfavourable economic climate and the application of stringent structural adjustment policies. All these macroeconomic factors have greatly reduced the possibilities of generating sufficient employment in other sectors and have induced many millions of workers to take refuge in the informal sector as the only means of survival for themselves and their families. It is clear that the problems presented by a large and growing informal sector can only be effectively tackled if there is a more favourable environment for growth and employment creation, and if efforts are made to redress the imbalances in general development policy. The latter would include much greater emphasis on the revitalisation of rural areas and equitable policies for rural development, which are essential prerequisites for stemming migration to the already crowded and congested urban areas.

The problems faced by informal-sector workers and producers will not, however, be overcome merely through a revival of economic growth or through a more favourable climate for employment creation. Specific measures are also required to help the informal sector improve its productive capacity, break out of its marginalised, vulnerable and semi-legal position in society and overcome the obstacles to ultimate integration into the rest of the economy.

Another major justification for policies being actually applied towards the informal sector rests on the need for poverty alleviation measures. There is usually a large pool of urban poor in most low-income countries. The existence of poverty is seen as part of a necessary transitional phase which these countries have to go through, since with very low income levels there is too little capital available to generate sufficient employment at wages above subsistence level. Income-sharing mechanisms such as informal-sector activities serve a useful social function by acting as a buffer against destitution. There is thus a need to tolerate the existence of informal-sector activities and to relax the rules of economic efficiency in viewing such activities. The efficiency loss in macroeconomic terms would not, in any case, be very significant since such activities are concentrated on the production of non-tradables and use resources which are non-scarce from the standpoint of the formal sector.

This rather pessimistic line of reasoning leads to the case for welfare-type poverty-alleviation policies. Since the prospects of achieving any significant breakthrough along a production-oriented route appear so bleak, measures to alleviate existing suffering are called for. The types of measure to be adopted would include the distribution of subsidised or free food to the poorest of the poor, the provision of basic amenities such as safe drinking water and sanitation, public-health measures, and housing-improvement schemes. Various forms of 'make-work' programme, as opposed to viable income-generating projects, would also fall within the category of welfare-oriented measures.

The primary aim of such measures is to reinforce the 'safety net' function of the informal sector and to mitigate the effects of a breakdown in the entitlements of the most vulnerable groups. But they also contain the potential for supporting more growth and production-oriented objectives. It could be argued that all these measures enhance the satisfaction of basic needs among the poorest and to that extent will also strengthen their capacity for productive effort. Greater impact could be ensured if welfare and production-oriented measures were integrated in a mutually supportive way. However, this is easier said than done in the context of the present lack of any institutional framework for handling the planning and implementation of anti-poverty programmes in most Third-World cities.

5 Urban Poverty and Access to Housing and Basic Social Services

URBAN POVERTY AND ACCESS TO HOUSING

The urban growth process and slum formation

As discussed earlier, the urban labour market in most developing countries is marked by structural dualism. The analysis also suggests that the existence of the informal sector has to be seen not merely as a short-term transitory phenomenon, but as a persistent one.

The persistence of trade- and service-dominated informal-sector activities and of slums must not be seen merely as two unrelated phenomena which happen to exist simultaneously, for the former is causally linked to the latter. The low levels of income accruing to workers in the informal sector do not enable them to face the challenges of urban life in general and the high cost of living in particular. In large cities where there is not enough scope for geographical expansion in the face of high population density, land scarcity leads to high land prices and speculation. In such situations, the dualistic economic structure of the cities in terms of employment further accentuates the level of inequality by limiting the access of informal-sector workers, particularly migrant workers, to housing and land. This therefore leads to the formation and growth of slums and squatter settlements in large cities (Mitra, 1987).

The National Commission on Urbanisation in India regards the proliferation of slums and squatter settlements in the urban areas as the most visible symbol of urban poverty and decay. It notes that between 1961 and 1981, while the Indian population increased by 50 per cent and the urban population doubled, in Bombay the squatter population recorded a tenfold increase from 400 000 to four million (National Commission on Urbanisation, 1987).

Although not all squatters earn their livelihood in the informal-sector, and not all informal sector workers live in squatter settlements, there is nevertheless a considerable overlap between the two. Some studies suggest that 70–80 per cent of squatter residents, depending on the location, would be unable to afford 'formal-sector' accommodation.

The data presented in Table 5.1 show that in many cities such as Bombay, Lagos and Rio, the rate of growth of the slum population is very high. In Rio, for example, the slum population increased at 11.3 per cent per annum during the 1970s. The table also shows that in many cities the rate of growth of the slum population was higher in the 1980s than in the 1970s. In Bombay the rate of growth of the slum population nearly doubled from 2.9 per cent in the 1970s to 5.6 per cent in the 1980s. In Mexico City, where a quarter of the city's population lives in slums, the rate of growth of the slum population increased from 1.5 per cent in the 1970s to 2.1 per cent in the 1980s. The number of rooms available per household also declined from 2.4 in 1970 to 2.1 in 1980, while the number of persons per room remained more or less stable. Among the African cities, 58 per cent of the population of Lagos live in slums while in Cairo 84 per cent of the population live in informal, illegal housing. Although Shanghai does not have the type of slum generally found in other Third-World mega-cities, nearly 20 per cent of the population in Shanghai has been identified as living in houses which have poor facilities and therefore need to be rebuilt. There has, however, been a slight improvement in the living floor space available for each person, which increased from 4.4 square metres in 1970 to 6.3 square metres in 1988.

In general, the data presented in Table 5.1 indicate that, despite marginal improvements in the number of rooms available per household in some cities, overcrowding still prevails. Only in Seoul, where the growth rate of the slum population (inadequate housing units) has been negative, has there been any significant improvement in this regard.

Even in Seoul, the housing situation is far from satisfactory. Table 5.2 shows that, despite some improvement, inadequate housing units (slums and squatter dwellings) accounted for 10.7 per cent of Seoul's total housing stock in 1985. The data also show that the problem of inadequate housing units is relatively more serious in Seoul than in the nation as a whole. Total housing units increased at 4.5 per cent per annum in the city during 1970–85 while the corresponding national figure was 7.1 per cent.

Housing policy issues are not related simply to meeting the basic need for shelter: they also have an important bearing on a host of other issues such as the informal sector, employment generation and resource

Table 5.1 Slum and housing indicators in selected cities, 1970–88

| City | Slum population | | | | Year | No. of rooms per household | No. of persons per room |
	In millions (1988)	As a proportion of city's population (1988) (%)	Rate of growth of slum population (%) 1971–81	1981–8			
Bombay	5.6	56.7	2.9	5.6	1971	1.4	4.0
					1981	1.4	3.6
Cairo	–	84.0[1]	–	–	1976	2.7	1.9
					1986	3.0	1.5
Lagos	1.5[2]	58.0[2]	–	9.5	1971	2.0	3.1
					1988	1.3	4.0
Mexico City	4.2	25.3	1.5	2.1	1970	2.4	2.0
					1980	2.1	1.9
Rio	1.7[3]	34.2[3]	11.3	–	1970	2.4	0.9
					1980	2.7	0.7
Seoul	1.3[4]	12.1[4]	–0.9	–2.6	1970	1.5	3.4
					1988	2.1	1.9
Shanghai	–	20.0[5]	–	–	1970	–	4.4[6]
					1988	–	6.3[6]

Notes: [1] Informal housing without licence (1986).
[2] 1981.
[3] 1980.
[4] Refers to inadequate housing.
[5] Housing units need to be rebuilt.
[6] Per capita living floor space (m²).

Source: ILO mega-city survey (1990).

Table 5.2   Inadequate housing stock in Seoul and the Republic of Korea, 1970–85

	Housing units (thousands)		Inadequate housing units (thousands)		Ratio of inadequate housing units to total units (%)	
	Seoul	Rep. of Korea	Seoul	Rep. of Korea	Seoul	Rep. of Korea
1970	597	1168	168	249	28.2	21.3
1975	803	1571	135	173	16.8	11.0
1980	936	2392	154	242	16.5	10.1
1985	1174	3374	125	248	10.7	7.3

Source: Kim *et al.*, 1991, table 3.10.

mobilisation. The construction of housing is clearly a source of both employment creation and income generation. But there is a widespread misconception in the way governments view investment in housing as investment in a durable consumer good, as opposed to investment in industry which they see as generative of economic development. Perlman (1986) notes that, as we come to understand the workings of the informal sector, the standard view of housing as a durable consumer good is seen to be way off the mark in relation to Third-World cities, where houses are often used for the making, storing and selling of goods. Yet because this is part of the conventional wisdom in official circles, it has led to misguided investments in 'finished product' homes and self-defeating codes, standards and zoning regulations (Singh, 1989).

Investments in public-housing projects do not satisfy even a small part of the needs that are identified. In fact, such investments often aggravate the housing problem for the majority of the poorer urban households, since they tie up scarce resources in a small number of housing units, usually for the benefit of the better-off. Moreover, public-housing projects have frequently involved the bulldozing of slums, and thus the destruction of valuable housing stock (Richards and Thomson, 1984).

Public-housing programmes have now given way to squatter-settlement upgrading and site-and-services schemes in most developing countries. Wadhwa (1988) notes that the success rate of these schemes has not been very high. In the case of squatter-settlement upgrading, the finance made available has been inadequate to improve living conditions significantly. The site-and-services schemes have suffered from many of the weaknesses of the earlier programmes such as faulty location and high costs. The locations preferred by the poor are generally in the vicinity of the city centre, close to employment opportunities. In these areas either vacant land is simply not available or, if it is available, not in large enough plots to make a site-and-services project feasible. Further, land near the city centre is very expensive. But even when governments have minimised the cost of land by locating projects in peripheral areas, the actual cost to the beneficiary has often turned out to be very high, either because of high transportation costs or because of the high cost of development of the sites (United Nations Center for Human Settlements, 1987). In most site-and-services projects, the cost to the beneficiary has also been increased by excessively high building and construction standards, by restrictions on the use of houses for commercial and informal-sector activities, and by limitations imposed on the way in which loans can be used.

Despite their many limitations, self-help and user-participation schemes are an important method of resource mobilisation. In their present form, however, they do not provide a long-term answer to the problems of accommodating the growing numbers of urban poor in decent housing. Virtually all the slum-upgrading and site-and-services projects undertaken so far in most developing countries have been supported by multilateral and bilateral aid agencies. Despite efforts to make projects replicable, the project approach ties up excessive resources and institutional effort in a few locations and has not been able to achieve the desired level of housing stock. The project approach is therefore unlikely to have a significant impact on solving the problem of shelter in most developing countries (United Nations, 1988).

There are several other unresolved issues which need urgent attention. One of the most contentious is security of tenure for squatters. The dominant view is that squatters cannot be expected to improve their housing conditions unless they are certain of being allowed to remain where they are. Another crucial issue is that of affordability: self-help schemes have little to offer the very poor and nothing to offer the destitute. If such people are to be reached, something more than squatter-settlement upgrading and site-and-services projects in their present form is required.

A recent evaluation of the site-and-services programme based on a field study at three locations in Bombay (Oshiwara, Dindoshi and Majaswadi) shows that the poor are least able to benefit from such programmes (Banerjee-Guha, 1990). Table 5.3 presents data on the distribution of households both at the time when sites and tenements were allotted and at the time of the survey conducted in 1988, three years after the initial allotment. Under the programme, it was envisaged that households belonging to economically weaker sections (EWS) and lower-income groups (LIG) would together constitute 70–80 per cent of the allottees. The data show that this objective was met only at Oshiwara. The Maharashtra Housing and Development Authority did not or could not check the veracity of the incomes reported by the applicants. Besides, the cost of the sites and tenements escalated between the time of allotment and actual occupation. Some of the original EWS and LIG allottees, unable to afford the extra costs, sold their allotments to richer individuals. The proportion of poor households was thus found to be much lower at the time of the survey than at the time of allotment in each location. In other words, the objective of the programme, namely to house the poor through cross-subsidies, was defeated by the workings of market mechanisms.

A unit of the Prime Minister's Grant Project implementing the Dharavi redevelopment scheme in Bombay priced a housing unit of

Table 5.3 Percentage distribution of households by income group in three site-and-services projects, Bombay, 1988

Income group	Distribution of household at allotment			Distribution of households at survey		
	Oshiwara	Dindoshi	Majaswadi	Oshiwara	Dindoshi	Majaswadi
EWS	20	9	11	3	6	9
LIG	70	26	47	31	20	39
MIG	10	53	36	20	50	40
HIG I	0	7	6	23	14	9
HIG II	0	5	0	23	10	3
Total	100	100	100	100	100	100

Notes: EWS = economically weaker sections. LIG = low-income group. MIG = middle-income group. HIG = high-income group.
Source: Banerjee-Guha, 1990, quoted and reproduced in Deshpande and Deshpande, 1991, table IV.4, p. 196.

16.7 square metres at Rs42 000, implying a monthly instalment of Rs180 if bought on hire purchase. The instalment would form 31 per cent of the average income of a household belonging to the EWS. An average household in the city, which spends 60 per cent of its income on food, would find it difficult to spare 31 per cent of its income for housing. Incomes in other slums are likely to be lower and the share of households belonging to EWS higher. Thus a large proportion of the population living in slums would not be able to afford even the cheapest of formal housing now offered to them (Deshpande and Deshpande, 1991).

Some governments, recognising these problems, have looked for low-cost alternatives. The Sudan and the United Republic of Tanzania, for example, have provided unserviced sites for the very poor and virtually abandoned the application of standards (United Nations Center for Human Settlements, 1987). The Tanzanian case is particularly interesting, since the application of site-and-services principles has undergone a marked transformation. The earliest schemes were built to too high a standard and were beyond the reach of the poor, but the latest schemes are based on the concept of progressive standards. This is a flexible scheme whereby standards are not viewed as fixed but assumed to improve over time as consolidation takes place.

One of the major problems in increasing the supply of housing for the poor is the availability of urban land. Frequently, more unused urban land could be made available for residential use if it were not for institutional constraints (Kundu, 1988). The subdivision of urban land and the conversion of land for different uses are often impeded by restrictive zoning regulations, cumbersome land-registration requirements, high land-transfer taxes and disputed land titles. The poor are least able to overcome these institutional barriers. If they are not willing to accept overcrowded living conditions, they must engage in various forms of illegal land deal. If they do so, they suffer from insecure tenure which in turn limits their ability and willingness to improve their accommodation.

Where land and services are available, lack of finance is probably the primary reason for the difficulties encountered by poor households in their efforts to build or improve housing. Financial markets are underdeveloped, particularly for housing finance, and hampered by government regulations on interest rates and on the conditions under which funds may be lent. The poor are the first to be excluded from such a capital market, especially where disputed land titles make it impossible to use land as collateral in borrowing.

An appropriate housing-finance system for a developing country would not be a replica of that found in the developed world, geared towards the purchase of a home. Instead, a system is needed that addresses the various facets of housing construction and upgrading. In metropolitan areas, large accretions to housing stock take place through the upgrading of existing dwelling units by petty landlords. Studies in low-income housing areas have indicated that the financing of such investments requires small loan amounts with short to medium repayment periods and flexible interest and repayment schedules. If the housing-finance system included home upgrading and rehabilitation within its scope, it would be able to serve a much larger proportion of lower- and middle-income households.

In a country where most private-sector housing for the higher-income groups is either more or less self-financed or involves privileged access to existing financial institutions, it is imperative that housing-finance institutions such as housing banks address themselves to the hitherto unserved group of the urban poor and broaden the scope of housing finance. Evaluations of housing-finance institutions in many developing countries have indicated that even a more liberal system of finance is unlikely to affect the quality and quantity of housing in any significant way as long as it is confined to the financing of home ownership alone.

Since many poor people rent accommodation, increasing the availability of housing sites, materials and credit for construction does little for them. The rental sector in most developing countries is large and growing steadily; it often constitutes at least 50 per cent of all urban housing stock. In view of its relative importance, particularly in low-income settlements, there is a need to promote investment in rented housing as an effective way of expanding options for shelter.

In Seoul at the end of 1982, the Co-operative Urban Redevelopment Plan was introduced with the objective of improving housing and reducing owners' share of the financial burden of redevelopment. Under this plan owners in each designated area create redevelopment associations which conduct redevelopment in concert with professional developers. If redevelopment association members who own land or buildings voluntarily decide to vacate and offer their property to developers, the developers build enough apartment units to house at least one and a half to two times the number of displaced owners. These owners each receive an apartment, and the developer sells the remaining units to the general public. As of June 1989, out of 212 areas (encompassing about 10 million square metres) designated for cooperative redevelopment, projects had been completed in 78 areas (2.3 million square metres). Projects were underway in 54 areas (3.3 million square metres), while projects had yet to be started in 80 areas (4.4 million square metres) (see Table 5.4).

Since 1987, new cooperative redevelopment projects have declined in number due to three major problems. First, in redeveloped areas, only ex-property owners receive compensation in the form of new apartments. People who had rented rooms or land from the owners have to pay rent, at considerably higher rates, to live in the newly constructed apartments. Thus, renters in the designated redevelopment areas object to the cooperative redevelopment plans, demanding construction of low-cost public-rented housing to protect their interests. In May 1989, construction of small rental units for displaced renters became a requirement of all cooperative redevelopment. This has contributed further to a decrease in project activity. Developers have reduced building activity not only because the requirement for rental units reduces the amount of regular apartment space which can be built for sale, but also because of concern that increases in the number of rental units drive down apartment prices and profits. Second, the government now requires a higher percentage of tenants to give their consent before redevelopment can proceed, which often leads to further complications and contributes to a reduction in the number of new projects. The third problem concerns the allocation of apartments among the ex-property owners. Since each owner surrenders a different amount of land in exchange for an apartment, disputes often break out within the redevelopment associations over the proper distribution of apartment space in relation to the amount of land surrendered, thus preventing the associations from reaching agreements with developers.

Table 5.4   Seoul housing redevelopment projects, June 1989

Status	No. of locations	Area under redevelopment (1000m²)	No. of buildings under redevelopment	Households involved
Completed	78	2 344	17 809	24 483
In progress	54	3 345	27 251	46 935
Not started	80	4 486	35 682	55 255
Total	212	10 175	80 742	126 673

Source: Adapted from Kim et al., 1991, table 4.7.

Investment in the housing sector should, in principle, be linked to the macro-economic performance of the nation's and the city's economy. It must be borne in mind, however, that housing expenditure accounts for a small proportion of cities' GDP, despite overall growth of the city's economy in most developing countries. With increasing demand for investible funds from other sectors of the city's economy, housing investment is unlikely to obtain a greater share in the near future.

Table 5.5 shows that housing expenditure generally accounts for less than 1 per cent of GDP in most cities, except in Seoul where the figure is close to 3 per cent. In Shanghai, the rate of growth of housing expenditure is quite high (7.1 per cent) but housing expenditure as a proportion of the city's GDP (0.8 per cent) is still low. In Bombay,

Table 5.5   Housing expenditure in selected cities, 1970–88

City	Housing expenditure				
	As a percentage of total expenditure	*As a percentage of city GDP*	*Period*	*Real rate of growth (%)*	*Real per capita rate of growth (%)*
Bombay					
1971	7.2	0.46	1971–81	1.5	−1.7
1988	3.9	0.35*	1981–88	4.2	1.5
Cairo					
1981	0.9	–	1981–85	4.5	3.3
1988	0.8	0.05	1985–88	−18.7	−23.1
Lagos					
1971	14.0	0.69	1971–81	−11.4	−19.1
1988	6.9	1.46	1981–88	3.4	−1.5
Mexico City					
1981	1.9	0.14	1981–85	6.8	3.8
1988	3.2	0.13	1985–88	−5.8	0.4
Rio					
1981	21.4	0.37	1981–88	6.7	4.5
1988	27.5	0.61			
Seoul					
1970	22.7	1.89	1970–80	13.4	9.2
1980	27.4	2.71	1980–88	11.8	9.2
Shanghai					
1981	12.2	0.36	1971–81	–	–
1988	13.0	0.80	1981–88	7.1	8.9

* 1985.
Source: ILO mega-city survey (1990).

although the share of housing expenditure in total public expenditure and as a proportion of GDP went down during the 1980s, the rate of growth of expenditure is at least positive (4.2 per cent). But in per capita terms, housing expenditure only increased at 1.5 per cent per annum during the 1980s, which is low, especially given the fact that almost 60 per cent of the city's population live in slums. Among African cities (Lagos and Cairo), the growth rate in per capita real expenditure on housing has been negative in more recent years. In both Latin American cities (Mexico City and Rio), housing expenditure as a proportion of GDP is very low, although more than 25 per cent of the population in these cities lives in slums. In Rio, however, the share of housing expenditure in total public expenditure rose from 21.4 per cent in 1981 to 27.5 per cent in 1988.

An important aspect of additional investment in the housing sector relates to its likely impact on employment and incomes. Housing compares favourably with other sectors in terms of income and employment multipliers. However, the available evidence also suggests that these effects are generally greater for low-income housing. Thus liberal housing finance for high-income groups alone is not likely to add significantly to employment generation in the economy at large. Recognising the employment potential of housing investment and the need for housing finance for low-income groups, the approach paper to India's Eighth Five Year Plan (1990–5), entitled *Towards Social Transformation*, stated: 'There is significant employment potential in housing activity in itself as well as in its backward and forward linkages'.[1] Notwithstanding the importance of employment generation through the housing sector, one must be aware of the transient nature of such employment. As Lall (1990) argues, 'While construction induced employment would be in the interest of employment generation, it has to be seen whether the employment generated through this mechanism is more desirable in the long run than through alternative mechanisms'. The employment created through development of microenterprises and promotion of self-employment schemes, for example, is likely to be of a less temporary nature. Moreover, while the housing sector will generate a limited range of jobs, basically unskilled and semi-skilled, self-employment and microenterprises will generate a wider range of jobs and skills and also provide an opportunity for skill upgrading as well as the emergence of new entrepreneurial talent from the workforce. Lall therefore suggests that a long-term perspective on employment generation through the development of microenterprises may be more relevant than a relatively short-term strategy of employment generation through the construction sector.

Another important issue related to housing is that of urban public transport, which plays a central role in the development of cities as the essential link between residence and employment, and between producers and users of goods and services. As cities grow, transport facilities are often not expanded enough to maintain mobility. Table 5.6 shows that the real rate of growth of per capita expenditure on transport was negative in most cities during the 1980s. The data also show that in many cities the share of transport expenditure in total public expenditure, as well as its share in the city's GDP, declined in the 1980s compared with the 1970s.

Table 5.6   Expenditure on transport in selected cities, 1970-88

City	Transport expenditure				
	As a percentage of total expenditure	As a percentage of City GDP	Period	Real rate of growth (%)	Real per capita rate of growth (%)
Bombay					
1971	24.5	2.83	1971–81	6.3	3.1
1988	18.9	3.74	1981–88	2.4	−0.3
Cairo					
1981	1.4	–	1981–85	8.9	−10.1
1988	0.8	0.04[1]	1985–88	−15.0	−15.7
Lagos					
1971	16.8	2.83	1971–81	−0.3	−8.0
1988	20.3	4.27	1981–88	−11.1	−22.1
Mexico City[2]					
1981	21.1	3.87	1981–85	−11.0	−13.9
1988	9.4	1.80[1]	1985–88	−6.4	−0.2
Rio de Janeiro			1981–88	−15.7	−17.9
1981	6.8	0.12			
1988	1.8	0.04			
Seoul					
1970	14.0	0.91	1970–80	11.4	7.3
1980	6.0	0.58	1980–88	1.2	−1.4
Shanghai					
1981	6.7	0.20	1971–81	–	–
1988	7.5	0.49	1981–88	12.6	11.4

Notes: [1] 1985.
[2] Includes only expenditure on roads and streets.
Source: ILO mega-city survey (1990).

The urban poor suffer disproportionately if urban transport services are inadequate, since they tend to be pushed to the locations to which access is most difficult, costly and time-consuming. For the very poor, such costs may become so high that in order to secure and keep employment, they must accept minimal standards of shelter (or no shelter, as in the case of street dwellers) in central locations. Whether a neighbourhood is accessible by road also determines to a considerable extent whether other urban services, such as water, electricity, sewerage and drainage, solid waste collection, and police and fire protection are made available, and whether schools and health care are within reach of the inhabitants. Building better roads for poor neighbourhoods therefore often has far-reaching effects on the welfare of the residents.

Prevailing policies in the cities of developing countries have generally done little to make their transport systems operate efficiently and meet the needs of the poor. Urban transport investments have served mainly to increase the road capacity for cars, often at the expense of modes of travel used by the poor. In the larger cities of South-East Asia, for example, cycle-taxis have progressively been banned to make way for cars. A few large cities – Buenos Aires, Mexico City, São Paulo and Seoul – have attempted to solve their transportation problems by constructing subways, but the capital and operating costs of these systems have been so high that the poor cannot afford to use them unless they are highly subsidised. Such subsidies in turn place severe burdens on public budgets.

Effects of urban land ceilings, rent-control laws and other interventions on the supply of housing and rational use of land

Urban land ceilings

Most large cities in developing countries have an Urban Land Act. The major objectives of such acts have been:

1. the imposition of a ceiling on vacant land in urban agglomerations;
2. the acquisition of land in excess of the ceiling;
3. the regulation of construction on such land;
4. the prevention of concentration of urban land in the hands of a few individuals;
5. the promotion of an equitable distribution of land in urban agglomerations to serve the common good.

The available evidence suggests, however, that in most cases such acts have not had any significant impact in mopping up excess vacant land. On the contrary, in many cases they have reduced the supply of urban land on the market and pushed up land prices in general, especially for those plots below the ceiling. In Bombay, for example, out of 166 192 hectares declared as excess vacant land in applications filed under the Urban Land (Ceiling and Regulation) Act, 1976, only 3852 hectares (2.32 per cent) had been taken possession of ten years after the act became operational. In contrast, 43 864 hectares of excess vacant land had been exempted from the purview of the act (National Commission on Urbanisation, 1987).

In economic terms, this means that the impact on the ownership pattern of urban land has been marginal. Except for 3852 hectares of excess vacant land already taken possession of, the rest (excluding exempted vacant land) is tied up in litigation; this has reduced the supply of urban land on the market and pushed up land prices.

The biggest setback to the implementation of the Urban Land Act in Bombay has probably been caused by Section 20. This section empowers the state government to exempt land in excess of the ceiling if it is necessary or expedient in the public interest or where it would cause undue hardship to any person. 'Public interest' and 'undue hardship' have not been clearly defined anywhere in the act and have become a matter of subjective interpretation.

A recent study of Bombay has shown that 55 per cent of vacant urban land is owned by 91 individuals (Deshpande and Deshpande, 1991). The situation becomes worse as additional land made available for urban use is cornered by relatively well-off households, thereby aggravating inequities. Moreover, when land emerges as a source of higher profits than can be obtained from any other form of investment, there is increasing demand for land for speculative purposes.

Rent-control legislation

Rent-control legislation has often been used to ensure reasonable rents and security of tenure for tenants. Its prime objective is to reconcile the interests of tenants and landlords in a situation of extreme scarcity of housing units. As a control on the price of an item of basic need, it is also seen as a welfare measure to help a disadvantaged group in society. Rent control, like any other price control, is also justified as an anti-inflationary measure.

Rent-control laws in most developing countries typically:

1. control the letting and leasing of vacant buildings in order to assist tenants in their search for desirable rented accommodation;
2. fix 'fair' or 'standard' rents;
3. protect tenants against indiscriminate eviction by unscrupulous landlords;
4. set out the obligations and duties of landlords vis-à-vis maintenance and upkeep of their rented properties;
5. set out the rights of landlords against tenants who default in paying rent or misuse the premises;
6. set out the rights of landlords in relation to the recovery of premises in specific cases such as for personal use.

The fair rent, usually fixed in relation to the cost of constructing the premises and the market price of land at the time of commencement/ completion of construction of the building (ensuring an annual rate of return varying from 6 per cent to 12 per cent of the cost), remains frozen at the original level. In some of the Acts, taxes on the property and the costs of repair and maintenance are also taken into account when determining a fair rent.

However, the enforcement of rent-control legislation is not always effective on account of:

1. the ability of landlords and tenants to circumvent the provisions;
2. complications in the fixing of standard rents;
3. problems associated with recovery of possession and eviction;
4. inadequate and ill-trained enforcement staff.

Although detailed procedures are often prescribed in the legislation for fixing fair rents, in practice it is a difficult task because of the lack of documentary evidence in respect of the required information base such as the cost of construction, the time of commencement/completion of construction, or the market value of the land at that time.

Among the grounds on which landlords can file a suit for recovery of possession, the most common are default in payment of rent, unlawful subletting and request for self-occupation. But the time-consuming and protracted nature of the litigation procedure often puts landlords to severe hardship. As a result, landlords who want tenants to vacate their premises often look upon the practice of harassing tenants as a shortcut to recovery of possession and thus a substitute for court procedures.

Most studies of the effects of rent controls on the housing market suggest that the positive effects in terms of the social objectives originally envisaged are far from being realised. On the other hand, several adverse economic effects are found to be present in varying degrees in almost all rent-controlled markets.

In Egypt, for example, according to the 1986 census, nearly 1.8 million housing units built after 1980 (250 000 in Cairo) are lying vacant, as noted earlier. It is also estimated that nearly 700 000 older housing units are unoccupied. This means that nearly 2.5 million housing units are currently not being used despite the housing shortage in Egypt. The rent freeze and the desire to keep a house for children and grandchildren are the basic reasons given for not renting these housing units. Many observers in Egypt believe that it is a waste of scarce resources to build new houses without using the existing stock.

One common adverse effect of rent control is therefore the reduced attractiveness of rental housing investment vis-à-vis other forms of investment. Although the supply of rental housing units is affected by many factors, rent control, by limiting returns on investment to a level lower than that in other sectors, often inhibits investment in housing. It may be argued that while considering returns on investment in real estate, one should also include capital appreciation. But capital appreciation in the case of urban property arises mainly in respect of land rather than the building. Housing construction for the rental market *per se* is therefore influenced more by returns on investment in the form of monthly rent than by the attraction of capital appreciation.

When rents are controlled the landlord's return is usually independent of 'operating investment', that is, expenditure in respect of repairs and maintenance. He has, therefore, no incentive to spend money on the upkeep of the housing unit. A part of such expenditure, which may be absolutely necessary, will probably be shifted to the tenant, thereby reducing the benefit the tenant gets from rent control. Lower standards of maintenance can directly shorten the life of a structure, and accelerated deterioration of the housing stock becomes inevitable.

The excessive protection given to tenants under rent-control legislation also makes landlords afraid of losing control of their property indefinitely; hence, they tend to withdraw vacant premises from the rental market. The alternatives open to landlords are:

1. to keep more accommodation for their personal use than they otherwise would;
2. to hold back the units for speculative purposes;

3. to sell the units and make capital gains for investment in alternative assets.

Rent control also distorts land-use patterns as scarce urban space is not allowed to respond to market-price signals. The exclusion of sites from competitive bidding in real estate markets prevents them from being used in the most productive and valuable manner in the light of their locational attributes. In consequence, dilapidated low-rent residential or commercial premises continue to stand in prime locations where high-rise apartment buildings or office-cum-shopping complexes might otherwise be built. The resulting land-use pattern thus becomes increasingly inefficient and sub-optimal.

Rent control can also distort the locational preferences of tenants and hamper labour mobility by creating incentives for people to stay where they are. Such incentives are due to the benefits derived from having procured a controlled unit at a reduced and frozen rent. The reduction in mobility of families that continue to live in controlled premises long after their children have grown up and left home also results in sub-optimal use of living space. This reduction in the mobility of labour may have implications for regional development and relocation plans.

Rent control limits the liquidity of real-estate assets in the market since it becomes very difficult to find buyers for premises that are occupied by tenants who are excessively protected by legislation. This gives rise to an additional risk factor in investment in housing and reduces the opportunities for making capital gains from such investment. Investment in housing thus becomes even more unattractive.

Perhaps one of the most undesirable effects of rent control is that it has often given rise to illegal transactions between landlords and tenants, and also between landlords (or tenants) and the rent-control administration. The landlord and the tenant, both wishing to avoid the law, often strike unofficial deals. The overall effect of such contracts is to keep the effective rent at a level in between the controlled rent and the market rent. Some of the ways through which rent-control provisions are circumvented are:

1. Tenancies are transferred for a large capital payment in black money. This payment represents part of the discounted present value of the difference between the economic rent and the controlled rent, and is shared between the outgoing tenant and the landlord. The outgoing tenant is usually the principal beneficiary in such deals, with the landlord getting a smaller share.

2. Many landlords compel their tenants to pay part of the rent in cash without any receipt. This helps them keep the apparent rent close to the standard rent and thus reduces the property-tax burden.
3. Landlords often do not report vacancies, claiming instead that the housing unit has been given to a paying guest or caretaker, converted into a lodging house, or is under a mortgage with possession.
4. Tenants who enjoy the protection of rent control sometimes sublet a part or the whole of the premises at a much higher rent than they pay to the landlord.

Finally, property tax levied by municipal bodies and the wealth tax levied by central government on housing property are based on frozen, historical rent levels, or, as is more often the case, linked to 'fair' or 'standard' rents as defined in rent-control laws. Municipal and other revenues therefore fall short of the full potential that could arise from a taxation system linked to real property values.

In view of the above considerations, there is an urgent need for rent control reforms which would improve the tax base of local authorities and attract investment in rental housing.

URBAN POVERTY AND ACCESS TO BASIC SOCIAL SERVICES

Goverment involvement in the provision of social services, especially those relating to education, health, nutrition and family planning, is a well-established practice in all developing countries. Serious policy issues arise in regard to the delivery of urban social services because of their significant effects on labour productivity and the welfare of the urban poor (Richards and Thomson, 1984). Absenteeism due to illness raises production costs in general, thereby reducing the surpluses available for investment. Frequent illnesses among children also lead to increased absenteeism among women who work. This prejudices employers against hiring women. It is also often observed that women with the same qualifications and doing the same work are usually paid much less than their male counterparts. Whereas some of this may be due to pure discrimination, part of the differential arises because of expectations of absenteeism from work and interruption in work careers due to child-bearing and child-rearing. Child-care facilities are generally inadequate in most Third-World mega-cities.

Where the city authorities in particular can make a much more direct and significant contribution to alleviating urban poverty is in relation to policies aimed at improving the quality and productivity of the labour force by increasing the access of the urban poor to social services. In principle, social services should be easier to provide in cities and towns, given their compact nature, than in rural areas. On average, urban households are in fact more educated, healthier, and better served by public and private education and health facilities than their rural counterparts. The urban poor, however, are often considerably worse off than the average statistics suggest. The main reason for this is usually the lopsided distribution of urban social services towards the better-off sections of urban society. In many cases, urban policies regarding infrastructure standards, subsidies, land tenure, land use, building codes, business licensing, and the distribution and pricing of urban services are seriously biased against the poor, not only depriving them of essential services but also raising significantly the costs of their daily existence.

Table 5.7 presents data on access to social infrastructure in the two areas of Rio – the capital city (relatively rich) and the peripheral

Table 5.7   Access to social infrastructure in the capital city and the peripheral areas, Rio de Janeiro, 1970–80

Indicator	Rio Metropolitan Area		Capital city		Periphery	
	1970	1980	1970	1980	1970	1980
Lack of access to electricity (%)	9.4	4.2	4.9	2.3	17.3	7.0
Persons per room	0.9	0.7	0.9	0.7	1.1	0.8
Dwellings without adequate running water (%)*	29.1 (37.3)	19.7 (43.7)	17.7 (26.8)	5.2 (30.3)	50.5 (56.5)	41.8 (64.1)
Dwellings without sewage disposal (%)	36.6	22.1	25.4	13.7	57.1	35.1
Persons per hospital bed (1987)	–	171	–	142	–	225
Persons per health professional	–	297	–	208	–	603
Illiterate age 5+ (%)	–	18.0	–	14.5	–	23.0

* Figures in brackets indicate percentage of households earning less than three minimum wages without adequate running water.
Source: Adapted from Tolosa *et al.*, 1991, Chapter 4.

(relatively poor) areas. The data show that access to social infrastructure is generally poorer in the periphery than in the capital city.
The level of education is considerably lower and housing conditions
much worse. More than one-third of the population in the periphery
does not have access to adequate sewage-disposal facilities compared
with only 13.7 per cent in the city. The availability of hospital beds
and medical professionals is 40 per cent and 70 per cent, respectively,
lower in the periphery than in the capital city. It is interesting to note
that even within the capital city the relatively poor households earning
less than three times the minimum wage have less access to an
adequate water supply than those earning more than three times the
minimum wage. This clearly shows that poverty and access to social
infrastructure are negatively correlated. During the 1980s, the centre–
periphery gap is expected to have risen as a consequence both of the
1981-83 recession and of the successive attempts at monetary reform
(Tolosa *et al.*, 1991).

Such differences in access to social infrastructure between centre and
periphery are a typical feature of large Brazilian cities. This may well be
true of large cities in many other Third-World countries. Another
aspect which deserves special attention relates to differences in access
to social infrastructure between poor and non-poor groups in the
metropolitan population.

Table 5.8 presents data on access to four facilities – water, sewerage,
garbage collection and education – among poor and non-poor groups
in the Rio de Janeiro Metropolitan Area. The data show that access
varies greatly between these two groups. Lack of access to piped water,
for example, is three times greater among poor dwellings and seems to
be improving at a much slower pace than among the non-poor group.
However, the data indicate that in general, in spite of the recession,
conditions of access did improve somewhat during the initial years of
the 1980s, but they worsened again in 1987–8.

The data presented in Table 5.9 show that even in Seoul the
educational infrastructure is not equally distributed between rich and
poor areas. The poorest district (Songdong) has fewer schools than the
richest district although it has a larger population. The poorest district
has 7.5 per cent of the city's population but only 5.2 per cent of its high
schools, while the richest district has only 4.4 per cent of the city's
population but 7.6 per cent of its high schools. Playground area per
student in the poorest district is 2.7 square metres compared with 5.1
square metres in the richest district. The number of students graduating
from middle to high school in the poorest district is only 60.7 per cent

Table 5.8   Access to social infrastructure among poor and non-poor groups, Rio de Janeiro metropolitan area, 1981–88 (%)

Access indicators	1981		1983		1985		1987		1988	
	P	NP	P	NP	P	NP	P	NP	P	NP
Dwellings lacking piped water	51.2	18.7	43.4	12.0	35.6	8.2	38.8	13.4	35.6	12.9
Dwellings without sewerage facilities	53.1	22.6	42.7	10.8	27.0	8.1	28.7	12.4	31.8	9.7
Dwellings not supplied with garbage collection services	59.7	27.0	54.1	20.3	52.0	17.8	48.8	21.5	51.5	23.5
Percent children aged 7–14 not attending school	17.2	6.6	15.3	4.1	15.7	3.2	17.9	5.8	17.1	5.1

Note: P = poor; NP = non-poor.
Source: Adapted from Tolosa *et al.*, 1991, table 4.14.

compared with 91.6 per cent in the richest district. The higher drop-out rate in the poorest areas has serious implications in terms of social unrest, crime, etc., in such areas.

This pattern of relatively few schools and unsatisfactory attendance and drop-out rates in poor urban areas is found in most Third-World mega-cities. Many children of school age in poor neighbourhoods perform a range of economic tasks such as helping with the family business or even babysitting at home, which permits the mother to work. The parents of these children may not be able to afford to send them to school unless schooling is available in the evenings near the home. In a study of slums in India, Singh and de Souza (1980) found that two-fifths of the children of school age belonging to slum households did not attend school not because schools were physically

Table 5.9   Distribution of educational facilities between rich and poor areas in Seoul, 1988

Characteristic	Richest district (Kangnam)	Poorest district (Songdong)
Share in city's population (%)	4.4	7.5
Share in city's total (%)		
Primary schools	5.3	7.1
Middle schools	6.0	6.0
High schools	7.6	5.2
Students graduating from		
middle to high school (%)	91.6	60.7
Playground area per student (m^2)		
Primary schools		
Middle schools	3.4	3.0
High schools	3.4	3.2
	5.1	2.7

Source: Adapted from Kim *et al.*, 1991, table 3.11.

inaccessible but because their parents were too poor to educate them. Of those who attended school, 58 per cent dropped out, even before completing four years of schooling. The opportunity cost of educating children over 10 years of age was high in relation to the income of households headed by illiterate and ill-educated people as these children contributed one-fifth of the household income. A survey-based study of Bombay reported by Deshpande and Deshpande (1991) also found that of the children enrolled in the first standard in 1970–1, 25 per cent dropped out before completing primary school while 61 per cent dropped out before completing secondary school. The drop-out rates were higher for girls, 31 per cent at primary and 74 per cent at secondary level. The corresponding rates for boys were 23 and 58 per cent, respectively. The study observes that high drop-out rates are essentially a problem for municipal schools that serve the poor, the working class and the lower-middle class. Coming from poor socio-economic backgrounds, students attending municipal schools are often irregular in attendance due either to poor health or to lack of attention from parents, who often fail to realise the importance of educating their children. At school, too, they fail to get enough attention from their teachers. The higher incidence of poor performance and eventual drop-out in municipal schools is clear evidence of the fact that the disadvantages of the economically and socially underprivileged in one generation are being passed on to the next generation.

There is, however, a growing realisation in most Third-World countries of the need to develop human capital for sustainable development and future welfare. As can be observed from the data presented in Table 5.10, there has been some improvement in literacy rates in most Third-World mega-cities over time. But the crucial question remains whether educational facilities are expanding fast enough to meet the growing demand for education resulting from the rapid growth of city populations. The data show that in almost all cities, there has been a decline in the number of schools, per hundred thousand population, at all levels (primary, secondary and higher).[2] This is not surprising since large capital expenditures are needed for

Table 5.10   Educational indicators in selected cities, 1970–88

City	Literacy rate	No. of schools/educational institutions per 100 000 population			Student–teacher ratio		
		Primary	*Secondary*	*Higher*	*Primary*	*Secondary*	*Higher*
Bombay							
1971	63.8	28.0	12.6	0.9	36.7	29.6	31.9
1988	68.2[1]	21.7	9.6	0.8	36.3	31.3	36.7
Cairo							
1976	65.7	30.7	5.6	0.1	34.3	18.2	5.4
1986	69.2	26.2	4.6	0.1	32.4	13.8	16.3
Lagos							
1971	–	20.1	5.7	0.6	34.2	22.6	22.7
1987	60.9[2]	12.7	5.4	0.2	51.2	29.7	18.3
Mexico City							
1970	89.9	23.7	6.6	3.1	46.0	16.7	13.9
1988	97.7	18.3	7.3	4.9	29.5	18.2	10.8
Rio de Janeiro							
1970	85.0	45.6	16.3	4.9	93.2	14.3	7.5
1988	87.0	46.9	6.9	–	21.0	12.2	–
Seoul							
1970	94.7	3.9	8.0	1.5	71.9	34.1	9.1
1988	–	4.4	5.8	1.6	42.7	28.8	16.4
Shanghai							
1971	–	44.2	8.7	0.2	23.6	16.0	–
1988	88.5[3]	22.7	5.9	0.4	17.6	11.2	4.7

Notes: [1] 1980.
              [2] 1981.
              [3] 1982.
Source: ILO mega-city survey (1990).

new buildings and related educational infrastructure, which most city authorities find difficult to undertake, especially when they cannot even meet the recurrent expenditures on most social services. Most city authorities have, however, used the softer option of developing human capital by improving teaching facilities, as reflected in the improvement in student-teacher ratios. But it should be borne in mind that if the number of schools drops to a very low level in relation to the number of students, then even with larger numbers of teachers it will not be possible to serve the growing needs of education, and literacy rates will suffer in the long term.

Table 5.10 also shows that higher-level education is more prevalent in Latin American cities than in cities in other regions. For example, the number of higher-level schools/educational institutions per hundred thousand population in Rio and Mexico City is close to five compared with less than one in most other cities except Seoul, where it is around 1.5. The student–teacher ratio in higher-level schools also shows some improvement in both Rio and Mexico City, but in Seoul it has worsened, largely because of the government's policy, already noted, of restricting the growth of higher-level schools in Seoul.

Table 5.11 provides data on educational expenditure in mega-cities. The data show that in the Asian cities (Bombay, Seoul and Shanghai) there has been a respectable growth in educational expenditure per capita, although in the case of Seoul the growth rate was lower in the 1980s than in the 1970s. In the African and Latin American cities, the real rate of growth of per capita expenditure on education has been negative, particularly in more recent years. This is likely to have adverse affects on human capital development.

The urban poor also usually have limited access to private or public health care due to the high costs of medical attention and drugs, lack of information, and the physical as well as cultural inaccessibility of modern curative care. Infant malnutrition and mortality in urban slums are aggravated by the fact that mothers increasingly switch from breast-feeding to commercial baby foods, frequently diluted with unsafe water. As long as the urban poor live in overcrowded housing with no access to safe water or disposal of human and solid waste, and with only limited access to preventive health care, they are likely to be seriously affected by ill health.

Table 5.12 includes data on selected health indicators in mega-cities. Although the data show that health facilities (numbers of doctors and hospital beds per thousand population) are somewhat better in large urban centres compared with the national level, they are still quite

Table 5.11   Expenditure on education in selected cities, 1970–88

	Educational expenditure				
City	As a percentage of total expenditure	As a percentage of city GDP	Period	Real rate of growth (%)	Real per capita rate of growth (%)
Bombay					
1971	14.4	1.67	1971–81	4.3	1.1
1988	11.7	1.77	1981–88	6.0	3.4
Cairo					
1981	53.4	–	1981–85	1.9	0.8
1988	54.5	2.90[1]	1985–88	−10.6	−12.2
Lagos					
1971	14.1	2.38	1971–81	−10.1	−17.7
1988	22.4	4.70	1981–88	1.4	−4.4
Mexico City[1]					
1981	1.4	0.11	1981–85	−0.3	−3.3
1988	1.5	0.07[2]	1985–88	−12.3	−6.1
Rio de Janerio					
1981	39.3	0.68			
1988	29.8	0.66	1981–88	−0.8	−3.0
Seoul					
1970	18.8	1.57	1970–80	15.3	11.2
1988	25.1	2.48	1980–88	10.6	8.0
Shanghai[3]					
1971	46.9	1.42	1971–81	5.0	4.1
1988	40.0	2.62	1981–88	8.7	7.6

Notes: [1] Data refer only to schools.
  [2] 1985.
  [3] Includes health and cultural expenditure.
Source: ILO mega-city survey (1990).

inadequate. There has, however, been some improvement in the availability of health facilities over time. In Bombay, the number of hospital beds per thousand population has more than doubled, while in Seoul it has increased almost eight times in just under two decades. In Cairo, although the number of medical professionals per thousand population has increased almost four times (from 2.1 to 8.2) since the beginning of the 1970s, the number of hospital beds available has stagnated at around four per thousand population. This shows that medical education is being spread without simultaneously increasing other health infrastructure. This has led to growing unemployment among medical professionals, as noted in a recent study (Farah, 1991). In Rio, too, although the number of doctors per thousand population

Table 5.12   Health indicators in selected cities, 1970–88

City	No. of doctors per 1000 population		No. of hospital beds per 1000 population	
	City	National	City	National
Bombay				
1971	–	0.28	1.53	0.66
1988		0.38	3.67	0.91
Cairo				
1971	2.1	1.8	3.9	2.1
1986	8.2	4.6*	3.9	2.0
Lagos				
1971	–	0.04	–	0.45
1987	–	0.13	–	2.20
Mexico City				
1970	2.0	0.5	–	–
1980	2.7	0.7	1.6	1.3
Rio de				
Janeiro				
1970	1.9	0.5	9.6	3.2
1980	2.5	1.1	6.7	4.1
Seoul				
1970	0.9	0.7	1.3	0.7
1988	1.4	1.2	10.0	2.9
Shanghai				
1971	1.8	1.1	4.1	1.9
1988	4.3	1.4	5.4	1.4

* 1981.
Source: ILO mega-city survey (1990).

has increased by almost 30 per cent in a decade, the health infrastructure has declined by a similar amount. In Seoul, the reverse seems to be the case. The number of doctors per thousand population has increased by about 55 per cent while the number of hospital beds per thousand population has grown almost eight times in less than two decades. The number of beds per thousand population in Seoul is far greater than that in most other mega-cities in developing countries.

Table 5.13 shows that most cities spend less than 1 per cent of their GDP on health. The data also show that in the Asian and African cities, health expenditure as a proportion of total public expenditure declined during the 1980s compared with the 1970s. There was a slight increase in the proportion of expenditure in Rio de Janeiro, although in

Table 5.13   Health expenditure in selected cities, 1970–88

City	Health expenditure				
	As a percentage of total expenditure	As a percentage of city GDP	Period	Real rate of growth (%)	Real per capita rate of growth (%)
Bombay					
1971	10.5	1.22	1971–81	5.0	1.8
1988	6.7	1.43	1981–88	1.7	−1.0
Cairo					
1981	15.8	–	1981–85	−1.0	−2.2
1988	14.7	0.76[1]	1985–88	9.9	−11.7
Lagos					
1971	3.5	0.60	1971–81	−0.6	−7.1
1988	0.7	0.15	1981–88	−29.6	−48.2
Mexico City					
1981	4.5	0.33	1981–85	7.0	23.3
1988	7.4	0.32	1985–88	−8.2	−2.0
Rio de Janerio[2]					
1981	11.8	0.20			
1988	14.9	0.33	1981–88	6.5	4.4
Seoul					
1970	6.2	0.52	1970–80	11.3	7.2
1988	5.4	0.53	1980–88	10.1	7.5

Notes: [1] 1985.
            [2] Includes water supply and sanitation.
Source: ILO mega-city survey (1990).

Mexico City the rate of growth of per capita expenditure dropped from 23.3 per cent per annum in the early 1980s to −2.0 per cent in the late 1980s. In Rio, there was a slight improvement in expenditure on health. In both Cairo and Lagos, per capita growth in health expenditure was negative during the 1980s. The same is true for Bombay. In Seoul, the real per capita growth rate of expenditure on health remained more or less the same during the 1980s as in the 1970s, although the share of health expenditure in total expenditure declined slightly.

The drop in per capita expenditure on health in many cities has serious implications for the future of health services in such cities. Lack of adequate access to health and education are also likely to hinder attempts to alleviate urban poverty.

6 Urban Poverty and Population Growth

Urban poverty has several causes, the most important being low levels of physical and human capital; unequal distribution of productive assets; inadequate access to social services; high fertility, particularly amongst the urban poor; and urban development strategies which are biased against labour absorption.

Rapid population and labour-force growth do not necessarily lead to increased unemployment and poverty in urban areas, particularly if the capital stock also grows and appropriate labour-intensive technologies are developed, but they often contribute to the decline in living standards of the urban poor. With rapid population growth there is usually a decline in the resources available for capital investment. As a result, urban economic growth is adversely affected. During the recent economic crisis, as discussed earlier, rapid urban population and labour-force growth was associated with rising urban unemployment, expansion of the low-productivity informal sector, declining real wages and increasing poverty.

FAMILY SIZE AND STRUCTURE AND URBAN POVERTY

At the household level, urban poverty is usually associated with employment and household characteristics such as family size and structure. A poor urban household is characterised by low (and often irregular) earnings of the principal income earner, and by a high dependency ratio because of the large household size relative to the number of earners (Sant'Anna et al., 1976). In a study of four selected slum pockets in Bombay, Mukerji and Ramesh (1991) have found that 'for every 100 adults in the age group of 15–59 years, there are about 64 dependants (persons in the age groups 0–14 and 60+ years). The corresponding figure for the general population of Bombay, according to the 1981 census, was 56.6'. Deshpande and Deshpande (1991), using data for Bombay from the 38th round of the National Sample Survey Organisation (NSSO), show that poor households have relatively fewer earners and more dependants than non-poor households (Table 6.1).

Table 6.1   Composition of poor and non-poor households (aged five and over), Bombay, 1983 (%)

Activity status	Poor	Non-poor
Workers	17.6	42.4
Unemployed	5.1	3.8
Students	38.8	27.4
Household duties	24.6	22.0
Dependants	13.9	4.4
Total	100.0	100.0
Ratio of non-workers to workers	4.7	1.4
Average size of household	5.1	3.7

Source: Adapted from Deshpande and Deshpande, 1991, table III.6.

As the authors note, the NSSO data do not bring out the full impact of demographic factors in explaining poverty because the NSSO sample excludes all those under five years of age. If this age group were included, it would further increase the dependency ratio among the poor since they generally have more children than the non-poor, as discussed below.

Several recent studies suggest that the following are generally more likely to be poor than others:

1.   those with little or no education;
2.   households headed by the very young, the very old and those in the 35–44 age group;
3.   large households with relatively more women and children.

The well-known positive association between education, skill, experience and earnings explains why those with little or no education and households headed by the very young are over-represented among the poor. At the same time, the income of many workers, especially those with little or no education, often does not rise much with age. This explains why households headed by someone in the 35–44 age group are more likely to be poor, as the children are still too young to work and the mother's ability to work is also limited because of child-care responsibilities. The larger the family the higher the over-representation among the poor of households headed by people in this age group, even if the earnings of the head of the household are otherwise 'reasonable'.

Thus, at the household level, an urban household with little or no physical capital may be poor for any of the following reasons:

1. Too many of its adult members cannot find work.
2. The jobs available to its members pay poorly.
3. There are too many children or other dependants even if total income is relatively high.

These alternative explanations of poverty are related, but they are not identical – and different explanations give rise to different ways of identifying the poor and of designing ways to help them. A study on ten cities in five Andean countries (Musgrove, 1980) attempts to separate the effects on relative poverty of household size, family composition, and the employment status of household members. Using three variables, Nw/N (proportion of members employed), Nw/Na (proportion of adult members employed) and Na/N (proportion of adults in household), the study found an association between the poverty measure C/N (consumption per head) and family composition and employment rates.[1] The proportion of households in poverty declined as Nw/N, Nw/Na or Na/N increased. The study therefore concluded that a family is less likely to be poor if it consists of more adults and fewer children, if more of the adult members work and, consequently, if more members out of the total work. The higher the dependency burden in the family, in any of these three senses, the more likely the family is to be poor. The study also found that if there are four or more children per adult (eight or more children in a complete nuclear family), the family has a high probability of being poor, over 70 per cent in six out of ten cities covered. Whatever the household composition, if more than one-third of the members work, then the chances of being poor drop, in most cities, to less than 20 per cent.

Two results of this study are worth noting. First, family composition is strongly related to poverty. Second, there is a weak association between poverty and the adult employment rate, Nw/Na. This is the variable to which the household presumably adjusts in the short run in relation to its composition, its consumption needs and its employment opportunities. Three effects can be distinguished here. As Nw/Na rises, other things being equal, income rises and poverty becomes less likely. However, as there is an increase in the income which a family would earn if all its adults were employed, part of the potential income will be taken as leisure, leading to a negative relation between Nw/Na and C/N. Finally, the presence of children not only increases N, making poverty more likely, but it may reduce adult employment by requiring at least one adult to stay home and care for the children, again leading to a negative relation between adult labour-force participation and family welfare. The positive effect of income appears, for these cities, to outweigh the negative effects, but only slightly.

The finding that large households are more likely to be relatively poor than small households, and that poverty is associated more with family composition than with employment rates, suggests that much relative poverty might be simply a life-cycle effect. As children are added to a family, consumption per person almost necessarily declines, so a family may pass through a period of relative poverty at one stage of the life cycle, although it would not have seemed poor before the children were born nor once they are old enough either to begin earning income or to leave home and reduce the family size.

Several points deserve attention here. First, such a life-cycle effect is still sensitive to the number of children; many families will show a decline in C/N as they add children, but how far C/N declines obviously depends on the maximum household size reached. Second, whether the life-cycle decline in C/N leads to relative poverty also depends on the income of the working members and on whether that income tends to rise significantly with age. Some families would never become poor, because their incomes start high or grow rapidly, unless they had an implausibly large number of children. Third, although income is positively associated with total family size, it may not be positively related to the number of children. If parents with low incomes tend to have more children than higher-income parents, their poverty is not necessarily a life-cycle phenomenon. Although C/N will decline as they add children, such parents may be poor all their lives. Finally, the fact that poverty may be 'temporary' for many families does not mean it is transitory or of no importance for welfare, since temporary poverty may last for a decade or two. This kind of life-cycle effect would be relatively unimportant only if families could save in anticipation of the trough or borrow during the years of low C/N and repay later, so as to maintain satisfactory levels of consumption per person. When they cannot do that, temporary poverty requires sacrifices which may fall particularly heavily on children: they may, for example, have to leave school early and take poorly paid jobs, thus perpetuating poverty.

By estimating life-cycle effects, Musgrove shows that if the household head has some secondary education, relative poverty will occur only if there are six or more children (Table 6.2). When the head is uneducated, relative poverty may occur as soon as there is one child in

Table 6.2   Predicted permanent income per person (Y^x/N) as a function of life-cycle stage, household size and education of the head, in Bogotá, Quito and Lima, 1968 (US dollars per year)

City/education	No children Age 12–34	Age 35–49: oldest child aged 8–18 years				
Secondary education	N = 2	N = 3	N = 4	N = 5	N = 6	N = 8
Bogotá[1]						
Head uneducated	658	557	418	335	278	209
Primary education	809	685	514	411	342	257
Secondary education	1 379	1 280	961	769	640	480
Quito[2]						
Head uneducated	424	313	235	188	156	117
Primary education	570	421	315	252	210	158
Secondary education	923	935	701	560	467	350
Lima[3]						
Head uneducated	655	454	341	273	227	170
Primary education	733	558	419	335	279	209
Secondary educated	1 108	1 031	773	618	515	387

Notes: N = family size.
[1] Poverty line – 40th percentile of C/N at US$421 per year.
[2] Poverty line – 40th percentile of C/N at US$355 per year.
[3] Poverty line – 40th percentile of C/N at US$416 per year.
Source: Adapted from Musgrove, 1980, table 9.

the family and will always occur once there are two children; for this group a definite life-cycle effect can be identified. Families whose heads have some primary education are also likely to pass through a stage of relative poverty in the life cycle, but only with a relatively larger number of children.

Two striking findings emerge from this study. First, poverty, defined as low levels of consumption per person, is not strongly associated with low average income, and it is hardly associated at all with low employment rates among adults. Both low wages and unemployment bear some relation to poverty, but neither relation is as strong as might be expected. Second, poverty is quite markedly associated with large household size and low overall employment rates, both of which reflect a large number of children per adult member. Low wages and high dependency levels together, of course, virtually guarantee that a family will be poor, but dependency alone can explain much of poverty.

An important implication which appears to follow is that it matters, for the distribution of welfare and the reduction of poverty, how employment is created. If families are poor because their adult members cannot find work, the important step is to create more jobs, even if they pay little. However, this strategy is of no help to poor households with no unemployed members: what they need is not more jobs but better-paid work. The evidence presented above suggests that the second situation may be more typical of families in poverty, despite the high rates of open unemployment characteristic of large Latin American cities. Open unemployment can be considered a luxury out of the reach of really poor families, who suffer from low productivity in the jobs they are forced to take. These two factors are not entirely separable, since low wages by themselves are a poor indicator of poverty; but low wages per family member (whether working or not) mean poverty almost by definition. Of course, this kind of evidence in favour of (possibly) fewer jobs but better pay runs counter to two pressures in favour of rapid expansion of employment even if wages are low: that such expansion is needed both to absorb increases in the labour force and to minimise capital requirements. The first of these pressures links the question of employment to that of population growth, since slower demographic growth could improve welfare directly and also make it easier to concentrate on raising labour productivity.

FAMILY SIZE AND FAMILY WELFARE

High fertility and resultant large family size have adverse economic consequences at the family level, as discussed above. Large family size also affects family welfare (the welfare of the individual child, the mother and the rest of the family) through changes in: (i) expenditures on education, health and shelter; (ii) amount of leisure time; and (iii) the work activities of family members. The lower the family income, the greater are the adverse effects of large family size, particularly on children's welfare.

Several studies show that children from smaller families generally tend to be more intelligent, more ambitious and more independent and to possess higher self-esteem than those from larger families. Children from smaller families also tend to have better health and higher survival probabilities (King, 1987).

When large families adjust to economic constraints, the burden of deprivation often falls heavily on the children. With increases in family size, there is usually a shift in family budgets towards more spending on food and less on education. Even increases in spending on food may not be in proportion to the number in the family. A study carried out in one Colombian town showed that the likelihood of malnutrition in pre-school children was directly related to the number of living children in their families (Birdsall, 1980).

The intellectual development of children is affected by the amount and quality of attention which they receive from parents and parent-substitutes in the first few years of life: a large number of children may strain not only parents' financial resources but their emotional and physical energies. Several time-use studies of mothers show that the time women spend on child-care is usually less per child in large families (Birdsall, 1980).

Large family size combined with poverty also has serious conse-quences for women's welfare. Poor women often have to walk long distances for cheap food products, fuel and water. The Bombay slum study referred to earlier noted that the 'majority of the households in slums on Central and State Government land have to walk almost one kilometre to fetch water, since they do not have any source of drinking water within the slum' (Mukerji and Ramesh, 1991). In a recent slum survey carried out in the Manila Metropolitan Area, Feranil (1990) found that nearly half of urban poor women spent more than one hour every day on fetching water/fuel for the household (Table 6.3).

Table 6.3   Percentage distribution of poor urban women by time spent on fetching water/fuel in selected slum areas in metropolitan Manila, 1990

Time spent	Slum area		Both areas
	Leveriza	*Payatas*	
< 1 hour	65.8	46.1	53.1
1–2 hours	22.5	28.8	26.6
2–3 hours	7.5	22.4	17.1
3–4 hours	4.2	2.3	2.9
4 + hours	–	0.4	0.3
Total	100.0	100.0	100.0
(No.)	(120)	(219)	(339)

Source: Adapted from Feranil, 1990, table 4.8

Sometimes domestic activities, as mentioned above, can be shared or taken over by other members of the household, particularly daughters, although this means that daughters are then hampered in their development with regard to education and job opportunities. In the Bombay slum study, the authors found that 'about 13 and 27 per cent of the boys and girls in the age group 15–19 years, respectively, do not attend schools. The majority of such boys are working, whereas the majority of girls not attending school are engaged in housework and child care.'

In large poor families, women often have to earn an income to support themselves and their family. Even children often have to make some contribution to the family budget for mere survival. The 'double function' weighs most heavily on poor working women, who have to combine their household duties with income-generating activities. Since working hours in formal-sector employment are rigid and not adapted to the double function of women, they are pushed into informal-sector activities where incomes are usually relatively low. But even here, not all women in the city can find work, particularly wage employment, in the neighbourhood, so travelling within the city becomes a necessity. However, this costs time and money, and for women who have neither it may be impossible to combine the two tasks if home and work are located far apart. This often results in the 'crowding' of women into certain informal sector activities (food processing, traditional crafts, etc.) where they compete with each other and thus have relatively low earnings.

The effect of children on women's labour supply depends on the type of work women are engaged in. Some types of work are more compatible with child-rearing than others. Usually wage employment away from home is less compatible with raising children than self-employment or unpaid family work, which generally have more flexible hours and can take place in or close to home. Ho (1979) found that mothers in the Philippines whose income-earning activity takes place at home or close to home devote as much time to the care of children as do mothers with no market activities.

In urban areas, particularly in large cities, there are often serious problems with arranging for child-care; a negative relationship between child-care and work away from home is thus obtained. The data presented in Table 6.4 suggest that a significant proportion of poor urban women in the slums of Manila were willing to work but could not do so because they had no one to take care of their young children. However, the presence of other household member(s) (for example a

Table 6.4   Willingness to work and reasons for not working among poor urban women who were unemployed/not working in Manila's slums, 1990 (%)

Indicator	Slum area		Both areas
	Leveriza	Payatas	
Willing to work			
Yes	73.9	74.9	74.6
No	21.0	20.9	21.0
Depends if husband allows	5.1	4.2	4.4
Total	100.0	100.0	100.0
(No.)	(119)	(215)	(334)
Reasons for not working			
Husband refuses	26.9	25.1	25.7
No financial need/cannot find suitable job	3.4	1.4	2.1
Have no special skills	2.5	0.9	1.5
No one to take care of young children	56.2	60.1	58.7
No one else to do housework	7.6	6.0	6.6
Others (health problems, still studying, etc.)	3.4	5.6	4.8
Total	100.0	100.0	100.0
(No.)	(119)	(215)	(334)

Source: Adapted from Feranil, 1990, table 4.4.

girl aged 10–19 or an older married woman) to provide child-care has the expected effect of reducing this negative relationship.

The effect of number of children on female labour supply is likely to vary over the life cycle. When children are young, parents with more children to support may have to work longer hours to increase the family income. At the same time, since child-care usually requires the input of time by parents, having a large family may decrease parents' leisure or work hours, and induce specialisation of work between husband and wife. In his study of the Philippines, Ho (1979) found that, except during the first year of the child's life, the time spent by mothers on child-care takes little time away from their labour-market employment, but significantly more time away from their leisure. During the child's infancy, however, the mother reduces both her leisure and her work time. Thus, the age distribution (spacing) of children as opposed to their number is a major determinant of the mother's time allocation.

While the above discussion suggests that high fertility contributes to urban poverty and adversely affects family welfare, several questions remain to be answered. For example, why do the urban poor usually have large families? Is their fertility higher because they want more children (for reasons of income security, etc.) or because they lack access to education, health facilities, family planning and other social services? Are efforts to reduce urban population growth less likely to succeed if the benefits of urban development do not reach the urban poor? The discussion that follows attempts to answer these questions.

URBAN POVERTY AND FERTILITY

The economic theory of fertility behaviour considers children as a form of consumer durable yielding a flow of services over time (children are a source of personal satisfaction, their labour adds to the family income, and they provide parents with economic and social security in old age). To set against this there are direct costs involved in rearing children and indirect costs, which involve the income-earning opportunities lost by parents in raising children. Families tend roughly to balance the utility of children against the cost of bearing and bringing them up (Becker, 1960; Leibenstein, 1974). Becker argues that people behave as regards children as they do in respect of consumer durables. In other words, increased income increases the family's demand for children (that is, the income effect is positive). How, then, does the theory account for the negative association between income and family size? Several reasons are given for this. First, as wage rates/income-earning opportunities increase, alternative uses of time – either to earn the higher wages/income or to enjoy purchased goods – increase the price of children relative to other goods. Because women are primarily responsible for child-rearing, the rising price of children operates chiefly through the increasing opportunity cost of the mother's time. Second, increases in income eventually lead parents to spend more on better clothing and housing, nutritious food, comfort, leisure and higher quality education. The raising of children therefore entails a greater expense. Third, rising income may bring changes in tastes and alter the economic utility of children to their parents. The utility of children as security in old age may decrease because the parents may begin to save more for their old age, thus reducing their dependence on children for support in adversity. Most poor urban families live in a low-wage/income environment, in which children entail low costs or even a net benefit. The children of the poor, as discussed above, often help at home and work outside the home at an early age. If children support their parents in their old age, the low current costs of raising children may be seen as a small premium to pay for insurance against future uncertainties. Where women command only low wages, the difference between children's and mothers' earnings may be small; work time lost by the mother during a child's infancy may be easily recaptured by the child in later years. Finally, in low-wage settings, much of women's traditional work – in traditional crafts and petty retailing – may be combined with the care of children, so that children do not involve much opportunity cost.

Two other factors contribute to the link between poverty at the household level and high fertility. One is the high rate of infant and child mortality in poor households. Poor parents often feel that they must have many children to ensure having enough grown-up children. They therefore tend to compensate, either by replacing children who die or by responding in advance with higher fertility in anticipation of the mortality threat. The second factor is much less well recognised as an integral part of the standard demand theory, but should not be overlooked. It is that poor households tend to be located in areas where basic social services and modern means to restrict fertility are not easily available or, if available, are costly.

Singh and de Souza (1980) have reviewed a number of studies on family planning acceptance and fertility among poor urban communities in India. A study based on a health survey in Calcutta found that:

> only 25 per cent of the *basti* [informal poor settlement] population practised family planning either regularly or irregularly compared to 47 per cent in the residential areas . . . the average number of live births was 3.3 in the residential areas and 4.0 in the *basti*, and the average number of surviving children per married woman was 2.8 and 3.5 respectively . . . while all women in the residential areas received antenatal care and their babies were delivered in institutions, 44 per cent of the women in *bastis* did not have any antenatal care and their babies were delivered at home by untrained *dais* [midwives] or relatives.

On the basis of their findings, Singh and de Souza conclude that ignorance of family-planning methods, high rates of infant and child mortality, and poor antenatal care and delivery services create special problems for the implementation of family-planning programmes among slum dwellers. Another factor mitigating against family planning, they argue, is the desire for sons. Studies reviewed by them have shown that, ideally, women would like to have two sons and one daughter. The desire and need for the economic security which sons can provide in old age among those who live at or below subsistence level is so great that women want to continue having children until they reach the ideal level of at least two sons.

Shaw (1984), on the basis of a study on wage labour in slum households in Calcutta, points out that there appears to be a definite economic rationality in family size decisions among slum households. This is illustrated in the way the number and spacing of children seem to be related to the availability within the household of earning members, which is in turn influenced by household structure. The study notes that:

> though the average size of non-nuclear families was larger with 6.3 members as compared to the 4.7 members of the nuclear families, the average number of children in the latter was higher (3.1 as compared to the 2.9 for the non-nuclear families). The proportion of children to total household members in the nuclear and non-nuclear families was 0.6 and 0.4 respectively. Expressed in percentage terms, this means that on an average, 65.9 per cent of the members of the nuclear families were less than 18 years of age as compared to 46.0 per cent for the non-nuclear families. Significant differences also existed in the spacing of children, with the spacing average for the non-nuclear families being 4.7 years and that for nuclear families being 3.4 years.

Explanations for these trends are sought in the urgent need of the urban poor to acquire a broad base of income sources in order to augment low individual earnings and somehow survive. In non-nuclear families, the number of earning adults being higher, the urgency to rapidly enlarge the family is less and the birth of children can be spaced over a longer period of time. In nuclear households, with only the parents as adult earning members, the need for children to augment household income is greater. Also, bunching up their births within a short span of the child-bearing years leaves the mother free to take up wage work in an uninterrupted manner later on. The presence of other female adults in the non-nuclear household allows women here to be more flexible in spacing the birth of their children.

Fong (1984) reports the findings of surveys carried out in poor urban areas in Peninsular Malaysia, and compares the results with those for rural land-settlement areas developed by the Federal Land Development Authority (FELDA). The comparison shows that the utilisation rate for modern health care facilities is relatively low among residents in poor urban areas. For example, only 57 per cent of the eligible poor urban women utilised post-natal care services compared with 78.9 per cent among the FELDA settlers.

With respect to family planning and fertility, the data gathered in the surveys show that about 29 per cent of poor urban households practise family planning. This is lower than the level of family planning prevalent in the country.

As regards access to public services, the surveys indicate that, with the exception of electricity, residents in the majority of poor urban areas have relatively limited access to utilities and public services. For example, only about 20.5 per cent of households have flush toilets, 46.7 per cent have regular garbage disposal services, 55.4 per cent have access to public water standpipes, and 57.6 per cent have access to mail delivery. The study notes that, in the context of thriving urban centres, these are low percentages and indicate the necessity to bring public utilities and services within reach of residents in the poor urban areas. On the basis of the results of the urban surveys, Fong concludes:

the relatively low rate of utilisation of health facilities indicates that residents in the urban poor areas may not have as much access to health facilities as residents in the more developed urban areas. This suggests the need for opening up more health centres in the poor areas. Health care is an essential need of every household, and steps must be taken to ensure that the health needs of these residents are met.

The results on fertility demonstrate the necessity for a campaign to encourage the residents in the urban poor areas to space out their children more optimally. Better spacing of children in a household will result in an economically more active mother, who can contribute towards the household income through participation in the workforce. This is especially important among the poor households, since the extra income earned by the housewives will result in higher per capita household income leading ultimately to improved family welfare.

Mohan and Hartline (1984), in a study of the poor in Bogotá, Colombia, observe that:

Large families are not poor because they have fewer workers; rather that the poor tend to have larger families. The fact that among the poor themselves larger families are somewhat better off, tends to indicate the holding together of larger households for insurance purposes. Banding together in larger families ensures some income flowing in even when one or two members are unemployed.

In a study of poverty in Indonesia, Chernichovsky and Meesook (1984) conclude:

poorer households are handicapped from a demographic perspective. They are larger and have a larger proportion of children who need to be supported. Although poor households also have more members in the labour force than non-poor households, this is not enough to make up for the higher dependency rates.

Mukerji (1988) has recently estimated the crude birth rate per thousand population (CBR), not only for the general population of Greater Bombay but also separately for the slum population, using data for 1984 and 1985 from the sample registration scheme (SRS).[2] Of the 53 sample units covered in Greater Bombay, 13 were predominantly slum areas. Table 6.5 shows that for both 1984 and 1985, the CBR for the slum units is much higher than in the other SRS units.

Table 6.5   Crude birth rates (CBR), Greater Bombay, 1984–5

	CBR	
Area	*1984*	*1985*
All SRS units	25.2	23.4
Slum SRS units	37.7	36.0

Note: SRS = sample registration scheme.
Source: Adapted from Mukerji, 1988.

A recent survey by the International Institute for Population Sciences and the ILO carried out in selected slum areas of Bombay also indicates that the slum dwellers have higher fertility levels than the general population of Bombay. Table 6.6 shows that the mean number of children ever born (CEB) in each age group, except in the 15–19 years group, was higher for the slum population in 1989 compared with the 1981 census results for the whole city.

A recent study based on a survey of 1000 women in Karachi (Sathar and Kazi, 1990) shows differentials in fertility between women working in the formal and informal sectors. The data presented in Table 6.7 show that after age and education are controlled for, women who have ever worked in the formal sector have about two-thirds the level of recent fertility (mean number of births in the last five years) of women who have ever worked in the informal sector and those who have never worked. With regard to desired family size, women working in the formal sector say they would like four children while women in the informal sector want five children.

Tolosa *et al.* (1991), in their study of Rio de Janeiro, notice large differences in fertility between the capital city and its relatively poor peripheral counties, which provide limited access to basic social services, as noted earlier. On the basis of the 1980 census data, the study finds that age-standardised fertility rates in the peripheries range from a minimum level of 2.4 (Niteroi) to a maximum of 4.4 (Itaborai). The data in Table 6.8 show that the Rio de Janeiro Metropolitan Area,

Table 6.6   Mean number of children ever born by age among women in selected slum areas (1989) and among the general population of Bombay (1981)

Age	Slum sample (1989)	Bombay's population (1981 census)
15–19	0.36	0.44
20–24	1.25	1.22
25–29	2.47	2.13
30–34	3.13	2.86
35–39	3.87	3.42
40–44	4.50	3.56
45–49	4.75	3.93
All	2.76	2.59

Source: Adapted From Mukerji and Ramesh, 1991.

Table 6.7 Mean number of children born in five years preceding survey, and mean desired family size, among ever-married women by type of employment, Karachi, 1987

Type of employment	No.	Mean number of births		No.	Mean desired family size	
		Unadjusted	Adjusted		Unadjusted	Adjusted
Formal sector	308	0.61	0.63	295	3.63	4.18
Informal sector	299	0.97	0.97	257	5.42	4.95
Unemployed	304	0.93	0.93	266	4.97	4.82
Beta value			0.16			0.15
F-value			11.49			7.73
R^2			0.12			0.203

Source: Adapted from Sathar and Kazi, 1990, table 4, p. 69.

Table 6.8 Fertility levels in selected areas in Brazil, 1940–86

Area	Family levels					
	1940	1950	1960	1970 urban	1980 urban	1983–6 urban
Rio state	4.41	4.38	4.53	3.50	2.82	2.6
Rio metropolitan area	–	–	–	–	2.81	–
Rio capital city area	–	–	–	–	2.43	–
São Paulo state	5.02	4.65	4.87	3.56	3.11	2.9
South–east region	5.69	5.45	6.34	3.83	3.17	–
Brazil	6.16	6.21	6.28	4.55	3.63	3.5

Source: Adapted from Tolosa *et al.*, 1991, table 1.10.

which includes several poor counties, has a relatively higher age standardised fertility rate (2.81) than the capital city (2.43).

The results of the studies reviewed above suggest that in general the urban poor have larger families than the urban non-poor, both because of their desire to have more children for reasons of economic security and because of their limited access to education, health facilities, family planning and other social services. Starting with education and its relation to other social services, higher levels of education tend to be associated with lower fertility in most societies, and it is widely recognised that family-planning programmes, to be more effective, need to be complemented by specific educational programmes. At the same time, reduced fertility lowers demands on the educational system because of the consequent decline in the school-age population. Education and training programmes are also useful in improving nutritional practices, especially in instructing women from low-income households on the value of breast-feeding and on the preparation of balanced and uncontaminated food for infants and children.

Women's education generally has a stronger and more consistently negative effect on fertility than does men's education. There are several plausible reasons for this. The opportunity cost of raising children is higher for women than men. Education delays marriage for both men and women and improves the likelihood that a woman will have knowledge of and be able to use modern contraceptives. The effect of female education on fertility thus provides an additional justification for rectifying the imbalance whereby boys attend school in greater numbers and for longer periods than girls.

The links between health, nutrition and family planning are particularly strong. On the one hand, improved health, as measured by a reduction in morbidity or an increase in life expectancy, is known to lead to reductions in fertility, albeit with a variable time lag. On the other hand, reductions in household size tend to increase overall family health; more specifically, a reduction in the number of births and increased spacing of children contribute to improved maternal and infant health and nutrition. Poor nutrition is a major cause of increasing susceptibility to illness, and malnutrition is itself a major cause of morbidity and death (Austin, 1980).

Besides the internal links between education, health, nutrition and family planning, there are important links between individual social services and other factors. Improved sanitation (water supply, sewerage and solid waste disposal), for example, has significant effects on the health of the urban population, but these benefits would be further enhanced if improved sanitation could be combined with educational measures aimed at improving the level of personal hygiene among urban dwellers. The quality of housing, in particular the extent of crowding, is closely related to health, since with high population densities the likelihood of disease transmission is considerably increased.

Finally, probably the most important external linkage of the education–health–nutrition-family planning complex is its relation to the level of income. Higher incomes – at the household, city and national levels – are associated with significantly improved levels of education, health, nutrition and family planning in a pattern of two-way causation. Better education, health, nutrition and family planning increase productivity and reduce the drain on household resources associated with poor health and large household size; in turn, higher incomes permit greater household, municipal and national expenditures to achieve and maintain good educational, health and nutritional levels, and may directly affect parental decisions regarding reproduction. Indeed, what for a poor family is a vicious cycle – where low income induces poor education, health, nutrition and family planning which leads again to low income – is for a high-income family a self-reinforcing cycle where high income yields good education, health, nutrition and family planning and thus perpetuates high income.

The synergistic interactions of education, health, nutrition and family planning, however, imply that both private and public efforts – in the areas of education, health and sanitation as well as family planning – are likely to be limited in their effectiveness unless a comprehensive and coordinated effort is made to assist the urban poor.

Urban health-care facilities in developing countries are usually provided by both the public and the private sector. The quality of services provided by each and the population they serve vary greatly. The best private services are generally available only to middle- and high-income households. Services provided by the public sector, on the other hand, are in principle available to all, but their general lack of quality means that poor and low-income households are their only clients. In most Third-World cities resources are limited, and even public health services remain out of reach for many households. To reach the urban poor and low-income households, primary health care facilities need to be improved. Primary health-care workers in urban slum communities can help reduce malnutrition and infant mortality, and help disseminate information about family planning. Primary health-care programmes specifically geared to the urban poor are thus not only likely to provide direct benefits in terms of lower mortality and a reduction in absenteeism at work but can also be expected to have some influence on fertility.

Improving access to other services such as water supply and transportation could release time for more productive and remunerative activities. For example, more convenient and dependable water supplies would reduce the time needed for fetching water and give women more time and energy for income-generating activities.

Economic, social and family-health programmes should be mutually supportive. Women's education can achieve a great deal in improving the health of their children if basic health needs are provided for by primary health-care services, including family planning. Non-formal education, particularly for working women, and the establishment of family planning and health clinics in poor urban areas should therefore become a priority. Income-generating programmes and the provision of knowledge concerning a balanced diet can help alleviate the nutritional problems of the poorest strata of urban society.

With regard to education, changing the balance in favour of primary education, attempting to reduce the drop-out rate, and increasing access to education may all directly or indirectly produce benefits for the poor, as long as care is taken in educational programmes to ensure that the poor are actually reached. The question of access to education and the net benefits to the poor that are expected from education are closely related. Unless there are physical constraints on mobility or discriminatory constraints on school entrance (based, for instance, on location, race or social status), the decision to seek or not seek education involves comparing the costs incurred with the benefits derived. Since budget constraints are particularly binding for the lowest-income groups, lowering the costs of education for them is a crucial concern. One important way to do this is by locating schools in poor urban neighbourhoods, thus reducing transport costs.

Physical distance is not, however, the only reason why the costs of education may be prohibitive for poor families. Expenditures on school uniforms, lunches, textbooks and materials may be considerable, not to mention the opportunity cost in terms of lost time that children (or adult students) could use for domestic chores (such as infant supervision) or income-earning activities.

In addition to lowering the costs of education for low-income groups, the benefits that the poor derive from education can also be increased. Returns from schooling for low-income groups depend significantly on the overall demand for skilled and semi-skilled labour. Unless demand for skilled and semi-skilled labour expands, increased schooling may do no more than push down the private and social returns on education.

7 Resource Mobilisation to Finance Urban Programmes

While the demand for shelter, services and infrastructure, and consequently for urban financing, has increased as a result of the rapid growth in urban populations in recent years, performance on the supply side of financial resources has been generally disappointing. The supply of resources in most large cities either declined or grew very slowly during the 1980s. There are three main reasons for this. First, the urban development sector, particularly in Africa and Latin America, was often accorded a low priority in the allocation of financial resources during the economic crisis (lower growth rates, declining export prices, rising debts, increasing interest rates and so on) of the 1980s. This is reflected, as we shall see later in this chapter, in a decline in intergovernmental transfers of resources. Second, urban local bodies have made little, if any, effort to change pricing policies or tax-collection procedures to exploit fully the revenue-raising powers that they already have under existing financial arrangements. Third, as noted earlier, an important factor which has seriously affected the overall availability of urban finance is the increasing number of poor in urban areas who are unable to pay for services and infrastructure. All these factors have meant that the resources available to urban local bodies for financing urban development are totally inadequate. This has contributed to the deteriorating urban environment.

Table 7.1 includes data on the real rate of growth of total as well as per capita revenue during the period 1970–88. The data show that most cities in Africa and Latin America experienced a larger decline in revenue in the 1980s than in the 1970s. It is interesting to note that this decline was sharper in per capita terms, which suggests that population growth has contributed to the resource constraint. The data also show that although Asian cities such as Bombay and Seoul have not suffered negative rates of growth of revenue, growth rates did decline in the 1980s compared with the 1970s largely because of the general economic recession. As in cities of other regions, the effect of population growth in Asian cities was to further depress revenue growth rates. In Bombay

164

Table 7.1 Total and per capita revenue in selected cities, 1970–88

	Total revenue in million US dollars (1988 prices)	Per capita revenue in US dollars (1988 prices)	Period	Real rates of growth of revenue (%)	
				Total revenue	Per capita revenue
Bombay					
1988	903.7	91.2	1971–81	8.1	4.9
			1981–88	5.8	3.2
Cairo					
1988	553.6	87.7	1981–85	8.0	6.8
			1985–88	−11.8	−13.5
Lagos					
1988	284.6	68.7	1971–81	−0.9	−8.7
			1981–88	−8.3	−14.7
Mexico City					
1988	2502.6	303.8*	1981–85	−1.9	−4.8
			1985–88	−8.1	−1.9
Rio de Janeiro					
1988	564.2	95.1	1981–88	−0.5	−2.6
Seoul					
1988	4899.0	475.2	1970–80	12.7	8.5
			1980–88	10.4	7.4
Shanghai					
1988	4344.6	344.2	1971–81	0.1	−0.8
			1981–88	−8.5	−1.0

* Relates to federal district only.
Source: ILO mega-city survey (1990).

during the 1980s, for example, while total revenue grew at 5.8 per cent, per capita revenue grew at only 3.2 per cent. This indicates the adverse effect of population growth on the city's financial resources.

THE STRUCTURE OF CITY REVENUE

Locally levied taxes are an important source of revenue for financing urban services. Non-tax revenues consisting of fees, fines, rents and user charges are another important component of total revenue. Intergovernmental fiscal transfers play a different, though not very significant, role in financing urban services in the majority of developing countries.

City taxation

City taxation often includes taxes on land and buildings, vehicles, professions, trades and employment, advertisements, entertainment and betting, and octroi (duty on goods entering the city). The data presented in Table 7.2 show that in Asian cities such as Bombay and Seoul, local taxes account for around one-quarter of total revenue. In China, local taxes now include the profits of state-owned enterprises and so account for a major proportion of total revenue. In African cities, local taxes contribute only 10-20 per cent of the city's financial resources. Among Latin American cities, Rio gets one-third of its revenue from local taxes, while local taxes account for less than 10 per cent of revenue in Mexico City. The data in Table 7.2 also show that revenue from local taxes either declined or remained static during the 1980s compared with the 1970s in most Third-World mega-cities.

As far as growth rates are concerned, revenue from local taxes in Bombay increased from 3.3 per cent in 1971–81 to 6.9 per cent in 1981–8. In Shanghai, the real growth rate of both total and per capita tax revenue showed a marked increase during the 1980s. In Cairo, however, the trend is reversed: in the 1980s the growth rate of tax revenue became negative after the positive growth trend of the 1970s.

While property tax is levied in most cities, its relative importance in the overall revenue structure of local governments has fallen in recent years. This is partly due to an increased reliance upon higher levels of government to provide the resources needed for cities' public services and partly due to the low growth in property tax revenues despite the rapid growth of urban populations and the rapid rise in property

Table 7.2 City revenue from local taxation, 1970–88

City	Proportion of revenue from local taxes (%)			Period	Real rate of growth of revenue from local taxes (%)		Real rate of growth of per capita revenue from local taxes (%)	
	Property tax	Other local taxes	Total local tax		Property tax	Total local taxes	Property tax	Total local taxes
Bombay								
1971	19.5	23.3	42.8	1971–81	−1.7	3.3	−4.8	0.1
1988	4.7	22.3	27.0	1981–88	0.2	6.9	−2.4	4.3
Cairo								
1981	2.2	8.4	10.6	1981–85	14.7	8.0	−4.6	5.9
1988	2.8	7.2	10.0	1985–88	−11.8	−11.8	–	−13.4
Lagos								
1971	–	19.0	19.0	1971–81	–	−1.1	–	−8.8
1988	–	19.0	19.0	1981–88	–	−8.1	–	−14.5
Mexico City								
1981	5.7	4.5	10.2	1981–85	−19.5	−21.2	−22.5	−24.2
1988	1.7	6.9	8.6	1985–88	−24.2	12.2	−18.0	18.2
Rio de Janeiro								
1981	14.4	26.3	40.7	1981–88	−9.3	−2.9	−11.5	−5.0
1988	7.7	26.7	34.4					
Seoul								
1970	3.3	26.4	29.7	1970–80	15.1	14.0	10.9	9.8
1988	3.0	23.3	26.3	1980–88	6.3	7.1	3.6	4.5
Shanghai								
1971	–	26.8	26.8	1971–81	–	−3.6	–	−5.5
1988	–	80.1	80.1	1981–88	–	34.6	–	32.4

Source: ILO mega-city survey (1990).

values. Even in Bombay and Rio, where property taxes accounted for nearly 15–20 per cent of total revenue in the 1970s, the share of such taxes dropped considerably during the 1980s (Table 7.2). In Bombay it declined from 19.5 per cent in 1971 to 4.7 per cent in 1988. In Cairo, although the share of property tax marginally increased during the 1980s, its overall contribution to total revenue remains low (2.8 per cent in 1988). In most cities, property tax contributes less than 5 per cent to total revenue. In terms of growth rates, the data in Table 7.2 indicate that the performance of property tax as a source of revenue has been rather disappointing.

It is generally expected that market forces will increase the value of property (either its rental or capital value) as population and incomes increase; however, the linkage may be less than perfect. This is particularly true if market forces are in some way subverted. Probably the most common form of interference in the workings of the property market is rent control, as noted earlier. To the extent that rent controls are effective, increases in the value of property may not result in improvements in the economic base of a community. The link between economic growth and increases in the tax base is, of course, also influenced by the definition of the base. Certain types of property, such as religious and government property, are commonly excluded from the taxable base; likewise, some countries exempt properties with particularly low market values, while in other countries owner-occupied parcels are given preferential status.

Linn (1983) argues that property tax in its basic form – that is, levied at rates proportional to the value of the real estate – can be quite progressive. However, statutory provisions and administrative practices often counteract and possibly eliminate its inherent progressiveness. Some of the features that reduce the progressiveness of urban property tax are regressively graduated tax rates, low assessment ratios for high-value properties, lower taxes on vacant lots, higher rates on improvements than on site value, and inadequate efforts to collect tax on high-value properties. In addition, owner-occupied properties are quite frequently given preferential treatment over rented properties, which further reduces the progressiveness of property tax and burdens the urban poor, who are more likely to rent.

Several observers have therefore suggested that, in those cities where regressive property tax practices are prevalent, an effort should be made to eliminate such practices, since their removal would improve revenues, efficiency, equity and administrative ease (Schroeder and Dalton, 1986). Measures such as higher tax rates on site value than on improvements, and higher than average tax rates for vacant lots, are also likely to increase progressiveness. Tax exemption for low-value or slum properties would improve efficiency and equity. It is also suggested that overall reliance on property tax can perhaps be increased in many cities in developing countries, particularly since average effective tax rates tend to be extremely low compared with those found in cities in industrialised countries.

One particularly attractive aspect of effective urban land taxation is that it can act as an instrument to appropriate for public use some of the windfall gains that urban landowners reap in the rapidly growing cities of developing countries. In most developing countries, however, the revenue potential of real-estate taxation is not fully utilised. The existing systems tend to suffer from poor assessment administration, substantial erosion of the tax base due to exemptions, and poor performance in terms of tax collection.

When a government decides to invest in roads and other physical and social infrastructure, there is a tendency for the value of land in the vicinity to rise. There could therefore be some mechanism by which a government could appropriate part of this increase in land value, which usually benefits only builders and private individuals.

Besides property tax, non-property taxes such as local sales taxes and octroi play a significant role in financing urban public services in some countries. On the one hand, octroi is regarded as the most liquid and elastic tax at the disposal of urban local bodies. On the other hand, it has been viewed as an 'inherently bad tax' on several grounds. First, it acts as a barrier to interregional and intercity trade and its impact falls on inputs which may get taxed repeatedly. It therefore tends to distort the pattern of location of industrial activity. Second, it has a high collection and enforcement cost. Third, it is often regressive in incidence. As a result, suggestions have frequently been made that this tax should be phased out. But, despite its inherent weaknesses, it has persisted since many urban local bodies find it an important revenue source. In fact, in Bombay the share of octroi in total revenue increased from 19.0 per cent in 1970–2 to 26.6 per cent in 1985–7 (Deshpande and Deshpande, 1991).

Municipal sales taxes also have certain shortcomings. Sales taxes place an administrative burden on retailers, who must collect and remit the tax to the government department levying the tax; furthermore, in the absence of an effective auditing system, it may be susceptible to evasion. On balance, however, a sales tax (general or selective) is superior to octroi as a source of revenue for urban local bodies. As a potential source of finance for urban services in developing countries, sales taxes merit careful consideration.

Car ownership and use provide an excellent but much neglected revenue source for many city governments. As noted earlier, the number of cars registered in cities in recent years has grown much faster than city populations, and in most developing countries car ownership is heavily concentrated in the largest cities. Furthermore, an overwhelming proportion of the urban vehicle fleet in developing countries consists of cars, and these are owned and operated mainly by the higher-income classes. Several observers have therefore suggested that, in the interests of both revenue and efficiency, a set of taxes directed at car ownership and fuel consumption makes good sense; the equity and environmental dimensions add additional force to the argument.

Local governments all over the world have also utilised admission tax, sometimes also known as entertainment or amusement tax, for raising revenue. This tax has several advantages. It does not impose a great burden since its administration is fairly simple. It is one of the few taxes that reaches non-residents and tourists who do not otherwise contribute directly to city revenues. The tax can provide a fair amount of revenue, especially in large cities. As it has no serious disadvantages, it is generally considered a good source of revenue for financing urban services in developing countries.

Some of the non-property taxes mentioned above are an important source of revenue for urban governments. However, proliferation and indiscriminate use of non-property taxes is not desirable because a number of them are regressive and cause hardship for those least able to pay. Careful consideration must therefore be given not only to their potential for raising revenue, but also to other aspects such as equity, collection costs and administrative ease.

Pricing of public services and the role of user charges in encouraging efficient allocation of demand

User charges belong to the family of non-tax revenues. Non-tax revenues consist of two major categories: (i) fees and fines and (ii) rents and prices or user charges. The former includes fees for licences and permits, and fines and forfeitures. These are not, however, a significant source of municipal revenue because income from them is usually small. Their main objective is to regulate certain activities in the broader interests of public health, social discipline and welfare. In most large cities, fees and fines account for only 1–3 per cent of total revenue (see Table 7.3). Rents and prices or user charges, on the other hand, account for a significant proportion of total revenue and accrue to local governments either through their ownership of real estate (lands, markets, houses, etc.) or through their operation of public utility services and semi-commercial undertakings (electricity, water supply, sewerage, city transport, etc.). User charges are theoretically based on the benefit principle and affect only those who really avail themselves of the service or benefit provided.

Table 7.3 shows that user charges contribute significantly to municipal resources in many Third-World mega-cities. In Bombay and Seoul, around 50 per cent of total revenue comes from user charges. In Shanghai, social services are highly subsidised so user charges do not play a significant role in raising resources for the city. Among Latin American cities, Mexico City put great emphasis on cost recovery during the economic crisis of the 1980s, and now over 40 per cent of its revenue comes from user charges. Rio de Janeiro, on the other hand, has depended less on user charges as a revenue source. In 1988, only 3.6 per cent of total revenue came from this source. In Cairo, although user charges have risen in recent years, their contribution to total revenue is still quite low (13.2 per cent).

The data in Table 7.3 also show that the proportional contribution of user charges to total revenue declined slightly during the period 1970–88 in Bombay, Rio de Janeiro and Seoul while it increased in Cairo, Mexico City and Shanghai. Looking at growth rates one finds that all mega-cities, except Mexico City and Seoul, experienced a decline in the real rates of growth of total as well as per capita revenue from user charges during the 1980s. As a result their dependence on loans and borrowings to finance urban programmes has increased, as we shall see later, thereby adding to their debt burden. In the case of Bombay, however, the real growth rates of user charges are positive both in total and per capita terms despite being somewhat lower during the 1980s (4.7 per cent and 2.0 per cent, respectively) than in the 1970s (8.9 per cent and 5.7 per cent, respectively).

In most large cities, urban services such as electricity, water and public transport have often been underpriced to benefit various groups. In many cases, prices have not covered the cost of production, and the agencies supplying these services have consequently been unable to meet operating costs or to make adequate investment without extensive state subsidies, which constitute a heavy drain on the public budget and are themselves a disincentive to efficient operation. The usual result has

Table 7.3 City revenue from non-tax sources, 1970–88

City	Proportion of revenue from non-tax sources (%)			Period	Real rate of growth of revenue from non-tax sources (%)		Real rate of growth of per capita revenue from non-tax sources (%)	
	User charges	Fees and fines	Total non-tax revenue		User charges	Total non-tax revenue	User charges	Total non-tax revenue
Bombay								
1971	50.5	5.6	56.1	1971–81	8.9	7.3	5.7	4.0
1988	49.0	2.8	51.8	1981–88	4.7	5.3	2.0	2.7
Cairo								
1981	4.1	4.5	8.6	1981–85	33.0	21.5	31.6	20.4
1988	13.2	3.8	17.0	1985–88	−5.3	−6.0	−6.0	−7.4
Lagos								
1971	13.3	–	13.3	1971–81	–	−1.1	–	−8.8
1988	13.3	–	13.3	1981–88	–	−8.1	–	−14.5
Mexico City								
1981	16.8	3.6	20.4	1981–85	5.3	0.9	2.4	−2.1
1988	40.7	1.0	41.7	1985–88	11.9	12.1	18.1	18.3
Rio de Janeiro								
1981	4.3	10.9	15.2	1981–88	−2.9	−16.4	−13.9	−18.6
1988	3.6	1.4	5.0					
Seoul								
1970	52.3	2.3	54.6	1970–80	12.0	9.6	4.2	5.4
1988	48.2	1.2	49.4	1980–88	13.4	12.9	18.2	10.3
Shanghai								
1971	1.4	–	1.4*	1971–81	–	0.3*	–	−1.3*
1988	5.0	–	5.0*	1981–88	–	−30.9*	–	−33.3*

* Includes income from state-owned enterprises.
Source: ILO mega-city survey (1990).

been excess demand and rationing, with all its attendant problems (Prakash, 1986).

Table 7.4 shows that in Bombay, domestic users pay only 30 per cent of the cost of supplying water, while those in neighbouring towns pay 30 per cent more than the real cost of providing the service in the city. Commercial users, however, pay 12 times the cost of production. The financial burden of supplying water therefore falls mainly on commercial users, who subsidise both households living in slums (which, by and large, do not pay for the water supply) and others not living in slums who pay much less than the cost. The rate structure is also flat so that households that use more water do not pay a progressively higher price. In Cairo, too, domestic users pay only 23 per cent of the cost of supplying water. With regard to transport, the railway authorities in Bombay have failed to cover their operating costs despite overcrowding on trains, largely because monthly or quarterly season tickets are priced unduly low.[1] The data presented in Table 7.4 show that first-class passengers pay only 12 per cent and second-class passengers 28 per cent of the average cost of providing the service. Thus, even on grounds of equity, such a subsidy can hardly be justified. The pricing of bus transport in Bombay follows a system of telescopic rates so that passengers travelling short distances subsidise those travelling long distances. Since the poor on average travel short distances, these telescopic rates do not contribute to equity. Inequity is further increased by cross-subsidy from the electricity department to the department of transport, as both services are provided by the same undertaking, BEST,[2] and electricity is consumed by a large section of the poor who cannot afford to commute on buses (Deshpande and Deshpande, 1991). In Shanghai, bus travellers with monthly season tickets pay only 50 per cent of the cost, while city dwellers pay only two-thirds of the cost of providing gas.

This failure to recoup the cost of urban services from users has frequently led to extensive subsidies, particularly to higher-income groups. Besides public utilities, other kinds of services for which subsidies are generally provided include public housing, urban road space, secondary and higher education, and modern hospital care. As Linn (1983) has argued, these subsidies on balance favour the wealthier groups, for several reasons. First, their greater political influence ensures them better access to public services such as housing, and the location of certain services in their neighbourhood. Second, the concentration of urban property ownership in the hands of the affluent means that they reap any benefits from the increase in land

Table 7.4 Prices and real costs of public utilities in selected cities

City	Public Utility	Unit	Price (A)	Real cost (B)	Cost recovery (%) (A/B)
Bombay (1980)	Water supply	Rs per 10000 litres	3 (domestic usage)	10	30
			120 (non-residential use)		1200
			13 (neighbouring towns)		
	Rail transport	Monthly ticket second-class first-class	14^1 6^1	50^2 50^2	28 12
Cairo (1985)	Water supply	Egyptian pounds per cubic metre	0.012	0.053	23
Shanghai (1989)	Gas	Yuan per cubic metre	0.10	0.15	67
	Water supply	Yuan per ton	0.12	0.11	109
	Transport (monthly ticket)	Yuan per ticket	6.00	12.00	50

Notes:
[1] Number of single journeys charged per month.
[2] Number of expected single journeys per month.
Source: Deshpande and Deshpande, 1991; Farah, 1991; Shanghai Planning Commission, 1991.

value which results when urban public services are provided in the vicinity of that land. Third, the poor are not able to benefit from some public services because of certain private costs they must incur, for example, out-of-pocket expenses and loss of income when attending school or visiting modern hospitals. Many observers have therefore suggested that the elimination of general subsidies for urban public services would provide additional public revenue, mainly by reaching and tapping the resources of the wealthier groups to a greater degree than before. Requiring users to pay for services would also curtail demand to more efficient levels (Prakash, 1986).

Some economic theorists, however, consider user charges inappropriate for financing what are defined as 'pure public goods' – services whose dominant characteristics are such that no one is denied their benefits regardless of whether they pay for them or not. It is further argued that in some cases, even when a particular public service is not a 'pure public good', user charges may be feasible but not desirable. User charges are also less justifiable where the service produces substantial public benefits in addition to those enjoyed by the individual user.

Notwithstanding the merits of these arguments, it is doubtful if this approach can be applied to developing countries in the initial stages of their development when the emphasis has to be on resource mobilisation, capital formation and cost recovery. Few developing countries can at present afford to provide, for example, drinkable water free of charge or at highly subsidised rates. If user charges are not related to the costs of public services, the community will have to finance them through taxation, which in most developing countries may well be regressive and unstable. User charges, unlike taxation, provide greater flexibility in that a citizen can choose not to utilise the service, or at least to economise on its use. Moreover, most user charges, when required, can be designed to favour underprivileged groups through cross-subsidisation, lifeline tariffs, etc. Thus, those who advocate cost recovery do not see any economic rationale in providing general subsidies to users, arguing instead that the supply price of services should be at least equal to their marginal, if not average, cost.

Economic theory dictates that the most efficient use of the economy's resources is achieved when the price of any product equals its marginal cost. In the case of urban services, marginal cost pricing would result in their use to the point at which the private benefits of using an additional unit would equal the cost of producing it. Thus, marginal cost pricing is expected to lead to more efficient allocation of demand among urban services.

Linn (1983) has argued that an additional benefit of marginal cost pricing is that it provides a guide for efficient investment decisions by public authorities. Since consumers are induced to consume according to their willingness to pay, public authorities have an incentive to provide a standard of service that reflects consumers' willingness to pay. User charges based on marginal costs would therefore aid in cost recovery. Greater equity would also be achieved since financing services through user charges would prevent redistribution from the poor to the rich.

Given this general prescription for financing urban services through user charges based on marginal costs, the question arises as to why the provision of these services is not left to the private sector. Economies of scale, externalities, and the possibilities of monopoly conditions in the private sector are often cited as arguments in favour of public intervention. Public provision of social services has often led to extensive cost reductions, subsidies, and benefits to low-income households. However, public intervention, particularly in the provision of housing, does not always lead to these benefits, as noted earlier.

Some observers also argue that it is not clear how user charges based on marginal costs can be justified in the presence of decreasing costs or externalities – two primary reasons for public intervention. When production occurs under decreasing cost conditions, marginal cost pricing will result in losses, and costs will not be covered. On the other hand, average cost pricing would cover costs, but result in lower than optimal consumption. It would thus be useful to see how user charges fit into the scheme of a public policy involving goods or services produced under decreasing cost conditions.

The other area of conflict concerns marginal cost pricing in the face of externalities. When positive externalities are associated with a given urban service, its marginal social benefits exceed its marginal private benefits. Thus, marginal cost pricing will result in a lower level of consumption than is optimal, since individuals will compare only their marginal private benefit with the marginal cost price. The market solution may therefore be inefficient and government intervention in the form of tax concessions, quotas and subsidies may be required. In the provision of water supply, for example, the use of the life-line tariff subsidises low-income consumers who could not otherwise afford it.

In general, the principle that price should equal marginal cost is alien to most urban local governments; besides, its implementation would be hampered by the non-availability of cost data on many services. Furthermore, the cost of a service often depends on the costs of complementary or related services, which presents enormous methodological problems when it comes to determining appropriate prices consistent with the principle of marginal cost pricing. The entire range of pricing questions therefore remains fuzzy. But even when the 'right' prices are known, they are often not adopted for political reasons. However, political considerations are all too often used as an excuse for failure to analyse the costs of not applying sound pricing policies, to see that such costs are adequately examined at the proper level of authority, or to ascertain whether the efficiency benefits forgone are clearly compensated by the political benefits obtained. Even when these steps are taken, implementing the 'right' decisions may be painful and call for strong political will.

Overall, the implications of the principle of full cost recovery through user charges have not been worked out sufficiently for the principle to be operationalised in developing countries. In most countries there is virtually no direct cost recovery for capital investment in urban services. The general policy has been that, as far as possible, recurrent expenditure should be recovered through user charges but the initial capital investment should be provided to users as a subsidy or grant. Even this policy is, however, posing problems, and policy-makers today face a choice between highly subsidised, low-quality services for many, and non-subsidised but high-quality services for a few.

In the face of increasing population and demand for services, greater efforts will have to be made to recover costs. The capital cost of supplying water, for example, can be recovered in two ways. If the land market is functioning well, part of the capital cost gets capitalised in land prices where water is supplied. Hence, some of the capital costs can be recovered through sales of land in new developments, or through taxes on land sales. The fee for initial water supply connection could also be set at a level which reflects the capital costs. The running costs of water supply can be recovered through user charges which vary according to the volume of water used.

Inter-governmental fiscal transfers and the borrowing powers of local bodies

A significant proportion of fiscal resources is usually controlled by national and provincial governments. The capabilities of urban local governments depend, therefore, not only upon their tax base and non-tax revenues, but also upon intergovernmental fiscal transfers from national and state governments. The national government may transfer funds, both for capital and current programmes, to local bodies directly and/or through the state or provincial governments. There are two major instruments for intergovernmental fiscal transfers and cooperation: (a) tax-sharing and (b) grants-in-aid. In fiscal terms, a grant is an appropriation of funds from the higher government's budget to local government. It is not, therefore, a tax or shared revenue. Although grants were conceived primarily as a measure of financial assistance, they have acquired a number of important features which add to their usefulness and put them in a distinct class of public revenues. For instance, grants are often used as measures of control and supervision over local governments. They are designed and employed to stimulate local public expenditure, to promote certain national objectives or to underwrite the supply of certain public goods provided locally. This is done either because there is a national interest in providing a minimum level of services for all citizens or because certain services carry external benefits or costs, giving rise to inequities or inefficiencies.

In the overall context of resource mobilisation, however, urban development projects must compete with other development programmes for scarce national capital resources. In the prevailing circumstances, their share is bound to be grossly inadequate despite their high priority needs. This means that urban local governments or development authorities need to make herculean efforts to mobilise additional resources of their own.

The data presented in Table 7.5 show that intergovernmental transfers account for only a small proportion of total revenue in Asian cities (Bombay, Seoul and Shanghai), while the proportion is relatively high in African and Latin American cities (Cairo, Lagos, Mexico City and Rio). In Mexico City and Rio, tax-sharing constitutes a major part of intergovernmental transfers. A substantial proportion of total revenue in these two cities (Mexico City, 46.9 per cent; Rio, 30.9 per cent) comes from tax-sharing. In Cairo and Lagos, grants from the state and central government are relatively more important. Excessive dependence on grants has, however, serious fiscal implica-tions, since during periods of economic difficulties, cities that are highly dependent on grants are likely to receive less resources. In Shanghai, the revenue structure is completely different. Here income from state-owned enterprises constitutes an important component of

Table 7.5 City revenue from intergovernmental transfers, loans, borrowings and other sources, 1970–88 (%)

| City | Total intergovernmental transfers | | | Loans and borrowings | Other revenue |
	Tax-sharing with state and national government	Grants from state government	Grants from central government		
Bombay					
1971	0.2	0.9	–	–	–
1988	0.3	1.2	–	19.7	–
Cairo					
1981	24.2	–	56.6	–	–
1988	16.3	35.0	10.4	7.1	4.0[1]
Lagos					
1971	–	24.2	42.4[2]	–	1.1
1988	–	24.2	42.4[2]	–	1.1
Mexico City					
1981	33.8	–	–	35.6	–
1988	46.9	1.8	–	1.0	–
Rio de Janeiro					
1981	34.1	–	3.0[3]	–	6.9[4]
1988	30.9	–	5.6[3]	8.7	15.4[4]
Seoul					
1970	3.8	–	10.9	1.0	–
1988	–	–	15.7	8.6	–
Shanghai					
1971	–	–	–	–	71.8[5]
1988	–	–	–	–	14.9[5]

Notes: [1] Foreign grant.
[2] Capital receipts.
[3] Transfer under the constitution.
[4] Indemnity, dividends, interest, etc.
[5] Income (or profits) from state-owned enterprises.

Source: ILO mega-city survey (1990).

total revenue. However, the importance of this component has declined over time from 71.8 per cent in 1971 to 14.9 per cent in 1988. In Cairo, intergovernmental transfers constituted more than 80 per cent of revenue in 1981 but this proportion had declined to 61.7 per cent in 1988. In Mexico City, revenue from intergovernmental transfers (particularly from tax-sharing) increased, while in Bombay, Rio and Seoul the contribution of intergovernmental transfers to total revenue remained more or less stable during the period 1970–88.

Loans and borrowings are another important source of funds to finance urban programmes. In Bombay, the proportion of funds from this source had increased to almost 20 per cent by 1988. This was largely due to heavy borrowings from the International Development Agency (IDA) in recent years to finance water supply and sewerage projects. Seoul has also been relying more on loans and borrowings to finance capital expenditure on underground and surface transportation systems. In Rio, too, loans and borrowings constituted almost 9 per cent of total revenue in 1988.

Table 7.6 provides data on rates of growth of intergovernmental transfers and loans and borrowings measured in real terms. The data show that in real terms, most cities have experienced a declining rate of growth of intergovernmental transfers. In Bombay, for example, the

Table 7.6　Growth of city revenue from inter-governmental transfers, loans and borrowings, 1970–88 (%)

| City | Period | Real rate of growth of revenue from | | Real rate of growth of per capita revenue from | |
		Intergovernmental transfers	Loans and borrowings	Intergovernmental transfers	Loans and borrowings
Bombay	1971–81	12.6	–	9.4	–
	1981–88	4.7	6.1	2.0	3.5
Cairo	1981–85	−2.1	–	−3.3	–
	1985–88	−4.5	−47.7	−6.2	−49.6
Lagos	1971–81	−8.4	−0.9	−16.1	−8.7
	1981–88	2.3	−8.3	−4.1	−14.8
Mexico	1981–85	3.6	−5.7	0.7	−8.7
City	1985–88	−3.3	−124.2	−3.0	−117.9
Rio	1981–88	−0.7	–	−2.9	–
Seoul	1970–80	12.7	36.1	8.5	31.7
	1980–88	11.1	8.7	8.5	6.1

Source:　ILO mega-city survey (1990).

growth rate of intergovernmental transfers dropped from 12.6 per cent in the 1970s to 4.7 per cent in the 1980s, while in Mexico City it declined from 3.6 per cent in 1981–5 to −3.3 per cent in 1985–8. This shows that most cities have had fewer resources made available from state and central governments, probably because of the worsening economic situation during the 1980s. With regard to loans and borrowings, the data show that in the case of Bombay, these were growing at a rate of 6.1 per cent per annum during the 1980s. In Seoul, also, borrowings grew at an annual rate of 8.7 per cent in the 1980s, although the growth rate had declined considerably from 36.1 per cent during the 1970s, when large sums of money were borrowed to finance infrastructure investment, particularly the development of subway systems. In most other cities, the growth rate of borrowings has been negative and declining. This is not necessarily a good sign. It may simply indicate that most cities in Africa and Latin America have been less able to raise money through borrowings due to the economic recession and debt crisis, or that they have abandoned investment in infrastructure development.

As pointed out earlier, urban local bodies in developing countries have inadequate powers to raise revenue relative to their financial needs. In many cases, however, they may not even be fully utilising the revenue powers already available to them. The much-needed devolution of revenue-raising powers to local governments will therefore have to be backed up with, or even preceded by, earnest efforts on their part to make use of their existing revenue-raising powers more fully.

An equally serious problem is the limited access of local governments to loans. With few exceptions, municipal bodies in very large cities are for various reasons unable to secure long-term financing against the issuance of their own bonds. Important among these reasons, apart from legal constraints on their borrowing power, are the weaknesses in their revenue bases and their unsatisfactory financial performance and housekeeping.

The limited borrowing power granted to city governments in most developing countries creates an extremely serious bottleneck, given the infrastructure investments that are needed, especially since a strong case can often be made in favour of urban governments engaging in the large-scale acquisition, development and disposal of land. Loans invariably have to be approved by provincial and national governments, and sometimes by the national banks of the country concerned. The interest rates on municipal borrowing are generally below the market rate, but the time allowed for the repayment of loans is generally much shorter than the useful physical life of the facilities financed through borrowing.

Many observers argue that if loans to urban local bodies in developing countries are to be provided largely by higher levels of government, it may be appropriate to set up special financial institutions, for example, revolving funds, both at state and national levels. Alternatively, a special national bank may be established to facilitate loan financing for urban-land and infrastructure-development projects. The revolving fund boards or the special bank can then loan funds to local bodies and charge them the interest that the former have to pay to the national or state governments, plus a nominal charge for management of the funds.

Overall, the fundamental principle for improving municipal finance systems is for cities to pay their own way. This must be accomplished gradually by replacing central-government contributions and grants with revenues raised from local sources. In this context, user charges offer some promise. Property-tax administration also needs to be improved. Property owners, particularly those holding vacant land, have resisted the tax, arguing that because their land does not generate income, they have no means of paying. One way to overcome this difficulty is to defer taxes on vacant land, with interest, until the land is sold – in effect, lending the tax to landlords and collecting later. This may also induce some action on the part of landowners who may otherwise merely wait for their land to appreciate and so restrict the supply of land on the market.

Taxes on urban wealth, and particularly on the gains from rising property values, could more than offset the cost of providing adequate services for urban areas. But such taxes are often difficult to collect, both because of evasion and because of inefficient tax administration.

Administrative capacity is the chief impediment to mobilising resources for urban services and infrastructure. This capacity is blunted by severe shortages of trained manpower, particularly trained accountants and financial managers, by low morale because of low wages and limited career opportunities, and by ineffective monitoring and evaluation systems.

8 Conclusions and Policy Implications

Rapid urbanisation and the concentration of economic activity in a few locations, particularly in large cities, are an inevitable outcome of economic and industrial development. Manufacturing industry flocks to major urban centres to benefit from economies of agglomeration. By the year 2000, nearly half the population of developing countries will be living in urban areas and more than one-quarter of the urban population is expected to be concentrated in large cities (with a population of more than four million). Urban population growth will be particularly high in African countries, both because of their lower initial level of urbanisation and because of their high rates of natural population growth.

The evidence suggests that most large cities today are growing more through natural population growth than through migration. Although migration is not a major source of urban population growth in most Third-World cities, the age selectivity of the migration process increases the proportion of the young in urban populations. This has enormous implications for the provision of urban employment opportunities and social services such as education.

In the absence of information on the relative costs and benefits of urban versus rural development, and of the growth of large versus small cities, it is difficult to determine the optimum rate of urbanisation and the best spatial distribution of economic activity in any given country. It is also difficult to determine the optimum size of a city at which the losses created by congestion and environmental deterioration begin to equal or exceed the benefits of agglomeration. However, economic efficiency is not the only aspect of urbanisation with which governments are concerned. In most developing countries, particularly those with distinct regional or ethnic interests, it is extremely important to maintain balance between regions and between rural and urban development; hence some attempt to reduce the pace of urbanisation and to spread economic development more evenly across regions may be politically necessary, even if its economic desirability is not entirely obvious.

The range of policy instruments available for controlling migration is quite limited. Attempts have been made to restrict the movement of people (in China, Poland, Cuba, Indonesia, the United Republic of Tanzania and Zaire, among other countries) through administrative and legal controls. The evidence suggests that such policies have by and large been unsuccessful, and they have also raised serious questions relating to human rights. Governments have also tried a number of less draconian methods to reduce rural–urban migration and the concentration of population in large cities, such as land-settlement schemes, administrative and industrial decentralisation, and rural development programmes designed to enhance the attractiveness of living in rural areas. These policies, too, have met with only limited success, and rural–urban migration has continued on a significant scale.

One major problem with population distribution policies as implemented in the past has been the tendency to adopt a somewhat narrow approach, which involves either controlling the growth of large cities or, at the other extreme, retaining the population in rural areas. Even strategies for developing secondary cities and small towns have often been promoted as a panacea to be substituted for one or the other approach. But a sound population distribution strategy does not involve this choice since all the strategies should be seen as complementary. A balanced development strategy should encourage settlement in small and intermediate cities, promote economic development in the rural areas, and at the same time improve employment and living conditions in large cities.

It would, indeed, be more cost-effective if instead of intervening directly in migration flows, governments could correct the urban bias of national development policies, which has implications not only for industrial-location patterns but also for regional income inequalities. The removal of this urban bias alone is, however, unlikely to have much impact on the concentration of population in large cities, at least in the short run. Policies designed to improve internal efficiency in large cities must therefore be vigorously pursued. In fact, measures to improve urban efficiency, in particular the pricing of public services at marginal cost and the elimination of subsidies for private investors, are more likely to have important, albeit indirect, effects on migration.

In China, rapid changes in the structure of agriculture due to the introduction of the household responsibility system and the dismantling of communes have resulted in greater efficiency in production and accelerated population growth in rural areas. This has created a vast and still growing rural surplus labour force, estimated at

approximately 100 million in 1988. Another 100 million is expected
to be added to that number by the year 2000. While concerned about
the productive absorption of rural surplus labour, the Chinese
government has also been determined to avoid the 'over-urbanisation' which it perceives as having had a negative affect on the quality
of life in many cities. The response of the government has been to
reduce permanent rural–urban migration and mega-city growth
through legal and administrative restrictions. But merely closing off
cities as alternative places of permanent residence and employment
cannot solve the problem of surplus rural labour. Furthermore,
restrictive migration policies often lead to imbalanced sex ratios and
an ageing urban population, which adversely affects labour productivity, as has been the case in Shanghai. Appropriate measures are
therefore needed to deal with both the rural labour surplus and the
negative effects of restrictive migration policies.

A part of the surplus rural labour force in China is now being
absorbed through diversification within agriculture: in addition to the
cultivation of basic crops, other activites such as the rearing of
livestock are being promoted. But, more importantly, attempts are
being made to transform a substantial proportion of agricultural
workers into non-agricultural workers through:

1. the development of non-agricultural activities in rural areas;
2. the development of small market towns as commercial, industrial
   and service centres for their rural hinterlands and as alternative
   destinations for those wishing to settle in urban places;
3. a much greater reliance on temporary migration as an alternative
   to permanent migration to cities and towns.

Temporary migration, it is believed, meets the special service needs of
cities in terms of flexible labour supply, helps to reduce rural surplus
labour, and avoids the need for cities to absorb the vast numbers of
rural-urban migrants into their permanent populations. This policy has
led to a 'floating population' of more than 50 million in Chinese cities.
Each of the three largest cities (Shanghai, Beijing and Tianjin) has
more than one million temporary migrants.

While it may be beneficial to both rural and urban areas to allow an
increasing number of temporary migrants in towns and cities in China,
the creation of two classes of people in urban areas, one class with
access to registration, housing and subsidised rations and the other
with no such benefits, may be difficult to justify, given the socialist

principle of equality. If such a dual structure is allowed to continue for long, it may prove a source of social and political instability.

Since natural increase now contributes more to population growth in Third-World cities than rural–urban migration, greater emphasis needs to be placed on bringing down birth rates in order to slow down population growth in general, and urban natural growth in particular. In sub-Saharan Africa and low-income areas of Asia, family-planning efforts in rural areas are important to reduce migration to urban areas. In Latin America, where the level of urbanisation is already very high, reducing the natural growth rate of the urban population holds the best hope for checking the explosive growth of cities. An important reason for high fertility amongst the urban poor, particularly those in slums, is their limited access to education, health and family-planning services. Most slum dwellers have limited access to social services because of their low productivity and incomes. Raising the productivity and incomes of the urban poor and thus increasing their access to social services is therefore likely to reduce population pressure in large cities.

To reduce population growth and pollution in large cities, attempts have been made to locate industry away from such cities. While such a strategy has obvious appeal, its implications for employment generation and poverty alleviation need to be carefully assessed. Unemployment in Seoul, for example, where industrial decentralisation policies were vigorously pursued, is twice as high as in the country as a whole, and the level would have been even higher if decentralisation of heavy industry had not been accompanied by a growth in the number of small-scale manufacturing units, which are more labour-intensive. Moreover, moving out highly productive manufacturing industries which have the capacity to pay for urban services may adversely affect the revenue base of the city. Thus, a policy of industrial decentralisation may need to be accompanied by policies to create alternative sources of revenue and employment generation. Since the services sector may not be able to absorb all the increase in the labour force, it may be more appropriate to adopt a policy of selective industrial decentralisation. Non-polluting light industries (electronics, clothing, etc.) which are market-oriented and labour-intensive can be promoted. In any case moving polluting industries out of the large cities may merely transfer rather than solve the problem of pollution. Successful implementation of an industrial-decentralisation policy requires complementary efforts at addressing pollution through appropriate pollution-control measures, as well as the creation of several new growth poles with adequate social and physical infrastructure. Otherwise industrial concentration may take place again in one or two locations and defeat the objectives of the policy.

With regard to dispersed urbanisation, there is certainly a need to divert migration away from large cities to smaller cities and towns. However, the conditions under which such a strategy is likely to succeed need to be examined. In Egypt, for example, several new towns (6th of October, 10th of Ramadan, 15th of May, Sadaat City) have been created in recent years. Although these towns have attracted some industries, they have failed to attract many people because of the lack of social infrastructure. Since the cost of living is artificially low in Cairo because of rent controls and highly subsidised urban services, many people prefer to live in the capital city and commute to suburban towns for work. Thus, commuting patterns appear to be exactly contrary to what one would normally expect. In Shanghai, too, new growth centres developed in the periphery have failed to attract enough people away from the city centre because of the inadequate amenities and social infrastructure.

With regard to employment, the evidence suggests that in spite of employment growth in recent years, the excess supply of labour has led to increased unemployment and/or expansion of the low-productivity informal sector in most Third-World mega-cities. Increasing labour-force participation rates, particularly among females, have also contributed to the rapid growth of the labour force. Although the crisis of the early 1980s affected the growth of the formal sector (in particular manufacturing) in all the regions of the developing world, the heavy burden imposed by the debt crisis on the Latin American and African economies was particularly detrimental for modern-sector employment in these regions. The rate of growth of manufacturing employment not only fell in all cities except Shanghai but in many cities, particularly in Latin America, it became negative.

Both in Bombay and Seoul, the shift in industrial structure from manufacturing to services has been accompanied by a shift in the demand for labour from unskilled to semi-skilled and skilled labour. The changing industrial structure in Shanghai and the growing liberalisation of its economy has also generated a demand for special skills and labour resources in industries such as electronics, telecommunications and banking. Educational and training programmes thus need to be adjusted accordingly to avoid disruptions in labour markets and an increase in unemployment. This can be done only if industrial development and restructuring policies are coordinated with human-resources development policies.

Most of the textile industry in Bombay is sick and in need of either modernisation or closure. However, it is difficult to close industries because of legislation protecting labour. Government intervention is therefore required to help break the deadlock. The industry, if allowed to appropriate part of the capital appreciation in land values through tax exemptions, could move out of Bombay or convert to some more productive activity. This could involve high training or retraining costs, but even if the employers are willing to bear these costs, the trade unions may prevent the restructuring taking place unless they are part of the negotiation process and obtain adequate compensation.

In China, appropriate policies are needed to promote efficiency and profitability in state and collective enterprises, for example, by encouraging contract systems of employment. Permanent systems of employment have led to inefficiency and hidden unemployment. There is also an urgent need to modernise industry in Shanghai and update technology. Small and medium-size industries which have lower labour costs also need to be developed and encouraged.

The increase in the rate of open unemployment in Latin American cities during the 1980s was accompanied by changes in the structure of unemployment, with more heads of household, men in the most active age groups and workers with previous experience amongst the unemployed.

Lower real wages in the formal sector combined with declining incomes in the informal sector have contributed to increased poverty. At the city level, budgetary constraints and structural-adjustment programmes have forced authorities to cut down social-service expenditures. This has led to worsening living standards for the urban poor and degradation of the environment. The deterioration in living conditions (poor housing, lack of waste-disposal facilities, etc.) and environmental degradation have also reinforced each other.

The negative effects of the urban environment (spread of disease, ill health, birth defects, accidents, increased mortality) lead not only to increased public expenditure but also to lower productivity and incomes. It is therefore surprising that in most developing countries, environmental concerns are not incorporated into human-settlement policies (industrial location and land settlement policies, urban infrastructure and development programmes, land-use planning, etc.) nor into population and human-resources development planning. Part of the problem is that the operational methodologies necessary for such incorporation of environmental concerns are not adequately developed. In addition, in most Third-World cities planning departments or agencies have inadequate resources and manpower to cope with the overwhelming magnitude of environmental problems. Policies of obtaining compensation for social costs stemming from private activities and taxing of private benefits due to government improvements in infrastructure are rarely implemented. Market forces thus contribute to a less socially optimal pattern of urban growth.

The existence of poor and vulnerable groups in urban areas calls into question the functioning of urban labour markets. Poverty and precarious and poorly paid work certainly exist, but it is by no means clear that it is the structure of labour markets as opposed to overall development and employment policies that are mainly at fault. In the case of Bombay, the decline in the rate of growth of employment in the 1970s and the absolute fall in the 1980s can be attributed partly to protective legislation. On the other hand, as discussed in Chapter 3, countries where GDP per capita fell, unemployment rose, real wages fell and poverty increased. It may therefore be argued that it is the pace and employment-intensive pattern of economic growth rather than labour-market interventions which have the largest potential impact on poverty alleviation.

While economic growth may be necessary to promote employment and incomes, it may not be sufficient to improve poverty conditions in Third-World mega-cities. In the case of Seoul, for example, poverty conditions did not improve during the 1970s even though economic growth was more rapid during this period than in the 1980s. As noted earlier, this was largely because wage restraint policies were strictly enforced in order to achieve competitiveness in export markets. But once international competitiveness had been achieved, wages were allowed to increase, which led to significant improvements in poverty conditions during the 1980s. Thus, it is not economic growth alone which leads to poverty alleviation: much depends on the nature of the growth process and whether or not supporting wage and employment-growth policies are implemented.

The comparison of city- and national-level figures also shows that despite relatively high productivity and growth rates in mega-cities, the incidence of poverty in most such cities is as high as in the countries as a whole. This may indicate that the pattern of economic development in large cities is characterised by marked income inequalities. In terms of policy, it implies that economic growth may not necessarily solve the problem of urban poverty. Active implementation of direct anti-poverty programmes to benefit the poor and vulnerable sections of the urban population is also required. Women and children are a particularly vulnerable group in this respect. Policies and measures for poverty alleviation should focus on their particular needs and give special attention to maternal and child health care and the education of children.

While direct poverty alleviation and urban welfare programmes (public-works projects and livelihood-protection programmes in Seoul, public-distribution systems in Bombay and subsidised rations in Cairo) are required, the focus of such programmes should not be on alleviating conditions of poverty alone, but on raising the productivity and earnings of the urban poor. The main emphasis of antipoverty programmes in the past has been on the mere provision of relief. Such relief measures are often costly and, once initiated, are politically difficult to scale down or abolish. The future direction of policy, therefore, should be to create more productive employment and self-reliance among the poor. In the long run this is the most effective way of reducing poverty. Efforts should also be made to ensure that poverty is not handed down from parents to children. In this respect, education and job training for the children of poor families need to be subsidised and adequate measures taken to provide these children with better nutrition and health care.

The promotion of self-employment should be a crucial component of anti-poverty programmes in Third-World mega-cities. City authorities can play an important role in employment generation by adopting more appropriate land-use planning and zoning regulations. Enhancing the capacity of the urban poor and informal-sector workers to engage in new income-generating activities (or to increase the productivity of existing activities) through the provision of productive assets, credit and training, infrastructure and access to markets is an important means of raising their income levels. Training programmes should emphasise the development of basic business and vocational skills and entrepreneurship. Likewise, technical-assistance programmes should aim to provide advice in the field of management development.

While local-level initiatives are important for employment generation, open unemployment and underemployment can only be significantly reduced by national macroeconomic policies. These can bring about a resumption of economic growth and remove obstacles to the growth of productive self-employment. Again, it is at the macroeconomic level, rather than at the level of the city administration, that it can be ensured that government economic policies as a whole do not retard growth by having a pro- or antiurban bias.

Increasing poverty associated with the growth of the informal sector is causally related to the proliferation of urban slums. Since many among the urban poor cannot afford to buy or rent a house, they squat on whatever land is available. This leads to the formation and growth of slums and squatter settlements in Third-World mega-cities. The urban poor also lack access to basic social services such as education, health care and family planning. Schools are generally scarce in squatter and slum areas, with low attendance and high drop-out rates. In addition, the urban poor usually have limited access to private or public health care due to the high costs of medical attention and drugs, lack of information, and the physical as well as cultural inaccessibility of modern curative care. Infant malnutrition and mortality in urban slums are aggravated by the fact that mothers increasingly switch from breast-feeding to commercial baby foods, frequently diluted with unsafe water. As long as the urban poor live in overcrowded housing with no access to safe water and disposal of human and solid waste, and with only limited access to preventive health care, they are likely to be seriously affected by ill health.

Lack of access to social services has negative effects on labour productivity and the welfare of the urban poor. Absenteeism due to illness raises production costs in general, thereby reducing the surpluses available for investment. Hence, apart from the intrinsic welfare reasons for providing safe water, sanitation and health services, the generation and maintenance of employment requires these services. Frequent illness among children also leads to increased absenteeism among working women. This in itself prejudices employers against hiring women.

Limited access to education, health care and family-planning services also leads to large family sizes. In the case of Rio de Janeiro, for example, large differences in fertility can be observed between the capital city and its relatively poor peripheries, where access to basic social services is limited, as discussed in Chapter 4. The urban poor want more children for reasons of economic security. They are thus trapped in a vicious cycle in which low incomes ensure poor education, nutrition and health, which in turn lead to low productivity and low incomes. The main policy question is therefore how to help the poor to break this vicious cycle.

There is a growing realisation in most Third-World countries of the need to develop human capital for sustainable development and future welfare. But in many cities in Africa and Latin America the real rate of growth of per capita expenditure on education has been negative, particularly in more recent years. This has led to a decline in the number of schools per thousand population. Governments have attempted to compensate for this decline by improving the teacher–student ratio, but there are obvious limits to how much this can help maintain educational standards. This is therefore likely to have adverse effects on human-capital development.

Where the city authorities can make a much more direct and significant contribution to alleviating urban poverty is in relation to policies aimed at improving the quality and productivity of the labour force by increasing the access of the urban poor to social services essential for health, and by providing a decent living environment. This can be done by redirecting public expenditure and social services from rich to poor households. Thus, even within existing budgets, the redirection of city services towards the poor should help to increase their productivity and earnings. The nature and form of such services will also have to change if the needs of the urban poor are to be adequately met. Many children of school age in poor neighbourhoods perform a range of economic tasks such as helping with the family business or even babysitting at home, which permits the mother to work. The parents of these children may not be able to afford to send them to school unless schooling is available in the evenings near home. In other areas, too, including the provision of information about nutrition, birth control and family size, delivery systems need to be similarly adapted to the specific needs of the urban poor. Special educational programmes are also needed to improve the urban environment. The mere provision of infrastructure for waste collection and disposal may not be enough. Even when waste-disposal bins are provided, the poor do not necessarily use them.

In order to reduce traffic congestion on city roads, additional capacity needs to be created. And since it is not possible to increase road capacity indefinitely, traffic has to be diverted to railroad and subway systems. The key to solving the transportation problem thus lies in increasing the capacity and improving the efficiency of the public-transport system.

The decline in per capita expenditure on health in many cities during the recent economic crisis raises concern over the future of health services in such cities. In some cities such as Cairo, the increase in the number of medical professionals has not been accompanied by a corresponding increase in medical infrastructure. There has therefore been no significant improvement in health care but only an increase in unemployment among medical personnel. In most Third-World cities, resources are limited and even public-health services remain out of reach for many households. To reach the urban poor more effectively, the focus must shift to primary health-care. This would also help reduce the burden on the curative medical system. Primary health-care workers in urban slums can help reduce malnutrition and infant mortality and disseminate information about family planning. Primary health care programmes are thus not only likely to provide benefits in terms of lower mortality and reductions in absenteeism at work but can also be expected to have a favourable influence on fertility behaviour.

In terms of the working environment, workplace health problems can be dealt with through relatively well-established systems of occupational health in which government, employers and trade unions all play an important role. But it is unorganised workers in the informal sector who face the highest risk. Occupational health problems in this sector cannot be dealt with, as in the formal sector, by unions and legislation alone. Many informal-sector activities are home-based family enterprises. The occupational health and working environment of workers in this sector therefore pose a challenge to city and health authorities, who must find new strategies to tackle the problem.

With regard to the housing problem, the evidence suggests that Urban Land Ceiling Acts have had little impact in mopping up excess vacant land. On the contrary, in many cases they have had a negative effect on the urban land market in that they have pushed up land prices, particularly of those parcels below the ceiling. The analysis of the effects of rent-control legislation in Chapter 5 also suggests that the intended social objectives of rent-control have not been realised. Instead, a number of adverse economic consequences have been felt in varying degrees in almost all rent-controlled housing markets. In Egypt, for example, 1.8 million housing units built after 1980 are simply locked up. Of these, 250 000 are in Cairo alone. The rent freeze and the desire to keep a house for children and grandchildren are cited as the basic reasons for not renting out these housing units. There is thus an urgent need for rent-control reforms, which would both improve the tax base of local authorities and attract investment in rental housing.

Investment in housing is generally less than 1 per cent of the city's GDP in most Third-World cities, except in Seoul where it is close to 3 per cent. Increased investment in housing would not only reduce the housing shortage but also generate more employment. There is ample evidence that investment in housing has a much greater employment multiplier effect than investment in other sectors. However, it should be borne in mind that employment generated in the housing sector is generally of a transient nature and provides only a limited range of jobs. Thus, it is worth examining whether employment generated in this way is less desirable in the long run than that generated through alternative mechanisms such as the development of microenterprises and the promotion of self-employment schemes.

In many cities such as Seoul, authorities have retained green-belts. While this has had a beneficial effect on the urban environment, it has further reduced the supply of land. This has contributed to over-crowding and land speculation. A possible solution to the problem of overcrowding would be to encourage people to live in the suburban areas of the city. This would, however, require the development of a massive and subsidised transport system. Seoul has, to an extent, been able to provide this, given its rapid economic growth, but for other resource-poor countries such infrastructure investment poses an enormous problem.

The efficient management of land and the control of land specula-tion are critical elements in improving the functioning of housing markets in mega-cities. Mechanisms intended to increase public control over land markets are not difficult to identify in individual cities. The problem has been implementation. Strong political will is required to introduce effective policies because powerful vested interests are always determined to maintain the status quo. Capital-gains taxes that aim to suppress housing speculation should be implemented in such a way as not to discourage housing investment, and taxes on housing units should be levied more heavily on holdings than on transactions.

In Shanghai, the housing allocation system is very unfair. Housing units are provided by the enterprise or institution where a person is employed. While the more prosperous enterprises are able to build new houses for their workers, workers in less successful enterprises are at a disadvantage. In other cities, governments should avoid showcase housing projects such as high-rise flats and expensive site-and-services projects, which benefit relatively few people at great expense to others. Redevelopment programmes such as those attempted in Seoul could, however, be promoted. These programmes aim to improve residential environments without burdening the owners with the costs. Profes-sional developers build a large number of apartments on land offered by redevelopment associations formed by property owners. These owners each receive an apartment and the developer sells the remaining units to the general public. Care should, however, be taken to protect the interests of any former tenants living in dwellings on the land, and to ensure a fair distribution of apartment space between owners, who may have surrendered differing amounts of land.

More public support should also be given to self-help projects and renovation schemes. Loans could be made available for house maintenance and repair in addition to existing loans for construction. This would increase the housing stock by upgrading old houses, and would greatly benefit the lower- and middle-income groups. Land tenure, too, is an important issue when it comes to encouraging the urban poor to participate in self-help projects. Of the estimated five million slum dwellers in Bombay, for example, only 14 000 covered by the slum-upgrading programme enjoy *de jure* tenure. The government and the Bombay Municipal Corporation (BMC) are reluctant to grant tenure and supply basic amenities to slum dwellers unless the latter form cooperatives and agree to undertake routine maintenance of the infrastructure. People living in slums lack the organisational skills to form and operate cooperatives. This catalytic role could, however, be performed by the BMC through its community development officers or through voluntary agencies.

If a lasting solution is to be found to the problem of housing in large cities, attention has to be focused on causes rather than on symptoms. The root causes of the housing problem in most developing countries are the low level of productivity and low incomes of the urban poor. In fact, at existing prices, the majority of the poor cannot afford even modest housing of acceptable standards. Clearly efforts have to be directed both towards improving the productivity and incomes of the poor and towards reducing the cost of housing.

While the demand for finance for housing, social services and infrastructure programmes has increased in recent years largely as a result of the rapid growth of urban populations, the availability of financial resources has not increased commensurately. The supply of such resources in most large cities, particularly in Africa and Latin America, either declined in absolute terms or grew very slowly during the economic crisis of the 1980s. The analysis presented in Chapter 7 shows that the decline in per capita revenue has been sharper than that in total revenue, which suggests that population growth has contributed to the resource constraint.

In most large cities, the performance of property tax as a source of revenue has been disappointing. On average it now contributes less than 5 per cent to total revenue. Even though user charges contribute significantly to municipal resources in many Third-World mega-cities, there is scope for further resource mobilisation through this source. Urban services such as electricity, water and public transport have often been underpriced in order to benefit the poorer groups. In many cases, prices do not cover even the marginal cost of production. In Bombay, for example, only 30 per cent of the cost of supplying water is recovered. In consequence, the agencies supplying urban services have been unable to meet operating costs and to undertake adequate investment in infrastructure. General subsidies often provide benefits to groups that are not in need and therefore impose excessive strains on government budgets. Such subsidies can also lead to a distortion of prices and may, as in the case of food, have adverse effects on incentives for domestic production. There is therefore an urgent need to remove or drastically reduce general subsidies. In most cities, the pricing structure for water and other urban services should also be made more equitable by charging a progressively higher price to households using more of such services. This would not only improve the revenue base of cities but would also lead to a more rational use of the services.

The evidence suggests that intergovernmental transfers account for only a small proportion of total revenue in Asian cities such as Bombay and Seoul. In Bombay, the state government does not even share with the municipal corporation the proceeds from motor vehicle tax and profession tax, normally levied by local governments. In African and Latin American cities (Cairo, Lagos, Mexico City and Rio) intergovernmental transfers account for a relatively large proportion of total revenue, although this share fell in the 1980s, probably because of the worsening economic situation. In the case of Shanghai in China, the transfers are in the reverse direction: more than 50 per cent of the finance raised by the city is transferred to the central government. This severely constrains the ability of city authorities to invest in housing and infrastructural development. As far as loans and borrowing are concerned, their growth rate was positive during the 1980s in Asian cities such as Bombay and Seoul. In most other cities, the growth rate of borrowing was negative and declining. This is not necessarily a good sign. It may simply indicate that African and Latin American cities were less able to raise money through borrowing due to the economic recession and the debt crisis, or had abandoned investment in infrastructural development. The limited borrowing power granted to city governments in most developing countries also makes it difficult for them to make the infrastructure investments that are needed.

Intergovernmental transfers and grants to city authorities from central and state governments are often erratic and unpredictable, which can undermine local budgeting and planning. National and state governments should therefore consider devolving more revenue-raising power to local governments in mega-cities. City authorities will also have to take considerable initiatives to improve tax collection, modify pricing structures, and devise new revenue instruments in order to increase financial self-reliance. In particular, cities should look towards reforms of property tax, motor vehicle tax, sales taxes and user charges for efficient, equitable, stable and growing sources of public revenue. Motor-vehicle tax is an important albeit neglected tax source for urban governments. Higher motor-vehicle tax would also reduce congestion by encouraging the use of public transport. Pricing policies may also have an extremely important role to play in the context of resource mobilisation. Imbalances between expenditure requirements and the resources available to urban local bodies are likely to continue and even worsen in the future. Non-tax revenues, especially user and beneficiary charges, can potentially provide more elastic sources of revenue. City authorities can also appropriate a part of the increase in land value resulting from infrastructural development in the vicinity of that land.

No lasting solution to the problems of urban environmental degradation, housing and inadequate access to social services can be envisaged without strengthening the resource base of cities and improving the productivity and incomes of the urban poor. Coping with employment and poverty problems in large cities is thus the major challenge facing developing countries. There is an urgent need to examine the scope and adequacy of current policies relating to employment promotion, particularly in the informal sector: the promotion of small-scale industry; employment generation through investments in housing and community infrastructure for the poor; and improvements in the productivity and working conditions of vulnerable groups in the urban labour market. Particular attention will need to be paid to the question of the adequacy of the existing institutional structure for dealing with employment and poverty problems at the city level. In most developing countries, city authorities are primarily oriented towards the provision and maintenance of urban infrastructure and services. They have little interest in, and no capacity to deal with, social and economic issues such as the promotion of employment and the alleviation of poverty. Unless this situation is changed it will be virtually impossible to find any viable means of initiating and implementing comprehensive antipoverty programmes in Third-World cities. The solution to the problems of employment and urban poverty cannot be found in an institutional vacuum.

Appendix 1

Table A1.1   Contrast between countries with expanding and mature urbanisation

	Expanding urbanisation	Mature urbanisation
(1) National population	Expanding well above the net reproduction rate. The average age of the population is young.	Current population-growth rates often below the net reproduction rate. The average age of the population is above 30 and a substantial proportion is above 60.
(2) Rural–urban migration	Significant factor in the growth of practically all cities of the national urban system. Urban amenities are not a major determinant of migration.	Has practically stopped. The growth of cities is entirely dependent on urban–urban migration. Because migrants are already completely urbanised, they are particularly sensitive to urban amenities. The only factor preventing urban growth from becoming strictly a zero-sum game among cities is international migration.
(3) Degree of economic and social integration	There are conspicuous constraints to economic and social mobility between sectors as well as regions.	Most of the constraints on locational mobility have been removed. Amenity-intensive regions have an edge.
(4) Level of income and complexity of the economy	Still not comparable with advanced economies. A major national objective is to reach comparability with advanced countries.	The leading sectors of the economy are highly human-capital-intensive and information-intensive. The majority of the population is employed in the services sector, which has reached high levels of productivity.
(5) Capital region and largest cities	Still growing at a substantial rate.	No longer growing. In fact there is evidence that the processes of deconcentration in the major urban region of the country have already started. A factor masking this new trend is the important role played by international migration in replacing the larger net out-migration of native urbanites from the capital region.

Source: World Bank, 1979, quoted in Singh, 1989.

Appendix 2

A TECHNICAL NOTE ON BASIC DATA COLLECTED FOR A
COMPARATIVE ANALYSIS OF THE PROBLEMS FACING LARGE
CITIES IN DEVELOPING COUNTRIES

In addition to data gathered for individual city case studies, all collaborating
individuals/institutions were requested to provide some core-city and national-
level data for attempting a comparative analysis of the problems facing large
cities in developing countries. The information was obtained from several
published and unpublished sources such as Population and Economic
Censuses, Annual Survey of Industries, Labour Force and Household Surveys
and Municipal records. Most data gathered related as close to the years 1970,
1980 and 1988 as possible to improve comparability across cities and countries.
The type of information collected included the following:

1. **Demographic indicators** (city, state/province and national level)

Population (male, female, total), urban population, net migration (persons),
number of households, household size, density of population (persons/square
kilometre), sex ratio (males per 100 females), age composition of population by
sex, crude birth rate (per 1000 population), crude death rate (per 1000
population), infant mortality rate (per 1000 births), total fertility rate (per
woman), mean age at marriage by sex, mean age of married women at first
birth, and life expectancy by sex.

2. **Labour force and employment** (city level only)

Economically active population (labour force) by sex and age group,
economically active population (15 years old and over) by sex and activity
status (employed, unemployed), employed labour force by sector (formal,
informal) and nature of employment (public, private), employed labour force
by sex, occupation and employment status (self-employed, wage-earner, unpaid
family worker), and employed labour force by sex, industry and employment
status.

3. **Income and output indicators** (city, state/province and national level)

Gross domestic product (current and constant prices), distribution of GDP at
current prices by sector[1] (agriculture, industry, manufacturing, services), GDP
per worker (current and constant prices), GDP per capita (current and constant
prices), net capital stock in manufacturing (current prices), net capital stock in
industry (current prices), distribution of value added in manufacturing (food
and agriculture, textile and clothing, machinery and transport equipment,
chemicals, other manufacturing), manufacturing value added per worker

(current and constant prices), percentage of households below poverty line, percentage share of household income (bottom 30 per cent, middle 40 per cent, top 30 per cent), minimum wage (current prices), annual rate of change of consumer prices, and rate of change of consumer prices between 1970–80 and 1980–8.

4. Social and other indicators (city level unless otherwise indicated)

Housing and land availability:	Slum and squatter population, number of housing units, number of rooms per household, number of persons per room, private-sector investment in housing (current prices), and public-sector investment in housing (current prices).
Water supply:	Percentage of households having access to piped water supply, and average daily water supply per household (litres).
Electricity:	Percentage of households having access to electricity, average daily supply of electricity (megawatts), and average daily consumption of electric power (domestic, industrial, other).
Waste disposal:	Percentage of households covered by underground sewerage, daily garbage production (metric tons), and daily garbage collection (metric tons).
Transport and communication:	Number of automobiles (buses, trucks, private cars, scooters and motor cycles, auto rickshaws, taxis), number of passengers carried by subway system, number of passenger kilometres (kms) travelled by public transport, number of traffic accidents (involving death and injury), number of passengers handled (domestic, international), and number of telephones (business, residence).
Education:	Primary, secondary and higher (number of schools/institutes, enrolment, number of teachers), literacy rate (male, female, total) for city, state and national level.
Health and family planning:	Number of hospitals, primary health centres, health clinics, dispensaries and family planning clinics (city, state/province

and national level data for indicators listed below). Number of hospital beds and doctors (per thousand population), and contraceptive prevalence rate (percentage of married women of child-bearing age using contraception).

Crime (city, state/province and national level):

Rioting, number of crimes against persons (murders, others), number of crimes against property (robbery, theft, housebreaking, etc.).

5. Public expenditure and revenue (city level only)

Local public expenditure and investment: (separate figures for current and capital expenditure):

General administration, shelter (housing, slum and squatter upgrading), primary infrastructure (electricity, water supply, roads and streets, sewage and drainage, etc.), and social services and amenities (health, education, solid waste management, parks, environmental hygiene, etc.).

Revenue:

Local taxes (property tax, municipal sales tax, entertainment tax, motor-vehicle tax, advertisement tax, passenger tax, residence tax, profession, trade and employment tax, octroi tax, etc.), non-tax revenue such as fees and fines (stamp and registration fee, fines) and user charges (rents from ownership of land, markets and houses, income from operation of public utility services such as electricity, water, sewerage, city transportation, etc.), intergovernmental transfers (tax supplements, tax credits and tax sharing from state and national taxes, grants from state governments, grants from central government), and loans and borrowings, etc.

The quality of data provided by the national research institutes was generally good although it varied across cities. The data from the Asian (except Shanghai) and Latin American cities were relatively more complete than from the African cities. In some cases national research institutes had to be contacted several times for checking accuracy/consistency of data. For some indicators, such as income (GDP) and modern-sector employment, data in some cases were not available in ready form particularly relating to the city level. These therefore required special tabulations from the concerned departments/

authorities or had to be estimated. For example, in some cases city level GDP was estimated as follows:

$$GDP_c = \sum_{i=1}^{N} EAP_{ic} \ \frac{GDP_i(R)}{EAP_i(R)}$$

Where GDP_c = gross domestic product of the city;
EAP_{ic} = economically active population (labour force) of the ith sector in the city;
$GDP_i(R)$ = gross domestic product of ith sector in the region (state) containing the city;
$EAP_i(R)$ = economically active population (labour force) of the ith sector in the region (state) containing the city;
i = 1, 2, 3, ... N (activity sectors: agriculture, industry, services ...);
R = region (state) containing the city for which GDP figures are available.

Percentage modern-sector employment (particularly for Cairo) was estimated from the distribution of economically active population by occupation and job status available in the following format:

	Employers and workers on own account	Salaried employees and wage-earners	Family workers	Other and status unknown	Total
Professional, technical and related workers	b_{01}	b_{02}	b_{03}	b_{04}	b_0
Administrative, executive and managerial workers	b_{11}	b_{12}	b_{13}	b_{14}	b_1
Clerical workers	b_{21}	b_{22}	b_{23}	b_{24}	b_2
Sales workers	b_{31}	b_{32}	b_{33}	b_{34}	b_3
Farmers, fishermen, hunters, loggers and related workers	b_{41}	b_{42}^2	b_{43}	b_{44}	b_4
Miners, quarrymen and related workers	b_{51}	b_{52}	b_{53}	b_{54}	b_5
Workers in transport and communications	b_{61}	b_{62}	b_{63}	b_{64}	b_6
Craftsmen, production workers and labourers	$b71$	b_{72}	b_{73}	b_{74}	b_7
Service, sport and recreation workers	b_{81}	b_{82}^2	b_{83}	b_{84}	b_8

$$\sum_{i=0}^{8} b_i = B$$

Percentage modern sector-employment was defined as

$$m^* = \frac{m_1^* + m_2^*}{B} \times 100$$

where m^* is the percentage of total employment in modern sector;

$m_1^* = (b_0 + b_1 + b_2)$ is the sum of all professional, administrative and clerical workers (both wage-earners and self-employed),

$m_2^* = (b_{32} + b_{52} + b_{62} + b_{72})$ is the sum of wage-earners among sales, mining, transport and production process workers;

B = economically active population.

Notes and References

Preface

1. The Nairobi case-study was later excluded from the analysis for lack of adequate information.
2. See Appendix 2 for a technical note on the type of basic data gathered for a comparative analysis of the problems facing Third-World mega-cities.

1 Introduction

1. See, for example, Oberai (1987) for a detailed assessment of migration-influencing policies.
2. Six city case studies (Abidjan, Bogotá, Calcutta, Jakarta, Lagos and São Paulo) were carried out by the ILO during the 1970s. The present studies (Bombay, Cairo, Lagos, Nairobi, Mexico, Rio de Janeiro, Seoul and Shanghai) although based on this experience differ from the earlier studies in the sense that these have been carried out in a comparative framework with a similar methodology. The Nairobi case study was later cancelled due to lack of appropriate data. For details of the earlier studies, see Lubell and McCallum (1978) and the references cited therein.
3. For a detailed discussion of these concepts, see World Bank, 1979.

2 Urbanisation and Spatial Concentration

1. The discussion on major trends in urbanisation is largely based on the updated version of Section II in Oberai (1987).
2. Countries use a wide variety of criteria for defining 'urban' population. United Nations (1987) notes: "The most common criterion for urban population is a minimum number of people but the figure differs from country to country, reflecting a variety of social and geographical conditions. For example, an urban population is defined as at least 200 persons in Denmark, Greenland, Iceland, Norway and Sweden, but as 20,000 in Mauritius and Nigeria, and as 30,000 in Japan; most countries choose a minimum between 2,000 and 5,000 persons. Other criteria that are used to define an urban area are the number of dwelling units in a locality and characteristics of settlement, such as population density, economic activity, and living facilities. There are also several ways to define "urban agglomeration". For example, it may be defined in terms of the administrative boundaries of cities or by areas of high population density'. The UN data cited in the tables in this section are based on national definitions of urban and rural populations. United Nations (1987) states: 'The practice was adopted, after lengthy study and discussion, on the grounds that the national statistical authorities were in the best position to distinguish the two populations in their own countries'.

3. For a detailed discussion of this debate, see Gilbert and Gugler, 1982.
4. See, for example, World Bank (1979) and the references contained therein.
5. For a more detailed discussion on the effectiveness of the population distribution policies discussed in this section, see Oberai, 1987.
6. The annual rate of resident tax in Seoul is 4000 won per person, and for medium-sized and large cities (with a population of 500 000 to 5 million), 2500 won. Small city residents pay 1500 won a year, and rural residents 800 won.
7. In China, 'small cities and towns' generally refers to those with a population of less than 200 000.
8. In many countries the types of incentive given are sometimes unsuitable: import duty rebates have little meaning for firms using domestic inputs; interest rate subsidies have no relevance if firms are denied access to credit; and tax rebates provide no benefit unless profits are made.
9. 60 per cent of the value of the fixed-capital investments of a large- or medium-scale unit is exempted from tax for a period of five years if located in region B, 75 per cent for seven years in region C, 90 per cent for nine years in region D and 100 per cent for ten years in the No Industry region. A small-scale unit is exempted from tax liability to the full extent of its fixed capital investments for five years if located in B, seven years in C, nine years in D and ten years in the No Industry region.
   A large- or medium-scale unit also receives a grant of 20 per cent of its fixed-capital investments but not exceeding Rs2 million if located in region B, 25 per cent but not exceeding Rs2.5 million in region C and 30 per cent but not exceeding Rs3 million in the D and No Industry regions. A small-scale unit receives a grant of 25 per cent of its fixed capital investments if located in region B, 30 per cent in C and 35 per cent in the D and No Industry regions, up to a maximum of Rs1 million, Rs1.5 million and Rs2 million, respectively.

3 Urban growth, Employment and Poverty

1. In 1979–80 prices, the mid-point was Rs76 in urban areas (Sixth Five Year Plan, 1980–5, Planning Commission, New Delhi, p. 51).
2. See studies quoted in Singh, 1989.

4 Scope for Employment Promotion and Poverty Alleviation in Third-World Mega-Cities

1. For an excellent discussion of these issues, see Mohan, 1990.
2. The discussion draws heavily on Lee, 1987. Also, see Sethuraman, 1981.

5 Urban Poverty and Access to Housing and Basic Social Services

1. *Towards social transformation*, Approach to the Eighth Five Year Plan 1990–95, Planning Commission, Government of India, May 1990, p. 25.
2. In Shanghai, the decline is partly due to the redefining of the city's boundaries to include some rural areas.

6 Urban Poverty and Population Growth

1. Consumption per person (C/N) is used as a welfare indicator. No adjustment is made for economies of scale in consumption or for differences in needs among different types of family member. The author argues that this is not only the easiest course statistically but is supported by two kinds of evidence. First, subsistence food needs, or the cost of a minimum adequate diet, do not differ greatly by age or sex for members older than five years, and even very young children represent about two-thirds of the cost of an adult. Citing several other studies, he notes that the cost of children aged 6–12 years, relative to an adult male, ranges from 0.91 to 1.0, that for adult women from 0.85 to 0.91, and that for adolescents from 1.05 to 1.09. Second, estimations of subsistence expenditures from observed behaviour, whether for food alone or for all categories of spending, show an elasticity with respect to household size of between 0.9 and 1.0. For details see Musgrove, 1980.
2. In the SRS, births and deaths are recorded continuously by actually visiting households in the selected sample units at periodic intervals and making enquiries.

7 Resource Mobilisation to Finance Urban Programmes

1. During peak hours, which extend from 8.30 a.m. to 11.00 a.m. and from 5.00 p.m. to 8.00 p.m., there are usually more than 3400 passengers on a train meant to carry 852 passengers seated and 876 standing (Deshpande and Deshpande, 1991).
2. Bombay Electric Supply and Transport Undertaking. The historical reasons for both electricity and transport being provided by the same undertaking are interesting. When the transport service was first established in 1873, the power supply for its trams was found to be so irregular that it decided to generate its own power. The organisation was soon providing electricity for the city.

Appendix 2

1. Because manufacturing is generally the most dynamic part of the industrial sector, its gross domestic product was obtained separately.
2. Since professional, administrative and clerical workers have already been included, the residual wage-employment in agriculture is predominantly composed of labourers in traditional agriculture. These two categories, although in wage-earning employment, are usually subject to traditional working conditions and are therefore excluded from the calculations of modern-sector employment.

Bibliography

Alonso, W. (1969) 'Urban and regional imbalances in economic development', in *Economic Development and Cultural Change*, vol. 17, no. 1, pp. 1–14.

Amjad, R. (1990) *Urban planning and employment generation in Asian Megalopolis*, paper presented at the Regional Technical Workshop on Employment Generation in the Asian Megalopolis, ILO, ARTEP, New Delhi, 6–7 Dec.

Anker, R. and C. Hein, (1985) 'Why Third World urban employers usually prefer men', *International Labour Review*, vol. 124, no. 1 (Jan.–Feb.) pp. 73–90.

Austin, J. (1980) *Confronting urban malnutrition* (Baltimore: Johns Hopkins University Press).

Banerjee-Guha, S. (1990) *Sites and services projects in Greater Bombay: Viable solutions to the housing problems of the poor?*, paper presented at the International Seminar on the Asian Urban Environment, Benares, Benares Hindu University, March.

Bardhan, P. (1989) 'Poverty and employment characteristics of urban households in West Bengal, India: An analysis of the results of the National Sample Survey, 1977–78', in Rodgers, 1989.

Becker, G. (1960) 'An economic analysis of fertility', in *Demographic and economic change in developed countries*, (Princeton University Press).

Birdsall, N. (1980) *Population and poverty in the developing world*, World Bank Staff Working Paper no. 404 (Washington, DC).

Blair, T. L. (1984) *Urban innovation abroad: Problem cities in search of solutions* (New York: Plenum Press).

Cairncross, S. (1990) 'Water supply and the urban poor', in S. Cairncross, J. E. Hardoy and D. Satterthwaite (eds), *The poor die young: Housing and health in the Third World* (London: Earthscan) pp. 109–26.

Camazon, D., G. Garcia-Huidobro and H. Morgado (1989) 'Labour market performance and urban poverty in Panama', in Rodgers, 1989.

Chen, J. and B. Hu (1989) *Multi-level transfers and comprehensive explorations: The way out for surplus agricultural labor*, paper presented at the International Conference on Urbanization in China, Honolulu, Hawaii, 23–27 Jan.

Chernichovsky, D. and O. A. Meesook (1984) *Poverty in Indonesia: A profile*, World Bank Staff Working Paper no. 671 (Washington, DC).

Cointreau, S. J. (1982) *Environmental management of urban solid wastes in developing countries: A project guide*, Urban Development Technical Paper no. 5 (Washington, DC: World Bank).

Deshpande S. and L. Deshpande (1991) *Problems of urbanisation and growth of large cities in developing countries: A case study of Bombay*, ILO, WEP 2-21, Working Paper no. 177 (Geneva: ILO).

Ebanks, G. E. and C. Cheng (1990) 'China: A unique urbanisation model', *Asia–Pacific Population Journal*, vol. 5, no. 3, pp. 29–50.

Farah, N. (1991) *Problems of urbanisation and growth of large cities in developing countries: A case study of Cairo*, report prepared for ILO, Cairo (mimeo).

Farooq, G. M. and Y. Ofosu (1992) *Population, labour force and employment: concepts, trends and policy issues*, background paper for Training in Population, Human Resources and Development Planning, no. 9 (Geneva: ILO).

Feranil, I. Z. (1990) *Childbearing, family survival and planning among the urban poor: A Metro Manila slum survey* (Manila: Population Institute, University of the Philippines), mimeo.

Fields, G. (1987) *The impact of policies on urban employment in small economies*, paper presented at the OECD Meeting on Evaluation of Urban Employment Research and Policies in Developing Countries, Paris, 2–4 Nov.

Fong, C. O. (ed.) (1984) *Urban poverty in Malaysia: Policies and issues* (Kuala Lumpur, Population Studies Unit, Faculty of Economics and Administration, University of Malaya).

Frankel, I. (1983) 'Socio-economic development and rural–urban migration in Poland', in A. S. Oberai (ed.), *State policies and internal migration: Studies in market and planned economies* (London and Canberra: Croom Helm; New York: St. Martin's Press).

Ghai, D. (1987) *Economic growth, structural change and labour absorption in Africa: 1960-85*, paper prepared for the OECD Meeting on Evaluation of Urban Employment Research and Policies in Developing Countries, Paris, 2–4 Nov.

Gilbert, A. G. (1974) 'Industrial location theory: Its relevance to an industrialising nation', in B. S. Hoyle (ed.), *Spatial aspects of development* (New York: John Wiley) pp. 271–90.

—— (1976) 'The arguments for very large cities reconsidered', *Urban Studies*, vol. 13, no. 1, pp. 27–34.

—— and J. Gugler (1982) *Cities, poverty and development: Urbanisation in the Third World* (Oxford University Press).

Goldstein, S. (1987) 'Forms of mobility and their policy implications: Thailand and China compared', *Social Forces*, vol. 65, pp. 915–42.

Griffin, K. (1977) review of book *Why poor people stay poor* by M. Lipton, *Journal of Development Studies*, vol. 14, no. 4, pp. 108–9.

—— and A. R. Khan (1978) 'Poverty in the Third World: Ugly facts and fancy models', *World Development*, no. 6, pp. 295–304.

Hardoy, J. E. and D. Satterthwaite (1991) 'Environmental problems of Third World cities: A global issue ignored?', *Public Administration and Development*, vol. 11, no. 4, pp. 341–61.

Harriss, J. (1989) 'Vulnerable workers in the Indian labour market', in G. Rodgers (ed.) 1989.

Ho, T. J. (1979) 'Time costs of child rearing in the rural Philippines', *Population and Development Review*, vol. 5, pp. 643–63.

ILO/JASPA (1989) *African Employment Report, 1988* (Addis Ababa).

ILO/PREALC (1986a) *Adjustment and social debt: A structural approach* (Santiago).

—— (1986b) *Creation of productive employment: A task that cannot be postponed* (Santiago).

— (1991) *Empleo y equidad: El desafío de los 90* (Santiago).
Jakobson, L. and V. Prakash (eds.) (1974) *Metropolitan growth: Public policy for South and Southeast Asia* (New York: Halsted Press).
Jamal, V. (1990) *Nature and magnitude of employment problems in Kenya*, background paper prepared for the Presidential Committee on Employment, 1990, (Geneva: ILO), mimeo.
Jin-Ho Choi (1990) 'Patterns of urbanisation and population distribution policies in the Republic of Korea', *Regional Development Dialogue*, vol. 11, no. 1 (Spring).
Kim, Jong-Gie, Kim Kwan-Young and Son Jae-Young (1991) *Problems of urbanisation and the growth of Seoul*, ILO, WEP 2-21, Working Paper no. 179, (Geneva: ILO).
Kim Won Bae (1990) 'Population distribution policy in China: A Review', *Regional Development Dialogue*, vol. 11, no. 1, pp. 159–87.
King, E. M (1987) 'The effect of family size on family welfare: What do we know?', in D. G. Johnson and R. D. Lee (eds), *Population growth and economic development: Issues and evidence* (University of Wisconsin Press).
Kirkby, R. J. R. (1985) *Urbanization in China: Town and country in a developing economy, 1949–2000 AD* (New York: Columbia University Press).
Knight, J. B. and R. Sabot (1982) 'Labour market discrimination in a poor urban economy', *Journal of Development Studies*, vol. 19 (1), pp. 67–87.
Kundu, A. (1988) 'Does national housing policy answer the housing question?', in *Economic and Political Weekly* (Bombay), 24 Sep.
Kuznets, S. (1971) *Economic growth of nations* (Cambridge, Mass.: Harvard University Press).
Lall, V. D. (1990) *Employment generation through informal sector delivery system: Policy issues and strategy for national and urban planning and development agencies*, paper presented at ARTEP meeting.
Lee, E. (1987) *The informal sector and aid policy*, paper presented for DANIDA meeting on The Informal Sector as an Integral Part of the National Economy: Research Needs and Aid Requirements, Copenhagen, 28–9 Sep.
Lee, J. A. (1985) *The environment, public health and human ecology* (Baltimore and London: World Bank and Johns Hopkins University Press).
Lefeber, L. (1978) *Spatial population distribution: Urban and rural development*, paper presented to the ECLA/CELADE Seminar on Population Redistribution, Aug. 1978.
Leibenstein, N. (1974) 'Socio-economic fertility theories and their relevance to population policy', *International Labour Review*, vol. 105 (May–June), pp. 443–58.
Lewis, A. (1954) 'Development with unlimited supplies of labour', *Manchester School of Economics and Social Studies*, vol. 20, pp. 139–92.
Linn, J. (1983) *Cities in the developing world* (New York: Oxford University Press).
Lipton, M. (1977) *Why poor people stay poor: A study of urban bias in world development* (London: Temple Smith).
Lubell, H. and J. McCallum (1978) *Bogotá: Urban development and employment* (Geneva: ILO).
Martin, J. T., I. Ness, and S. T. Collins (1986) *Book of world city rankings* (London: Free Press [Macmillan]).

Mazumdar, D. (1979) *Paradigms in the study of urban labour markets in LDCs: A measurement in the light of an empirical survey in Bombay City*, World Bank Staff Working Paper no. 366 (Washington, DC).

Mitra, A. (1987) *Duality, employment problem and poverty incidence: Slum perspective* (Delhi School for Economics), mimeo.

Mohan, R. (1990) *Issues in urban employment planning*, paper presented at the Regional Technical Workshop on Employment Generation in the Asian Megalopolis, ILO/ARTEP, New Delhi, 6–7 Dec.

— and N. Hartline (1984) *The poor of Bogotá: Who they are, what they do and where they live*, World Bank Staff Working Paper no. 635 (Washington, DC).

Mukerji, S. (1988) *Fertility and mortality rates for Greater Bombay based on sample registration scheme* (Bombay: International Institute for Population Sciences [IIPS]), mimeo.

— and B. M. Ramesh (1991) *Study of urban poor living in slums of Bombay*, report prepared for the ILO, Bombay (mimeo.).

Murphey, R. (1988) 'Shanghai', in M. Dogan and J. D. Kasarda, (eds), *The metropolis era: Mega-cities* (Newbury Park, Calif.: Sage Publications), pp. 157–83.

Musgrove, P. (1980) 'Household size and composition, employment and poverty in urban Latin America', *Economic Development and Cultural Change*, vol. 28, no. 2, pp. 249–60.

National Commission on Urbanisation (1987) *Interim Report* (New Delhi: Government of India).

Nuqui, W. G. (1989) *The Philippine Development Plan: Population program and poverty alleviation*, Research Paper series no. 51 (Tokyo: Population Research Institute, Nihon University), p. 8.

Oberai, A. S. (1978) *Changes in the structure of employment with economic development* (Geneva: ILO).

— (1987) *Migration, urbanisation and development* (Geneva: ILO).

— (1988) *Problems of urbanisation and growth of large cities in developing countries: A conceptual framework for policy analysis,*, WEP 2-21, Working Paper no. 169, (Geneva: ILO).

— (1989) *Rapid population growth, employment and housing in mega-cities in developing countries*, paper presented at the IUSSP XXIst General Conference, New Delhi, 20–27 Sep.

— (1990) *Urban population growth, employment patterns and their implications for health: The large metropolis in the Third World*, paper presented at the WHO Expert Committee on Environmental Health in Urban Development, Geneva, 17–23 Apr.

— and H. K. M. Singh (1983) *Causes and consequences of internal migration: A study in the Indian Punjab* (New Delhi: Oxford University Press).

Perlman, J. (1986) 'Six misconceptions about squatter settlements', *Development Seeds of Change*, no. 4, pp. 40–4.

Prakash, V. (1986) 'Role and structure of user charges in financing urban services in developing countries', *Regional Development Dialogue*, vol. 7, no. 2, pp. 1–24.

Renaud, B. (1981) *National urbanisation policy in developing countries* (New York: Oxford University Press).

Richards, P. J. and A. M. Thomson (eds) (1984) *Basic needs and the urban poor: The provision of communal services* (London: Croom Helm).

Richardson, H. W. (1973) *Economics of urban size* (Farnborough: Saxon House).

Robinson, G. and B. Salih (1971) 'The spread of development around Kuala Lumpur', *Regional Studies*, no. 5, pp. 303–14.

Rocca, C.A. (1970) 'Productivity in Brazilian manufacturing', in Bergsmann (ed.), *Brazil: Industrialisation and trade policies* (Oxford University Press), pp. 22–41.

Rodgers, G. (ed.) (1989) *Urban poverty and the labour market: Access to jobs and incomes in Asian and Latin American cities* (Geneva: ILO).

Sant'Anna, A., *et al.* (1976) *Income distribution and the economy of the urban household: The case of Belo Horizonte*, World Bank Staff Working Paper no. 237 (Washington, DC).

Sathar, Z. A. and S. Kazi (1990) 'Women, work and reproduction in Karachi', *International Family Planning Perspectives*, vol. 16, no. 2 (June), pp. 66–9.

Schroeder, L. and E. Dalton (1986) 'Local government tax revenue buoyancy and stability in developing countries', *Regional Development Dialogue*, vol. 7, no. 2, pp. 32–64.

Schteingart, M. (1989) 'The environmental problems associated with urban development in Mexico City', *Environment and Urbanization*, vol. 1, no. 1, pp. 40–9.

Sethuraman, S. V. (1978) *Jakarta: Urban development and employment* (Geneva: ILO).

— (1981) *The urban formal sector in developing countries: Employment, poverty and environment* (Geneva: ILO).

Shanghai Planning Commission (1991) *A Study on urban development of Shanghai*, report prepared for the ILO, Shanghai (mimeo).

Shaw, A. (1984) 'Wage labour in slum households of Calcutta', *Labour, Capital and Society*, vol. 17, no. 1 (April) (Centre for Developing-Area Studies, McGill University, Canada).

Singh, A. (1989) *Urbanisation, poverty and employment: The large metropolis in the Third World*, ILO, WEP 2-21, Working Paper no. 165 (Geneva: ILO).

Singh, A.M. and A. de Souza (1980) *The urban poor: Slums and pavement dwellers in the major cities of India* (New Delhi: Manohal).

Squire, L. (1981) *Employment policy in developing countries* (New York: Oxford University Press).

Stolnitz, G. J. (1984) *Urbanisation and rural-to-urban migration in relation to LDC fertility* (Bloomington, Indiana University).

Todaro, M. P. (1969) 'A model of labour migration and urban unemployment in less developed countries', *American Economic Review*, vol. 59, no. 1, pp. 138–48.

Tokman, V. (1987) *Evaluation of research and policies on employment problems in Latin America*, paper prepared for the OECD Meeting on Evaluation of Urban Employment Research and Policies in Developing Countries, Paris, 2–4 Nov.

Tolosa, H. C., A. V. Villela, J. B. Figueiredo and L. A. Villela, (1991) *Problems of urbanisation and growth of large cities in developing countries: The Rio de*

Janeiro Metropolitan Area case study, report prepared for the ILO, Rio, (mimeo.).

UNICEF (1987) *Adjustment with a human face* (New York).

United Nations (1980) *Patterns of urban and rural population growth* (New York).

— (1985a) *Estimates and projections of urban and rural city population 1950-2025: 1982 assessment* (New York).

— (1985b) *Migration, population growth and employment in metropolitan areas of selected developing countries* (New York).

— (1987) *The prospects of World Urbanisation: Revised as of 1984-85* (New York).

— (1988) *Global strategy for shelter to the year 2000,* report of the Commission on Human Settlements, Forty-third Session, General Assembly, 6 June, New York.

— (1990a) *Population growth and policies in mega-cities: Cairo* (New York: Department of International Economic and Social Affairs, ST/ESA/SER.R/ 103).

— (1990b) *Population growth and policies in mega-cities: Mexico* (New York: Department of International Economic and Social Affairs, ST/ESA/SER.R/ 105).

— (1991) *World urbanisation prospects, 1990* (New York).

United Nations Center for Human Settlements (HABITAT) (1987) *Global report on human settlements 1986* (Oxford University Press).

United Nations Development Programme (1990) *Human Development Report: 1990* (Oxford University Press).

Wadhwa, K. (1988) 'Housing programmes for the urban poor', *Economic and Political Weekly* (Bombay), 20 Aug.

World Bank (1979) *National urbanisation policies in developing countries,* Working Paper no. 347 (Washington, DC).

— (1991) *Urban policy and economic development: An agenda for the 1990s,* World Bank Policy Paper (Washington, DC).

Wu, Youren (1981) *On the question of China's socialist urbanisation,* paper presented at the Symposium on Chinese Population Science (Beijing: Academic Press), quoted in Ebanks and Cheng, 1990.

Yap, L. (1977) 'The attraction of cities: A review of the migration literature', in *Journal of Development Economics,* no. 4(3), pp. 239–64.

Yeung, Yeu-Man (1988) 'Great cities of Eastern Asia', in M. Logan and J. D. Kasarda (eds), *The metropolis era, Vol. 1: A world of giant cities* (Beverly Hills: Sage Publications).

Zhao, Y. (1989) *Strategy and choice: Review of China's road towards urbanization,* paper presented at the International Conference on Urbanization in China, Honolulu, Hawaii, 23–7 Jan.

Author Index

Subject Index